Date Due

THE COMPLETE WORKS

OF

JAMES WHITCOMB RILEY

IN SIX VOLUMES

Crayon sketch by Clay

THE COMPLETE WORKS

OF

JAMES WHITCOMB RILEY

IN WHICH THE POEMS, INCLUDING A NUMBER HERETOFORE UNPUBLISHED,
ARE ARRANGED IN THE ORDER IN WHICH THEY WERE WRITTEN,
TOGETHER WITH PHOTOGRAPHS, BIBLIOGRAPHIC NOTES,
AND A LIFE SKETCH OF THE AUTHOR

COLLECTED AND EDITED BY

EDMUND HENRY EITEL

BIOGRAPHICAL EDITION
VOLUME FIVE

INDIANAPOLIS
THE BOBBS-MERRILL COMPANY
PUBLISHERS

PRESS OF
BRAUNWORTH & CO.
BOOKBINDERS AND PRINTERS
BROOKLYN, N. Y.

CONTENTS

CONTENTS

CONTENTS

CONTENTS

CONTENTS

CONTENTS

CONTENTS

CONTENTS

THE COMPLETE WORKS

OF

JAMES WHITCOMB RILEY

IN SIX VOLUMES

"THEM OLD CHEERY WORDS"

PAP he allus ust to say,
   "Chris'mus comes but onc't a year!"
Liked to hear him thataway,
   In his old split-bottomed cheer
By the fireplace here at night—
Wood all in,—and room all bright,
Warm and snug, and folks all here:
"Chris'mus comes but onc't a year!"

Me and 'Lize, and Warr'n and Jess
   And Eldory home fer two
Weeks' vacation; and, I guess,
   Old folks tickled through and through,
Same as *we* was,—"Home onc't more
Fer another Chris'mus—shore!"
Pap 'ud say, and tilt his cheer,—
"Chris'mus comes but onc't a year!"

1

Mostly Pap was ap' to be
   Ser'ous in his "daily walk,"
As he called it; giner'ly
   Was no hand to joke er talk.
Fac's is, Pap had never be'n
Rugged-like at all—and then
Three years in the army had
Hepped to break him purty bad.

Never *flinched!* but frost and snow
   Hurt his wownd in winter. But
You bet *Mother* knowed it, though!—
   Watched his feet, and made him putt
On his flannen; and his knee,
Where it never healed up, he
Claimed was "well now—mighty near—
Chris'mus comes but onc't a year!"

"Chris'mus comes but onc't a year!"
   Pap 'ud say, and snap his eyes . . . .
Row o' apples sputter'n' here
   Round the hearth, and me and 'Lize
Crackin' hicker'-nuts; and Warr'n
And Eldory parchin' corn;
And whole raft o' young folks here.
"Chris'mus comes but onc't a year!"

Mother tuk most comfort in
  Jes' a-he'ppin' Pap: She'd fill
His pipe fer him, er his tin
  O' hard cider; er set still
And read fer him out the pile
O' newspapers putt on file
Whilse he was with Sherman—(She
Knowed the whole war-history!)

Sometimes he'd git het up some.—
  "Boys," he'd say, "and you girls, too,
Chris'mus is about to come;
  So, as you've a right to do,
Celebrate it! Lots has died,
Same as Him they crucified,
That you might be happy here.
Chris'mus comes but onc't a year!"

Missed his voice last Chris'mus—missed
  Them old cheery words, you know!
Mother helt up tel she kissed
  All of us—then had to go
And break down! And I laughs: "Here!
'Chris'mus comes but onc't a year!'"
"Them's his very words," sobbed she,
"When he asked to marry me."

"Chris'mus comes but onc't a year!"—
  "Chris'mus comes but onc't a year!"
Over, over, still I hear,
  "Chris'mus comes but onc't a year!"
Yit, like him, I'm goin' to smile
And keep cheerful all the while:
Allus Chris'mus *There*—And here
"Chris'mus comes but onc't a year!"

A DUBIOUS "OLD KRISS"

US-FOLKS is purty pore—but Ma
  She's waitin'—two years more—tel Pa
He serves his term out. Our Pa he—
He's in the Penitenchurrie!

Now don't you tell!—'cause *Sis,*
The *baby, she* don't know he is.—
'Cause she wuz only four, you know,
He kissed her last an' hat to go!

Pa alluz liked Sis best of all
Us childern.—'Spect it's 'cause she fall
When she 'uz ist a *child,* one day—
An' make her back look thataway.

Pa—'fore he be a burglar—he's
A locksmiff, an' maked locks, an' keys,
An' knobs you pull fer bells to ring,
An' he could ist make *anything!*—

'Cause our Ma *say* he can!—*An'* this
Here little pair of crutches Sis
Skips round on—Pa maked *them*—yes-sir!—
An' silivur-plate-name here fer her!

Pa's out o' work when Chris'mus come
One time, an' stay away from home,
An' 's drunk an' 'buse our Ma, an' swear
They ain't no "Old Kriss" anywhere!

An' Sis she alluz say they *wuz*
A' Old Kriss—an' she alluz does.
But ef they *is* a' Old Kriss, why,
When's Chris'mus, Ma she alluz *cry?*

This Chris'mus *now,* we live here in
Where Ma's rent's alluz due ag'in—
An' she "ist slaves"—I heerd her say
She did—ist them words thataway!

An' th'other night, when all's so cold
An' stove's 'most out—our Ma she rolled
Us in th' old feather-bed an' said,
"To-morry's Chris'mus—go to bed,

"An' thank yer blessed stars fer this—
We don't *'spect* nothin' from old Kriss!"
An' cried, an' locked the door, an' prayed,
An' turned the lamp down. . . . An' I laid

There, thinkin' in the dark ag'in,
"Ef *wuz* Old Kriss, he can't git in,
'Cause ain't no chimbly here at all—
Ist old stovepipe struck frue the wall!"

I sleeped nen.—An' wuz dreamin' some
When I waked up an' mornin' 's come,—
Fer our Ma she wuz settin' square
Straight up in bed, a-readin' there

Some letter 'at she'd read, an' quit,
An' nen hold like she's huggin' it.—
An' diamon' ear-rings she don't *know*
Wuz in her ears tel I say so—

An' wake the rest up. An' the sun
In frue the winder dazzle-un
Them eyes o' Sis's, wiv a sure-
Enough gold chain Old Kriss bringed to 'er!

An' *all* of us git gold things!—Sis,
Though, say she know it *"ain't"* Old Kriss—
He kissed her, so she waked an' saw
Him skite out—an' it wuz her Pa."

YOUR HEIGHT IS OURS

TO RICHARD HENRY STODDARD, AT THE STODDARD
BANQUET BY THE AUTHORS CLUB, NEW
YORK, MARCH 25, 1897

O PRINCELY poet!—kingly heir
  Of gifts divinely sent,—
Your own!—nor envy anywhere,
  Nor voice of discontent.

Though, of ourselves, all poor are we,
  And frail and weak of wing,
Your height is ours—your ecstasy—
  Your glory, when you sing.

Most favored of the gods, and great
  In gifts beyond our store,
We covet not your rich estate,
  But prize our own the more.—

The gods give as but gods may do—
  We count *our* riches thus,—
They gave their richest gifts to you,
  And then gave you to us.

HYMN EXULTANT

VOICE of Mankind, sing over land and sea—
   Sing, in this glorious morn!
The long, long night is gone from Calvary—
   The cross, the thong and thorn;
The sealed tomb yields up its saintly guest,
No longer to be burdened and oppressed.

Heart of Mankind, thrill answer to His own,
   So human, yet divine!
For earthly love He left His heavenly throne—
   For love like thine and mine—
For love of us, as one might kiss a bride,
His lifted lips touched death's, all satisfied.

Soul of Mankind, He wakes—He lives once more!
   O soul, with heart and voice
Sing! sing!—the stone rolls chorus from the door—
   Our Lord stands forth.—Rejoice!
Rejoice, O garden-land of song and flowers;
Our King returns to us, forever ours!

9

"O LIFE! O BEYOND!"

STRANGE—strange, O mortal Life,
   The perverse gifts that came to me from you!
From childhood I have wanted *all* good things:
      You gave me few.

You gave me faith in One—
   Divine—above your own imperious might,
O mortal Life, while I but wanted you
      And your delight.

I wanted dancing feet,
   And flowery, grassy paths by laughing streams;
You gave me loitering steps, and eyes all blurred
      With tears and dreams.

I wanted love,—and, lo!
   As though in mockery, you gave me loss.
O'erburdened sore, I wanted rest: you gave
      The heavier cross.

I wanted one poor hut
   For mine own home, to creep away into:
You gave me only lonelier desert lands
      To journey through.

10

Now, at the last vast verge
  Of barren age, I stumble, reel, and fling
Me down, with strength all spent and heart athirst
      And famishing.

Yea, now, Life, deal me death,—
  Your worst—your vaunted worst! . . . Across
    my breast
With numb and fumbling hands I gird me for
      The best.

OUR QUEER OLD WORLD

Fer them 'at's here in airliest infant stages,
  It's a hard world:
Fer them 'at gits the knocks of boyhood's ages,
  It's a mean world:
Fer them 'at nothin's good enough they're gittin',
  It's a bad world:
Fer them 'at learns at last what's right and fittin',
  It's a good world.
                              —THE HIRED MAN

IT'S a purty hard world you find, my child—
  It's a purty hard world you find!
You fight, little rascal! and kick and squall,
And snort out medicine, spoon and all!
  When you're here longer you'll change your mind
And simmer down sort o' half-rickonciled.
      But *now*—Jee!-
      My!-mun-nee!
It's a purty hard world, my child!

It's a purty mean world you're in, my lad—
  It's a purty mean world you're in!
We know, of course, in your schoolboy-days
It's a world of too many troublesome ways
  Of tryin' things over and startin' ag'in,—

12

Yit *your* chance beats what your *parents* had.
     But *now*—Oh!
     Fire-and-tow!
It's a purty mean world, my lad!

It's a purty bad world you've struck, young chap—
    It's a purty bad world you've struck—
But *study* the cards that you hold, you know,
And your hopes will sprout and your mustache
     grow,
    And your store-clothes likely will change your
       luck,
And you'll rake a rich ladybird into your lap!
     But *now*—Doubt
     All things out.—
It's a purty bad world, young chap!

It's a purty good world this is, old man—
    It's a purty good world this is!
For all its follies and shows and lies—
Its rainy weather, and cheeks likewise,
    And age, hard-hearin' and rheumatiz.—
We're not a-faultin' the Lord's own plan—
     All things 's jest
     At their best.—
It's a purty good world, old man!

ON A YOUTHFUL PORTRAIT OF STEVENSON

A FACE of youth mature; a mouth of tender,
    Sad, human sympathy, yet something stoic
In clasp of lip: wide eyes of calmest splendor,
    And brow serenely ample and heroic:—
The features—all—lit with a soul ideal . . .
    O visionary boy! what were you seeing,
What hearing, as you stood thus midst the real
    Ere yet one master-work of yours had being?

Is it a foolish fancy that we humor—
    Investing daringly with life and spirit
This youthful portrait of you ere one rumor
    Of your great future spoke that men might hear
        it?—
Is it a fancy, or your first of glories,
    That you were listening, and the camera drew you
Hearing the voices of your untold stories
    And all your lovely poems calling to you?

14

RUBÁIYÁT OF DOC SIFERS

PROEM

We found him in that Far-away that yet to us seems
   near—
We vagrants of but yesterday when idlest youth
   was here,—
When lightest song and laziest mirth possessed us
   through and through,
And all the dreamy summer-earth seemed drugged
   with morning dew:

When our ambition scarce had shot a stalk or blade
   indeed:
Yours,—choked as in the garden-spot you still de-
   ferred to "weed":
Mine,—but a pipe half-cleared of pith—as now it
   flats and whines
In sympathetic cadence with a hiccough in the lines.

Ay, even then—O timely hour!—the High Gods did
   confer
In our behalf:—And, clothed in power, lo, came
   their Courier—
Not winged with flame nor shod with wind,—but
   ambling down the pike,
Horseback, with saddle-bags behind, and guise all
   human-like.

17

And it was given us to see, beneath his rustic rind,
A native force and mastery of such inspiring kind,
That half unconsciously we made obeisance.—Smil-
*   ing, thus*
His soul shone from his eyes and laid its glory
*   over us.*

.   .   .   .

Though, faring still that Far-away that yet to us
*   seems near,*
His form, through mists of yesterday, fades from
*   the vision here,*
Forever as he rides, it is in retinue divine,—
The hearts of all his time are his, with your hale
*   heart and mine.*

RUBÁIYÁT

OF

DOC SIFERS

I

IF you don't know Doc Sifers I'll jes' argy,
  here and now,
You've bin a mighty little while about here, any-
    how,
'Cause Doc he's rid these roads and woods—er
    swum 'em, now and then—
And practised in this neighberhood sence hain't no
    tellin' when!

II

In radius o' fifteen mil'd, all p'ints o' compass round,
No man er woman, chick er child, er team, on top o'
    ground,
But knows *him*—yes, and got respects and likin'
    fer him, too,
Fer all his so-to-speak dee-fects o' genius showin'
    through!

III

Some claims he's absent-minded; some has said
    they wuz afeard
To take his powders when he come and dosed 'em
    out, and 'peared
To have his mind on somepin' else—like County
    Ditch, er some
New way o' tannin' mussrat-pelts, er makin' butter
    come.

IV

He's cur'ous—they hain't no mistake about it!—but
    he's got
Enough o' extry brains to make a *jury*—like as not.
They's no *describin'* Sifers,—fer, when all is said
    and done,
He's jes' *hisse'f Doc Sifers*—ner they hain't no
    other one!

V

Doc's allus sociable, polite, and 'greeable, you'll
    find—
Pervidin' ef you strike him right and nothin' on his
    mind,—
Like in some *hurry,* when they've sent fer Sifers
    quick, you see,
To 'tend some sawmill-accident, er picnic jamboree;

VI

Er when the lightin' 's struck some harebrained
  harvest-hand; er in
Some 'tempt o' suicidin'—where they'd ort to try
  ag'in!
I've *knowed* Doc haul up from a trot and talk a'
  hour er two
When railly he'd a-ort o' not a-stopped fer
  "Howdy-do!"

VII

And then, I've met him 'long the road, *a-lopin'*,—
  starin' straight
Ahead,—and yit he never knowed me when I
  hollered *"Yate,*
Old Saddlebags!" all hearty-like, er *"Who you goin'*
  to kill?"
And he'd say nothin'—only hike on faster, starin'
  still!

VIII

I'd bin insulted, many a time, ef I jes' wuzn't shore
Doc didn't mean a thing. And I'm not tetchy any
  more
Sence that-air day, ef he'd a-jes' a-stopped to jaw
  with *me,*
They'd bin a little dorter less in my own fambily!

IX

Times *now*, at home, when Sifers' name comes up, I
  jes' *let on,*
You know, 'at *I* think Doc's to *blame,* the way he's
  bin and gone
And disapp'inted folks—'Ll-*jee*-mun-*nee!* you'd ort
  to then
Jes' hear my wife light into me—*"ongratefulest o'*
  men!"

X

'Mongst *all* the women—mild er rough, splendifer-
  ous er plain,
Er them *with* sense, er not enough to come in out
  the rain,—
Jes' ever' shape and build and style o' women, fat
  er slim—
They all like Doc, and got a smile and pleasant word
  fer *him!*

XI

Ner hain't no horse I've ever saw but what'll neigh
  and try
To sidle up to him, and paw, and sense him, ear-
  and-eye:
Then jes' a tetch o' Doc's old pa'm, to pat 'em, er to
  shove
Along their nose—and they're as ca'm as any cooin'
  dove!

XII

And same with *dogs,*—take any breed, er strain, er
pedigree,
Er racial caste 'at can't concede no use fer you er
me,—
They'll putt all predju-dice aside in *Doc's* case and
go in
Kahoots with him, as satisfied as he wuz kith-and-
kin!

XIII

And Doc's a wonder, trainin' pets!—He's got a
chicken-hawk,
In kind o' half-cage, where he sets out in the
gyarden-walk,
And got that wild bird trained so tame, he'll loose
him, and he'll fly
Clean to the woods!—Doc calls his name—and he'll
come, by and by!

XIV

Some says no money down 'ud buy that bird o'
Doc.—Ner no
Inducement to the *bird*, says I, 'at *he'd* let *Sifers*
go!
And Doc *he* say 'at *he's* content—long as a bird o'
prey
Kin 'bide *him,* it's a *compliment,* and takes it
thataway.

XV

But, gittin' back to *docterin'*—all the sick and in
    distress,
And old and pore, and weak and small, and lone
    and motherless,—
I jes' tell *you* I 'preciate the man 'at's got the love
To "go ye forth and ministrate!" as Scriptur' tells
    us of.

XVI

Dull times, Doc jes' *mi*anders round, in that old rig
    o' his:
And hain't no tellin' where he's bound ner guessin'
    where he is;
He'll drive, they tell, jes' thataway fer maybe six er
    eight
Days at a stretch; and neighbers say he's bin clean
    round the State.

XVII

He picked a' old tramp up, one trip, 'bout eighty
    mil'd from here,
And fetched him home and k-yored his hip, and kep'
    him 'bout a year;
And feller said—in all *his* ja'nts round this
    terreschul ball
'At no man wuz a *circumstance* to *Doc!*—he topped
    'em all!—

XVIII

Said, bark o' trees 's a' open book to Doc, and vines
    and moss
He read like writin'—with a look knowed ever' dot
    and cross:
Said, stars at night wuz jes' as good's a compass:
    said, he s'pose
You couldn't lose Doc in the woods the darkest
    night that blows!

XIX

Said, Doc'll tell you, purty clos't, by underbresh and
    plants,
How fur off *warter* is,—and 'most perdict the sort
    o' chance
You'll have o' findin' *fish;* and how they're liable to
    bite,
And whether they're a-bitin' now, er only after
    night.

XX

And, whilse we're talkin' *fish,*—I mind they formed
    a fishin'-crowd
(When folks *could* fish 'thout gittin' *fined,* and
    seinin' wuz allowed!)
O' leadin' citizens, you know, to go and seine "Old
    Blue"—
But hadn't no big seine, and so—w'y, what wuz they
    to do? . . .

XXI

And Doc he say he thought 'at *he* could *knit* a stitch
    er two—
"Bring the *materials* to me—'at's all I'm astin' you!"
And down he sets—six weeks, i jing! and knits
    that seine plum done—
Made corks too, brails and ever'thing—good as a
    boughten one!

XXII

Doc's *public* sperit—when the sick's not takin' *all*
    his time
And he's got *some* fer politics—is simple yit
    sublime:—
He'll *talk* his *principles*—and they air *honest;*—but
    the sly
Friend strikes him first, election-day, he'd 'commo-
    date, er die!

XXIII

And yit, though Doc, as all men knows, is square
    straight up and down,
That vote o' his is—well, I s'pose—the cheapest one
    in town;—
A fact 'at's sad to verify, as could be done on oath—
I've voted Doc myse'f—*And I was criminal fer
    both!*

XXIV

You kin corrupt the *ballot-box*—corrupt *yourse'f*,
   as well—
Corrupt *some* neighbers,—but old Doc's as oncor-
   ruptible
As Holy Writ. So putt a pin right there!—Let
   Sifers be,
I jucks! he wouldn't vote ag'in' his own worst
   inimy!

XXV

When Cynthy Eubanks laid so low with fever, and
   Doc Glenn
Told Euby Cynth 'ud haf to go—they sends fer
   Sifers then! . . .
Doc sized the case: "She's starved," says he, "fer
   warter—yes, and *meat!*
The treatment 'at she'll git from *me's* all she kin
   drink and eat!"

XXVI

He orders Euby then to split some wood, and take
   and build
A fire in kitchen-stove, and git a young spring-
   chicken killed;
And jes' whirled in and th'owed his hat and coat
   there on the bed,
And warshed his hands and sailed in that-air
   kitchen, Euby said,

XXVII

And biled that chicken-broth, and got that dinner—
    all complete
And clean and crisp and good and hot as mortal
    ever eat!
And Cynth and Euby both'll say 'at Doc'll git as
    good
Meals-vittles up, jes' any day, as any *woman* could!

XXVIII

Time Sister Abbick tuk so bad with striffen o' the
    lung,
P'tracted Meetin', where she had jes' shouted,
    prayed, and sung
All winter long, through snow and thaw,—when
    Sifers come, says he:
"No, M'lissy; don't poke out your raw and cloven
    tongue at me!—

XXIX

"I know, without no symptoms but them *injarubber-
    shoes*
You promised me to never putt a fool-foot in ner
    use
At purril o' your life!" he said. "And I won't save
    you *now*,
Onless—here on your dyin' bed—you consecrate
    your vow!"

XXX

Without a-claimin' *any creed,* Doc's rail religious
    views
Nobody knows—ner got no *need* o' knowin' whilse
    he choose
To be heerd not of man, ner raise no loud, vain-
    glorious prayers
In crowded marts, er public ways, er—i jucks,
    *any*wheres!—

XXXI

'Less'n it *is* away deep down in his own heart, at
    night,
Facin' the storm, when all the town's a-sleepin' snug
    and tight—
Him splashin' hence from scenes o' pride and sloth
    and gilded show,
To some pore sufferer's bedside o' anguish, don't
    you know!

XXXII

Er maybe dead o' *winter*—makes no odds to *Doc,*—
    he's got
To face the weather ef it takes the hide off! 'cause
    he'll not
Lie out o' goin' and p'tend he's sick hisse'f—like
    some
'At I could name 'at folks might send fer and they'd
    never come!

XXXIII

Like pore Phin Hoover—when he goes to that last
    dance o' his!
That Chris'mus when his feet wuz froze—and Doc
    saved all they is
Left of 'em—"'Nough," as Phin say now, "to
    track me by, and be
A adver*tise*ment, anyhow, o' what Doc's done fer
    me!—

XXXIV

"When *he* come—knife-and-saw"—Phin say, "I
    knowed, ef I'd the spunk,
'At Doc 'ud fix me up *some* way, ef nothin' but my
    trunk
Wuz left, he'd fasten *casters* in, and have me,
    spick-and-span,
A-skootin' round the streets ag'in as spry as any
    man!"

XXXV

Doc sees a patient's *got* to quit—he'll ease him down
    serene
As dozin' off to sleep, and yit not dope him with
    mor*pheen*.—
He won't tell *what*—jes' 'lows 'at he has "airnt the
    right to sing
'O grave, where is thy victory! O death, where is
    thy sting!'"

XXXVI

And, mind ye now!—it's not in scoff and scorn, by
    long degree,
'At Doc gits things like that-un off: it's jes' his
    shority
And total faith in Life to Come,—w'y, "from that
    Land o' Bliss,"
He says, "we'll haf to chuckle some, a-lookin' back
    at this!"

XXXVII

And, still in p'int, I mind, one *night o' 'nitiation* at
Some secert lodge, 'at Doc set right down on 'em,
    square and flat,
When they mixed up some Scriptur' and wuz
    funnin'-like—w'y, he
Lit in 'em with a rep'imand 'at ripped 'em, A to Z!

XXXVIII

And onc't—when gineral loafin'-place wuz old Shoe-
    Shop—and all
The gang 'ud git in there and brace their backs
    ag'inst the wall
And *settle* questions that had went onsettled long
    enough,—
Like "wuz no Heav'n—ner no torment"—*jes' talkin'
awful rough!*

XXXIX

There wuz Sloke Haines and old Ike Knight and
　　Coonrod Simmes—all three
Ag'inst the Bible and the Light, and scoutin' Deity.
"Science," says Ike, "it DIM*onstrates*—it takes
　　nobody's word—
Scriptur' er not,—it *'vestigates* ef sich things could
　　occurred!"

XL

Well, Doc he heerd this,—he'd drapped in a minute,
　　fer to git
A tore-off heel pegged on ag'in,—and, as he stood
　　on it
And stomped and grinned, he says to Ike, "I s'pose
　　now, purty soon
Some lightin'-bug, indignant-like, 'll 'vestigate the
　　moon! . . .

XLI

"No, Ike," says Doc, "this world hain't saw no
　　brains like yourn and mine
With sense enough to grasp a law 'at takes a brain
　　divine.—
I've bared the thoughts of brains in doubt, and felt
　　their finest pulse,—
And mortal brains jes' won't turn out omnipotent
　　results!"

XLII

And Doc he's got respects to spare the *rich* as well
    as *pore*—
Says he, "I'd turn no *millionnaire* onsheltered from
    my door."—
Says he, "What's wealth to him in quest o' *honest*
    friends to back
And love him fer *hisse'f?*—not jes' because he's
    made his jack!"

XLIII

And childern.—*Childern?* Lawzy-day! Doc *wor-
    ships* 'em!—You call
Round at his house and *ast* 'em!—they're
    a-*swarmin'* there—that's all!—
They're in his *Lib'ry*—in best room—in kitchen—
    fur and near,—
In office too, and, I p'sume, his operatin'-cheer!

XLIV

You know they's men 'at *bees* won't sting?—They's
    plaguy *few,*—But Doc
He's one o' *them.*—And same, i jing! with
    childern;—they jes' flock
Round Sifers *natchurl!*—in his lap, and in his
    pockets, too,
And in his old fur mitts and cap, and *heart* as warm
    and true!

XLV

It's cur'ous, too,—'cause Doc hain't got no childern
  of his own—
'Ceptin' the ones he's tuk and brought up, 'at's
  bin left alone
And orphans when their father died, er mother,—
  and Doc he
Has he'pped their dyin' satisfied.—"The child shall
  live with me

XLVI

"And Winniferd, my wife," he'd say, and stop right
  there, and cle'r
His th'oat, and go on thinkin' way *some* mother-
  hearts down here
Can't never feel *their own* babe's face a-pressin'
  'em, ner make
Their naked breasts a restin'-place fer any baby's
  sake.

XLVII

Doc's *Lib*'ry—as he calls it,—well, they's ha'f-a-
  dozen she'ves
Jam-full o' books—I couldn't tell *how* many—count
  yourse'ves!
One whole she'f's Works on Medicine! and most the
  rest's about
First Settlement, and Indians in here,—'fore we
  driv 'em out.—

XLVIII

And Plutarch's Lives—and life also o' Dan'el
    Boone, and this-
Here Mungo Park, and Adam Poe—jes' all the *lives*
    they is!
And Doc's got all the *novels* out,—by Scott and
    Dickison
And Cooper.—And, I make no doubt, he's read 'em
    ever' one!

XLIX

Onc't, in his office, settin' there, with crowd o' eight
    er nine
Old neighbers with the time to spare, and Doc
    a-feelin' fine,
A man rid up from Rollins, jes' fer Doc to write
    him out
Some blame' p'scription—done, I guess, in minute,
    nigh about.—

L

And *I* says, "Doc, you 'pear so spry, jes' write me
    that recei't
You have fer bein' *happy* by,—fer that 'ud shorely
    beat
Your *medicine!*" says I.—And quick as *s'cat!* Doc
    turned and writ
And handed me: "Go he'p the sick, and putt your
    heart in it."

LI

And then, "A-talkin' furder 'bout that line o'
thought," says he,
"Ef we'll jes' do the work cut out and give' to you
and me,
We'll lack no joy, ner appetite, ner all we'd ort to
eat,
And sleep like childern ever' night—as puore and
ca'm and sweet."

LII

Doc *has* bin 'cused o' *offishness* and lack o' talkin'
free
And extry friendly; but he says, "I'm *'feard* o'
talk," says he,—
"I've got," he says, "a natchurl turn fer talkin' fit
to kill.—
The best and hardest thing to learn is trick o'
keepin' still."

LIII

Doc *kin* smoke, and I s'pose he *might* drink licker—
jes' fer fun.
He says, *"You* smoke, *you* drink all right; but *I*
don't—neether one"—
Says, "I *like* whisky—'good old rye'—but like it in
its place,
Like that-air warter in your eye, er nose there on
your face."

LIV

Doc's bound to have his joke! The day he got that
off on me
I jes' had sold a load o' hay at "Scofield's Livery,"
And tolled Doc in the shed they kep' the hears't in,
where I'd hid
The stuff 'at got me "out o' step," as Sifers said
it did.

LV

Doc hain't, to say, no *"rollin' stone,"* and yit he
hain't no hand
Fer *'cumulatin'.—Home's* his own, and scrap o'
farmin'-land—
Enough to keep him out the way when folks is tuk
down sick
The suddentest—'most any day they want him
'special quick.

LVI

And yit Doc loves his practise; ner don't, wilful,
want to slight
No call—no matter who—how fur away—er day er
night.—
He loves his work—he loves his friends—June,
Winter, Fall, and Spring:
His *lovin'*—facts is—never ends; he loves jes'
*ever'*thing. . . .

LVII

'Cept—*keepin' books*. He never sets down no
    accounts.—He hates,
The worst of all, collectin' debts—the worst, the
    more he waits.—
I've knowed him, when at last he *had* to dun a
    man, to end
By makin' him a loan—and mad he hadn't more to
    lend.

LVIII

When Pence's Drug Store ust to be in full blast,
    they wuz some
Doc's patients got things frekantly there, charged
    to *him*, i gum!—
Doc run a bill there, don't you know, and allus when
    he squared,
He never questioned nothin',—so he had his feelin's
    spared.

LIX

Now sich as that, I hold and claim, hain't *'scusable*
    —it's not
Perfessional!—It's jes' a shame 'at Doc hisse'f
    hain't got
No better *business*-sense! That's why lots 'd respect
    him more,
And not give him the clean go-by fer *other* doctors.
    Shore!

LX

This-here Doc *Glenn,* fer instance; er this little
  jack-leg *Hall;*—
They're *business*—folks respects 'em fer their
  business more'n all
They ever knowed, er ever *will,* 'bout *medicine.*—
  Yit they
Collect their money, k-yore er kill.—They're
  business, anyway!

LXI

You ast Jake Dunn:—he's worked it out in
  figgers.—He kin show
Stastistics how Doc's airnt about *three* fortunes in
  a row,—
Ever' ten-year' hand-runnin' straight—*three* of 'em
  —*thirty* year'
'At Jake kin count and 'lucidate o' Sifer's practise
  here.

LXII

Yit—"Praise the Lord," says Doc, "we've got our
  little home!" says he—
"(It's railly *Winniferd's,* but what she owns, she
  sheers with me.)
We' got our little gyarden-spot, and peach and
  apple trees,
And stable, too, and chicken-lot, and eighteen hive'
  o' bees."

LXIII

You call it anything you please, but it's *witchcraft*
  —the power
'At Sifers has o' handlin' bees!—He'll watch 'em
  by the hour—
Mix right amongst 'em, mad and hot and swarmin'!
  —yit they won't
Sting *him,* er *want* to—'pear to not,—at least I
  know they *don't.*

LXIV

With *me* and bees they's no *p'tense* o' socialbility—
A dad-burn bee 'ud climb a fence to git a whack
  at *me!*
I s'pose no thing 'at's *got* a sting is railly satisfied
It's *sharp* enough, ontel, i jing! he's honed it on
  my hide!

LXV

And Doc he's allus had a knack *inventin'* things.—
  Dee-vised
A windlass wound its own se'f back as it run down:
  and s'prised
Their new hired girl with *clothes-line,* too, and
  clothes-pins, all in *one:*
Purt' nigh all left fer *her* to do wuz git her
  primpin' done!

LXVI

And onc't, I mind, in airly Spring, and tappin'
sugar trees,
Doc made a dad-burn little thing to sharpen *spiles*
with—these-
Here wood'-spouts 'at the peth's punched out, and
driv' in where they bore
The auger-holes. He sharpened 'bout *a million*
spiles er more!

LXVII

And Doc's the first man ever swung a *bucket* on a
tree
Instid o' *troughs;* and first man brung *grained*
sugar—so's 'at he
Could use it fer his coffee, and fer cookin', don't
you know.—
Folks come clean up from Pleasantland 'fore they'd
believe it, though!

LXVIII

And all Doc's stable-doors *on*locks and locks
theirse'ves—and gates
The same way;—all rigged up like clocks, with
pulleys, wheels, and weights,—
So, 's Doc says, "Drivin' *out,* er *in,* they'll *open;*
and they'll *then,*
All quiet-like, shet up ag'in like little gentlemen!"

LXIX

And Doc 'ud made a mighty good *detective.*—
    Neighbers all
Will testify to *that*—er *could,* ef they wuz legal call:
His theories on any crime is worth your listenin'
    to.—
And he has hit 'em, many a time, long 'fore
    established true.

LXX

At this young druggist Wenfield Pence's trial fer
    his life,
On *primy faishy* evidence o' pizonin' his wife,
Doc's testimony saved and cle'red and 'quitted him
    and freed
Him so's he never even 'peared cog-*niz*ant of the
    deed!

LXXI

The facts wuz—Sifers testified,—at inquest he had
    found
The stummick showed the woman *died* o' pizon, but
    had downed
The dos't *herse'f,*—because *amount* and *cost* o'
    drug imployed
No *druggist* would, on *no* account, 'a' lavished and
    distroyed!

LXXII

Doc tracked a blame-don burglar down, and *nailed*
the scamp, to boot,
But told him ef he'd leave the town he wouldn't
prosecute.
He traced him by a tied-up thumb-print in fresh
putty, where
Doc glazed it. Jes' *that's* how he come to track him
to his lair!

LXXIII

Doc's jes' a *leetle* too inclined, *some* thinks, to
overlook
The criminal and vicious kind we'd ort to bring to
book
And punish, 'thout no extry show o' *sympathizin'*,
where
They hain't showed none fer *us,* you know. But he
takes issue there:

LXXIV

Doc argies 'at "The Red-eyed Law," as *he* says,
"ort to learn
To lay a mighty leenient paw on deeds o' sich
concern
As only the Good Bein' knows the wherefore of,
and spreads
His hands above accused and sows His mercies on
their heads."

LXXV

Doc even holds 'at *murder* hain't no crime we got
     a right
To *hang* a man fer—claims it's *taint* o' *lunacy,* er
     quite.—
"Hold *sich* a man responsibul fer murder," Doc
     says,—"then,
When *he's* hung, where's the rope to pull them
     sound-mind jurymen?

LXXVI

"It's in a nutshell—*all* kin see," says Doc,—"it's
     cle'r the *Law's*
As ap' to err as you er me, and kill without a cause:
The man most innocent o' sin *I've* saw, er *'spect* to
     see,
Wuz servin' a life-sentence in the penitentchury."

LXXVII

And Doc's a whole hand at a *fire!*—directin' how
     and where
To set your ladders, low er higher, and what first
     duties air,—
Like formin' warter-bucket-line; and best man in
     the town
To chop holes in old roofs, and mine defective
     chimblies down:

LXXVIII

Er durin' any public crowd, mass-meetin', er big
    day,
Where ladies ortn't be allowed, as I've heerd Sifers
    say,—
When they's a suddent rush somewhere, it's Doc's
    voice, ca'm and cle'r,
Says, "Fall back, men, and give her air!—that's
    all she's faintin' fer."

LXXIX

The sorriest I ever feel fer Doc is when some show
Er circus comes to town and he'll not git a chance
    to go.
'Cause he jes' natchurly *de*lights in circuses—clean
    down
From tumblers, in their spangled tights, to trick-
    mule and Old Clown.

LXXX

And ever'body *knows* it, too, how Doc is,
    thataway! . . .
I mind a circus onc't come through—wuz there
    myse'f that day.—
Ring-master cracked his whip, you know, to start
    the ridin'—when
In runs Old Clown and hollers *"Whoa!*—Ladies
    and gentlemen

LXXXI

"Of this vast audience, I fain would make
    inquiry cle'r,
And learn, find out, and ascertain—*Is Doctor Sifers*
    here?"
And when some fool-voice bellers down: "He is!
    He's settin' in
Full view o' ye!" *"Then,"* says the Clown, *"the*
    circus may begin!"

LXXXII

Doc's got a *temper;* but, he says, he's learnt it
    which is boss,
Yit has to *watch* it, more er less. . . . I never seen
    him cross
But onc't, enough to make him swear;—milch-cow
    stepped on his toe,
And Doc ripped out *"I doggies!"*—There's the
    only case I know.

LXXXIII

Doc says that's what your temper's fer—to hold
    back out o' view,
And learn it never to occur on out ahead o' *you.*—
"You lead the way," says Sifers—"git your *temper*
    back in line—
And *furdest* back the *best,* ef it's as mean a one as
    mine!"

LXXXIV

He hates contentions—can't abide a wrangle er
    dispute
O' any kind; and he 'ull slide out of a crowd and
    skoot
Up some back-alley 'fore he'll stand and listen to a
    furse
When ary one's got upper-hand and t'other one's
    got worse.

LXXXV

Doc says: "I 'spise, when pore and weak and
    awk'ard talkers fails,
To see it's them with hardest cheek and loudest
    mouth pervails.—
A' all-one-sided quarr'l 'll make me *biassed,* mighty
    near,—
'Cause ginerly the side I take's the one I never
    hear."

LXXXVI

What 'peals to Doc the most and best is "seein'
    folks *agreed,*
And takin' ekal interest and universal heed
O' ever'body *else's* words and idies—same as we
Wuz glad and chirpy as the birds—jes' as we'd
    ort to be!"

LXXXVII

And *paterotic!* Like to git Doc started, full and fair,
About the war, and why 't'uz fit, and what wuz
    'complished there;
"And who wuz *wrong,*" says Doc, "er *right,* 't'uz
    waste o' blood and tears,
All prophesied in *Black* and *White* fer years and
    years and years!"

LXXXVIII

And then he'll likely kind o' tetch on old John
    Brown, and dwell
On what *his* warnin's wuz; and ketch his breath and
    cough, and tell
On down to Lincoln's death. And *then*—well, he
    jes' chokes and quits
With "I must go now, gentlemen!" and grabs his
    hat, and *gits!*

LXXXIX

Doc's own war-rickord wuzn't won so much in line
    o' fight
As line o' work and nussin' done the wownded, day
    and night.—
His wuz the hand, through dark and dawn, 'at
    bound their wownds, and laid
As soft as their own mother's on their forreds when
    they prayed. . . .

XC

His wuz the face they saw the first—all dim, but
    smilin' bright,
As they come to and knowed the worst, yit saw the
    old *Red-White-*
And-Blue where Doc had fixed it where they'd see
    it *wavin'* still,
Out through the open tent-flap there, er 'crost the
    winder-sill.

XCI

And some's a-limpin' round here yit—a-waitin'
    Last Review,—
'Ud give the pensions 'at they git, and pawn their
    crutches, too,
To he'p Doc out, ef he wuz pressed financial'—
    same as he
Has *allus* he'pped them when distressed—ner never
    tuk a fee.

XCII

Doc never wuz much hand to pay attention to
    p'tense
And fuss-and-feathers and display in men o' promi-
    nence:
"A railly *great* man," Sifers 'lows, "is not the
    out'ard dressed—
All uniform, salutes and bows, and swellin' out his
    chest.

XCIII

"I *met* a great man onc't," Doc says, "and shuk his
    hand," says he,
"And *he* come 'bout in *one*, I guess, o' disapp'intin'
    me—
He talked so common-like, and brought his mind so
    cle'r in view
And simple-like, I purt' nigh thought, '*I'm* best man
    o' the two!' "

XCIV

Yes-*sir!* Doc's got convictions and old-fashioned
    kind o' ways
And idies 'bout this glorious Land o' Freedom; and
    he'll raise
His hat clean off, no matter where, jes' ever' time he
    sees
The Stars and Stripes a-floatin' there and flappin'
    in the breeze.

XCV

And tunes like old "Red-White-and-Blue" 'll fairly
    drive him wild,
Played on the brass band, marchin' through the
    streets! Jes' like a child
I've saw that man, his smile jes' set, all kind o' pale
    and white,
Bareheaded, and his eyes all wet, yit dancin' with
    delight!

XCVI

And yit, that very man we see all trimbly, pale and
    wann,
Give him a case o' *surgery,* we'll see another man!—
We'll do the trimblin' then, and *we'll* git white
    around the gills—
He'll show us *nerve* o' nerves, and he 'ull show us
    skill o' skills!

XCVII

Then you could toot your horns and beat your
    drums and bang your guns,
And wave your flags and march the street, and
    charge, all Freedom's sons!—
And Sifers *then,* I bet my hat, 'ud never flinch a
    hair,
But, stiddy-handed, 'tend to that pore patient layin'
    there.

XCVIII

And Sifers' *eye's* as stiddy as that hand o' his!—
    He'll shoot
A' old-style rifle, like he has, and smallest bore, to
    boot,
With any fancy rifles made to-day, er expert shot
'At works at shootin' like a *trade*—and all *some* of
    'em's got!

XCIX

Let 'em go right out in the *woods* with Doc, and
  leave their "traps"
And blame' glass-balls and queensware-goods, and
  see how Sifers draps
A squirrel out the tallest tree.—And 'fore he fires
  he'll say
Jes' where he'll hit him—yes, sir-*ee!*. And he's hit
  thataway!

C

Let 'em go out with him, i jucks! with fishin'-pole
  and gun,—
And ekal chances, fish and ducks, and take the *rain,*
  er *sun,*
Jes' as it pours, er as it blinds the eyesight; *then* I
  guess
'At they'd acknowledge, in their minds, their
  disadvantages.

CI

And yit *he'd* be the last man out to flop his wings
  and crow
Insultin'-like, and strut about above his fallen
  foe!—
No-*sir!* the hand 'at tuk the wind out o' their sails
  'ud be
The very first they grabbed, and grinned to feel
  sich sympathy.

CII

Doc gits off now and then and takes a huntin'-trip
  somewhere
'Bout Kankakee, up 'mongst the lakes—sometimes'll
  drift round there
In his canoe a week er two; then paddle clean on
  back
By way o' old Wabash and Blue, with fish—all he
  kin pack,—

CIII

And wild ducks—some with feathers on 'em yit,
  and stuffed with grass.
And neighbors—all knows he's bin *gone*—comes
  round and gits a bass—
A great big double-breasted "rock," er "black," er
  maybe *pair*
Half fills a' ordinary crock. . . . Doc's *fish*'ll give
  out there

CIV

Long 'fore his *ducks!*—But folks'll smile and
  blandish him, and make
Him tell and *tell* things!—all the while enjoy 'em
  jes' fer sake
O' pleasin' *him;* and then turn in and la'nch him
  from the start
A-tellin' all the things ag'in they railly know by
  heart.

CV

He's jes' a *child,* 's what Sifers is! And-sir, I'd
    ruther see
That happy, childish face o' his, and puore
    simplicity,
Than any shape er style er plan o' mortals
    otherwise—
With perfect faith in God and man a-shinin' in his
    eyes.

TAMÁM

WHERE THE CHILDREN USED TO PLAY

THE old farm-home is Mother's yet and mine,
  And filled it is with plenty and to spare,—
But we are lonely here in life's decline,
  Though fortune smiles around us everywhere:
      We look across the gold
      Of the harvests, as of old—
The corn, the fragrant clover, and the hay;
      But most we turn our gaze,
      As with eyes of other days,
To the orchard where the children used to play.

O from our life's full measure
And rich hoard of worldly treasure
  We often turn our weary eyes away,
And hand in hand we wander
Down the old path winding yonder
    To the orchard where the children used to
    play.

Our sloping pasture-lands are filled with herds;
  The barn and granary-bins are bulging o'er;
The grove's a paradise of singing birds—
  The woodland brook leaps laughing by the door;
      Yet lonely, lonely still,
      Let us prosper as we will,

Our old hearts seem so empty every way—
  We can only through a mist
  See the faces we have kissed
In the orchard where the children used to play.

O from our life's full measure
And rich hoard of worldly treasure
  We often turn our weary eyes away,
And hand in hand we wander
Down the old path winding yonder
  To the orchard where the children used to
  play.

MR. FOLEY'S CHRISTMAS

There's nothing sweet in the city
But the patient lives of the poor.
            —John Boyle O'Reilly

I

SINCE pick av them I'm sore denied
    'Twixt play or work, I say,
Though it be Christmas, I decide
    I'll work whilst others play:
I'll whustle, too, wid Christmas pride
    To airn me extry pay.—
It's like the job's more glorified
    That's done a-holiday!

Dan, dip a coal in dad's pipe-bowl;
    Kate, pass me dinner-can:
Och! Mary woman, save yer sowl,
    Ye've kissed a workin'-man—
Ye have, this Christmas mornin',
    Ye've kissed a workin'-man!

57

II

Whisht, Kate an' Dan!—ten thousan' grates
  There's yon where ne'er a charm
Av childer-faces sanctuates
  The city-homes from harm:
It's cold out there the weather waits
  An' bitter whirls the storm,
But, faith! these arms av little Kate's
  'Ll kape her fayther warm!

Ay, Danny, tight me belt a mite,—
  Kate, aisy wid the can!—
Sure, I'd be comin' home to-night
  A hungry workin'-man—
D'ye moind, this Christmas avenin'—
  A howlin'-hungry man!

III

It's sorry for the boss I be,
  Wid new conthracts to sign
An' hire a sub to oversee
  Whilst he lave off an' dine:
It's sorry for the Company
  That owns the Aarie Line—
What vasht raasponshibility
  They have, compared wid mine!

There, Katy! git me t'other mitt,
    An' fetch me yon from Dan—
(Wid aich one's "Christmas" hid in it!)
    Lave go me dinner-can!—
Ye'll have me docked this mornin'—
This blessed Christmas mornin',—
    A dishgraced workin'-man!

TO SANTA CLAUS

MOST tangible of all the gods that be,
O Santa Claus—our own since Infancy!—
As first we scampered to thee—now, as then,
Take us as children to thy heart again.

Be wholly good to us, just as of old;
As a pleased father, let thine arms infold
Us, homed within the haven of thy love,
And all the cheer and wholesomeness thereof.

Thou lone reality, when O so long
Life's unrealities have wrought us wrong:
Ambition hath allured us,—fame likewise,
And all that promised honor in men's eyes.

Throughout the world's evasions, wiles, and
    shifts,
Thou only bidest stable as thy gifts:—
A grateful king re-ruleth from thy lap,
Crowned with a little tinseled soldier-cap:

A mighty general—a nation's pride—
Thou givest again a rocking-horse to ride,
And wildly glad he groweth as the grim
Old jurist with the drum thou givest him:

The sculptor's chisel, at thy mirth's command,
Is as a whistle in his boyish hand;
The painter's model fadeth utterly,
And there thou standest,—and he painteth
    thee:—

Most like a winter pippin, sound and fine
And tingling-red that ripe old face of thine,
Set in thy frosty beard of cheek and chin
As midst the snows the thaws of spring set in.

Ho! Santa Claus—our own since Infancy—
Most tangible of all the gods that be!—
As first we scampered to thee—now, as then,
Take us as children to thy heart again.

CHRISTMAS ALONG THE WIRES

Scene—Hoosier railway station, Washout Glen

Night—Interior of Telegraph Office—Single oper-
ator's table in some disorder—lunch-basket, litter
of books and sheet-music—a flute and a guitar—
Rather good-looking young man, evidently in
charge, talking to commercial traveler.

*J*UNCTION-Station—Pilot Knob—
  Say "the operator there
Is a *girl*—with auburn hair
And blue eyes, and purty, too,
As they make 'em!"—That'll do!—
They *all* know her 'long the Line—
Railroad men, from President
Of the road to section-hand!—
And she knows *us*—the whole mob
Of us *lightnin'-slingers*—Shoo!—
Brownie's got us all down fine!
Though she's *business,* understand,
Brownie she just beats the band!
Brownie she's held up that job
Five or six years anyhow—
Since her *father's* death, when all

62

The whole road decided now
Was no time for nothin' small,—
It was *Brownie's* job! Since ten
Years of age she'd been with *him*
In the office. Now, I guess,
She was sixteen, more or less—
Just a girl, but strong and trim,
And as independent, too,
And *reliable* clean through
As the old man when he died
Two mile' up the track beside
His red-light, one icy night
When the line broke down—and yet
He got there in time, you bet,
To shut off a wreck all right!
Yes, *some* life here, and romance—
Pilot Knob, though, and Roachdale,
And this little eight-by-ten
Dinky town of Washout Glen
Have to pool inhabitants
Even for enough young men
To fill out a country dance,—
All chip in on some joint-date,
And whack up and pony down
And *combine* and celebrate,—
Say, on Decoration Day—
Fourth o' July—Easter, or
Circus-Day, or *Christmas,* say—
All *three* towns, and right-o'-way
Fer two extrys,—one from here—
One down from the Knob. Well, then

Roachdale is herself again!
Like *last* Christmas, when all three
Towns collogued, and far and near
Billed things for a Christmas-Tree
At old Roachdale.   Now mark here:—
I had leave, last Holidays,
And was goin' home, you see,
Two weeks—and the Company
Sent a man to fill my place—
An old *chum* of mine, in fact,
I'd been coaxin' to arrange
Just to have his dressin'-case
And his latest music packed
And come on here for a change.
He'd been here to visit me
Once before—in *summer then,*—
Come to stay "just two or three
Days," he said—and he stayed *ten.*
When he left here *then*—Well, he
Was clean gone on Brownie—wild
And plum silly as a child!
Name—MacClintock.   Most young men
Stood 'way back when Mac was round.
Fact is, he was *fine,* you know—
Silver-tenor voice that went
Up among the stars, and sent
The girls back to higher-tone'
Dreams than they had ever known!
A good-looker—stylish—slim—
And wore clothes that no man downed—
Yes, and smoked a good cigar

And smelt right; and used to blow
A smooth flute—And a *guitar*
No man heard till he heard *him!*—
Say, some midnight serenade—
Oomh! how drippin'-sweet he played!
Boys, though, wasn't stuck on Mac
So blame' much,—especially
Roachdale operator.—He
Kind o' had the inside-track
On *all* of us, as to who
Got most talk from Brownie, when
She had nothin' else to do
But to buzz us now and then
Up and down the wires, you know;
And we'd jolly back again
'Bout some dance—and "Would she go
With *us* or her *Roachdale* beau?"
(Boys all called him "Roachy"—see?)—
Wire her, "Was she 'Happy now'?"
And "How's 'Roachy,' anyhow?"
Or, "Say, Brownie, who's the jay
You was stringin' yesterday?"
And I've sat here when this key
Shot me like a battery,
Just 'cause Brownie wired to say
That "That box o' fruit, or flowers,
That 'I'd' sent her came O. K.,—
To beguile the weary hours
Till we met again!"—Then break
Short off—for the Roachdale cuss
Callin' her, and on to us.

'Course *he'd* sent 'em—no mistake!
Lord, she kept that man awake!
Yet he kept *her* fooled: His cheek
And pure goody-goody gall
Hid from *her*—if not from all—
A quite vivid *"yellow streak."*—
Awful' jealous, don't you see?—
Felt he had a *right* to be,
Maybe, bein' *engaged.*—And they
Were engaged—that's straight.—"G A!"*—
Well: MacClintock when *he* come
Down from York to take this job,
And stopped off at Pilot Knob
For "instructions," there was some
Indications of unrest
At *Roachdale* right from the start,—
"Roachy" wasn't *awful'* smart,
Maybe, but he done his best—
With such brains as he possessed.—
Anyway he made *one* play
That was brilliant—of its kind—
And *maintained* it.—From the day
That MacClintock took my key
And I left on Number Three,
"Roachy" opened up on Mac
And just *loved* him!—purred and whined
'Cross the wires how tickled he
Was to hear that *Mac* was back,
And how glad the *girls* would be
And the young-folks everywhere,

---

* Telegraphers' abbreviation for "Go ahead."

As he'd reason to believe,—
And how, even *then*, they were
"Shapin' things at old Roachdale
For a blow-out, Christmas-eve,
That would turn all others pale!—
First a *Christmas-Tree,* at old
Armory Hall, and then the floor
Cleared, and—"

    "Come in out the cold!"
Breaks MacClintock—"Don't I know?—
Dancin', say, from ten till four—
Maybe *daylight* 'fore we go!—
With Ben Custer's Band to pour
Music out in swirlin' rills
And back-tides o' waltz-quadrilles
Level with the window-sills!—
Roachy, you're a *bird!*—But, say,—
How am I to get away
From the office here?"

    Well, then
"Roachy" wires him back again:—
"That's O. K.,—I call a *man*
Up from *Dunkirk;* got it all
Fixed.—So Christmas-eve, you can
Collar the seven-thirty train
For Roachdale—the same that *he*
Comes on.—Leave your office-key
In the door: he'll do the rest."
Then "old Roachy" rattled through
A long list of who'd be there,—
Boys and girls that Mac knew best—

One name, though, that had no bare
Little mention anywhere!
Then he shut off, as he said,
For his supper. . . . About ten
Minutes *Mac* was *called again*—
With a click that flushed him red
As the signal-flag—and then
Came like music in the air—
"Yes, and *Brownie* will be there!"

———

Folks tell *me,* that Christmas-Tree,
Dance and whole blame' jamboree,
Looked like it was goin' to be
A blood-curdlin' tragedy.
People 'long the *roads,* you know—
Well, they've had experience
With all sorts of *accidents,*
And they've learnt *some* things,—and so
When an accident or wreck
Happens, they know *some man's "break"*
Is responsible, and hence—
Well—they want to *break* his *neck!*
So it happened, Christmas-eve,
At *Roachdale,*—MacClintock there
Cocked back in the barber-chair
At eight-forty, and no train
Down yet from the Knob, and it
Due at eight-ten sharp.   The strain
Was a-showin' quite a bit

On the general crowd; and when
Purty soon the rumor spread—
Wreck had probably occurred—
Some one said somebody said
That he'd heard somebody say,
"*Operator* at the *Glen*
Was to blame for the delay—
Fact is, he had run away
From his office—Even then
Was in *Roachdale*—there to be
Present at the Christmas-Tree
And the 'shindig' afterward,
Wreck or *no* wreck!" . . . *Mac* sat up,
Whiter than the shavin'-cup. . . .
Back of *his* face in the glass
He stared into he could see
A big crowd there—and, alas!
Not in all that threatening throng
One friend's face of sympathy—
One friend knowin' right from wrong!
He got on his feet—erect—
Nervy;—faced the crowd, and then
Said: "*I* am MacClintock from
The Glen-office, and I've come
To your Christmas festival
By request of one that all
Of you honor, gentlemen,—
Your most trusted citizen—
Your own operator here
At the station-office—where
He'll acquit *me* of neglect,

And will make it plain and clear
Who the sub. is he sent there
To my office at the Glen—
Or, if *not* one there,—who then
Is indeed the criminal? . . .
I am going now to call
On him.—Join me, gentlemen—
I insist you come with me."
Well, a sense of some respect
Caught 'em,—and they followed, all,
Silently, though sullenly.

Fortunately, half a square
Brought 'em to the station and
The crowd there that packed the small
Waiting-room on every hand,
With a kind o' general stand
Round the half-door window through
Which "old Roachy," in full view,
Sat there, smilin' in a sick
Sort o' way, yet gloryin', too,
In the work he had to do.
Mac worked closer, breathin' quick
At the muttered talk of some
Of the toughest of the crowd;
Till, above the growl and hum
Of the ominous voices, he
Heard the click of "Roachy's" key,—
And his heart beat 'most out 'loud
As he heard him wirin':—"Yes,
Trouble down at *Glen*, I guess.

Glen's fool-operator *here*—
What's-his-name?—MacClintock.—Fear
Mob will hang him.—Mob knows he
Left his office.—And no doubt
Wreck there on account of it.
People worked-up here—and shout
Now and then to 'Take him out!'—
'Hang him!'—and so forth." . . . Mac lit
Through the half-door window at
"Roachy's" table like a cat:—
He was *white,* but *"Roachy's"* face
Made a brunette out o' *his!* . . .
Mac had pinned him in his chair
Helpless—and a message there
Clickin' back from Pilot Knob.—
"Tell these people, word-for-word,"
Mac says, "what this message is!—
"Tell 'em.—Hear me?" "Roachy" heard
And obeyed:—" 'We sized your job
On MacClintock.—*Knob* here sent
A sub. there.—And all O. K.
At Glen-office.—Tie-up *here*—
One hour's wait—all fault of *mine.*
"Hang MacClintock," did you say?
"Hang MacClintock?"—Certainly,—
Hang him on the Christmas-Tree,
With a label on for *me,*—
I'll be there on Number Nine.' "

TO THE BOY WITH A COUNTRY

DAN WALLINGFORD

DAN WALLINGFORD, my jo Dan!—
  Though but a child in years,
Your patriot spirit thrills the land
  And wakens it to cheers,—
You lift the flag—you roll the drums—
  We hear the bugle blow,—
Till all our hearts are one with yours,
  Dan Wallingford, my jo!

To — ALMON KEEFER.

THIS first book that I ever knew
Was read aloud to me by you. —
Friend of my boyhood, therefore take
It back from me, for old=times' sake —
The selfsame "Tales" first read to me,
Under "the old sweet=apple=tree,"
Ere I myself could read such great
Big words, — but listened all elate,
At your interpreting, until
Brain, heart and soul were all athrill
With wonder, awe, and sheer excess
Of wildest childish happiness.

So take the book again — Forget
All else, — long years, lost hopes, regret;
Sighs for the joys we ne'er attain,
Prayers we have lifted all in vain,
Tears for the faces seen no more,
Once as the roses at the door! . . .
Take the Enchanted book — And, lo,
On grassy swards of Long Ago,
Sprawl out again, beneath the shade
The breezy old=home orchard made,
The veriest barefoot boy indeed. —
And I will listen as you read.

— James Whitcomb Riley.

X=mas
1895

AT CROWN HILL

LEAVE him here in the fresh greening grasses
    and trees
And the symbols of love, and the solace of these—
The saintly white lilies and blossoms he keeps
In endless caress as he breathlessly sleeps.
The tears of our eyes wrong the scene of his rest,
For the sky's at its clearest—the sun's at its best—
The earth at its greenest—its wild bud-and-bloom
At its sweetest—and sweetest its honey'd perfume.
    Home! home!—Leave him here in his lordly
        estate,
    And with never a tear as we turn from the gate!

Turn back to the home that will know him no
        more,—
The vines at the window—the sun through the
        door.—
Nor sound of his voice, nor the light of his
        face! . . .
But the birds will sing on, and the rose, in his place,
Will tenderly smile till we daringly feign
He is home with us still, though the tremulous rain

Of our tears reappear, and again all is bloom,
And all prayerless we sob in the long-darkened
    room.
    Heaven portions it thus—the old mystery dim,—
    It is midnight to us—it is morning to him.

SNOW IN THE AIR

SNOW is in the air—
　　Chill in blood and vein,—
Winter everywhere
　　Save in heart and brain!
Ho! the happy year will be
　　Mimic as we've found it,—
Head of it—and you, and me—
　　With the holly round it!

Frost and sleet, alack!—
　　Wind as bleak as wrath
Whips our faces back
　　As we foot the path;—
But the year—from there to here—
　　Copy as we've found it,—
Heart up—like the head, my dear,
　　With the holly round it!

THE NAME OF OLD GLORY

1898

I

OLD Glory! say, who,
    By the ships and the crew,
And the long, blended ranks of the gray and the
      blue,—
Who gave you, Old Glory, the name that you bear
With such pride everywhere
As you cast yourself free to the rapturous air
And leap out full-length, as we're wanting you
      to?—
Who gave you that name, with the ring of the same,
And the honor and fame so becoming to you?—
Your stripes stroked in ripples of white and of red,
With your stars at their glittering best overhead—
By day or by night
Their delightfulest light
Laughing down from their little square heaven of
      blue!—
Who gave you the name of Old Glory?—say, who—
    Who gave you the name of Old Glory?

The old banner lifted, and faltering then
In vague lisps and whispers fell silent again.

76

II

Old Glory,—speak out!—we are asking about
How you happened to "favor" a name, so to say,
That sounds so familiar and careless and gay
As we cheer it and shout in our wild breezy way—
We—the *crowd,* every man of us, calling you that—
We—Tom, Dick, and Harry—each swinging his hat
And hurrahing "Old Glory!" like you were our kin,
When—*Lord!*—we all know we're as common as
     sin!
And yet it just seems like you *humor* us all
And waft us your thanks, as we hail you and fall
Into line, with you over us, waving us on
Where our glorified, sanctified betters have gone.—
And this is the reason we're wanting to know—
(And we're wanting it *so!*—
Where our own fathers went we are willing to
     go.)—
Who gave you the name of Old Glory—Oho!—
    Who gave you the name of Old Glory?

The old flag unfurled with a billowy thrill
For an instant, then wistfully sighed and was still.

III

Old Glory: the story we're wanting to hear
Is what the plain facts of your christening were,—
For your name—just to hear it,
Repeat it, and cheer it, 's a tang to the spirit

As salt as a tear;—
And seeing you fly, and the boys marching by,
There's a shout in the throat and a blur in the eye
And an aching to live for you always—or die,
If, dying, we still keep you waving on high.
And so, by our love
For you, floating above,
And the scars of all wars and the sorrows thereof,
Who gave you the name of Old Glory, and why
     Are we thrilled at the name of Old Glory?

Then the old banner leaped, like a sail in the blast,
And fluttered an audible answer at last.—

IV

And it spake, with a shake of the voice, and it
     said :—
By the driven snow-white and the living blood-red
Of my bars, and their heaven of stars overhead—
By the symbol conjoined of them all, skyward cast,
As I float from the steeple, or flap at the mast,
Or droop o'er the sod where the long grasses nod,—
My name is as old as the glory of God.
    . . . So I came by the name of Old Glory.

ONE WITH A SONG

FRANK L. STANTON

HE sings: and his song is heard,
　　Pure as a joyous prayer,
Because he sings of the simple things—
　　The fields, and the open air,
The orchard-bough, and the mocking-bird,
　　And the blossoms everywhere.

He sings of a wealth we hold
　　In common ownership—
The wildwood nook, and the laugh of the
　　　　brook,
　　And the dewdrop's drip and drip,
The love of the lily's heart of gold,
　　And the kiss of the rose's lip.

The universal heart
　　Leans listening to his lay
That glints and gleams with the glimmering
　　　　dreams
　　Of children at their play—
A lay as rich with unconscious art
　　As the first song-bird's of May.

Ours every rapturous tone
  Of every song of glee,
Because his voice makes native choice
  Of Nature's harmony—
So that his singing seems our own,
  And ours his ecstasy.

Steadfastly, bravely glad
  Above all earthly stress,
He lifts his line to heights divine,
  And, singing, ever says,—
This is a better world than bad—
  God's love is limitless.

He sings: and his song is heard,
  Pure as a joyous prayer,
Because he sings of the simple things—
  The fields, and the open air,
The orchard-bough, and the mocking-bird,
  And the blossoms everywhere.

INDIANA

OUR Land—our Home!—the common home
    indeed
  Of soil-born children and adopted ones—
  The stately daughters and the stalwart sons
Of Industry:—All greeting and godspeed!
O home to proudly live for, and, if need
  Be, proudly die for, with the roar of guns
  Blent with our latest prayer.—So died men
    once. . . .
Lo, Peace! . . . As we look on the land THEY
    freed—
Its harvests all in ocean-overflow
  Poured round autumnal coasts in billowy gold—
  Its corn and wine and balmèd fruits and
    flow'rs,—
We know the exaltation that they know
  Who now, steadfast inheritors, behold
    The Land Elysian, marveling "This is ours!"

CHRISTMAS AFTERTHOUGHT

AFTER a thoughtful, almost painful pause,
Bub sighed, "I'm sorry fer old *Santy Claus:*—
They *wuz* no Santy Claus, ner *couldn't* be,
When *he* wuz ist a little boy like me!"

THE CHRISTMAS LONG AGO

COME, sing a hale Heigh-ho
    For the Christmas long ago!—
When the old log-cabin homed us
    From the night of blinding snow,
    Where the rarest joy held reign,
    And the chimney roared amain,
With the firelight like a beacon
    Through the frosty window-pane.

Ah! the revel and the din
From without and from within,
The blend of distant sleigh-bells
    With the plinking violin;
    The muffled shrieks and cries—
    Then the glowing cheeks and eyes—
The driving storm of greetings,
    Gusts of kisses and surprise.

EXCEEDING ALL

LONG life's a lovely thing to know,
    With lovely health and wealth, forsooth,
And lovely name and fame—But O
    The loveliness of Youth!

CLAUDE MATTHEWS

STEADFASTLY from his childhood's earliest
hour—
From simplest country life to state and power—
His worth has known advancement,—each new
height
A newer glory in his fellow's sight.

So yet his happy fate—though mute the breath
Of thronging multitudes and thundrous cheers,—
Faith sees him raised still higher, through our
tears,
By this divine promotion of his death.

THE SERMON OF THE ROSE

WILFUL we are, in our infirmity
  Of childish questioning and discontent.
Whate'er befalls us is divinely meant—
Thou Truth the clearer for thy mystery!
Make us to meet what is or is to be
  With fervid welcome, knowing it is sent
  To serve us in some way full excellent,
Though we discern it all belatedly.
The rose buds, and the rose blooms, and the rose
  Bows in the dews, and in its fulness, lo,
    Is in the lover's hand,—then on the breast
Of her he loves,—and there dies.—And who knows
  What fate of all a rose may undergo
    Is fairest, dearest, sweetest, loveliest?

Nay, we are children: we will not mature.
  A blessed gift must seem a theft; and tears
  Must storm our eyes when but a joy appears
In drear disguise of sorrow; and how poor
We seem when we are richest,—most secure
  Against all poverty the lifelong years
  We yet must waste in childish doubts and fears
That, in despite of reason, still endure!

Alas! the sermon of the rose we will
  Not wisely ponder; nor the sobs of grief
    Lulled into sighs of rapture, nor the cry
Of fierce defiance that again is still.
  Be patient—patient with our frail belief,
    And stay it yet a little ere we die.

O opulent life of ours, though dispossessed
  Of treasure after treasure! Youth most fair
  Went first, but left its priceless coil of hair—
Moaned over, sleepless nights, kissed and caressed
Through drip and blur of tears the tenderest.
  And next went Love—the ripe rose glowing
      there,
  Her very sister! . . . *It* is here, but where
Is *she,* of all the world the first and best?
And yet how sweet the sweet earth after rain—
  How sweet the sunlight on the garden-wall
    Across the roses—and how sweetly flows
The limpid yodel of the brook again!
  And yet—and yet how sweeter, after all,
    The smoldering sweetness of a dead red rose!

THE ONWARD TRAIL

MYRON W. REED, DENVER, JANUARY 30, 1899

JUST as of old,—with fearless foot
   And placid face and resolute,
He takes the faint, mysterious trail
That leads beyond our earthly hail.

We would cry, as in last farewell,
But that his hand waves, and a spell
Is laid upon our tongues: and thus
He takes unworded leave of us.

And it is fitting:—As he fared
Here with us, so is he prepared
For any fortuning the night
May hold for him beyond our sight.

The moon and stars they still attend
His wandering footsteps to the end,—
He did not question, nor will we,
Their guidance and security.

88

So, never parting word nor cry:—
We feel, with him, that by and by
Our onward trails will meet and then
Merge and be ever one again.

TO LESLEY

BURNS sang of bonny Lesley
  As she gaed o'er the border,—
Gaed like vain Alexander,
To spread her conquests farther.

I sing another Lesley,
Wee girlie, more alluring,
Who stays at home, the wise one,
Her conquests there securing.

A queen, too, is my Lesley,
And gracious, though blood-royal,
My heart her throne, her kingdom,
And I a subject loyal.

Long shall you reign, my Lesley,
My pet, my darling dearie,
For love, oh, little sweetheart,
Grows never old or weary.

THE NATURALIST

OLIVER DAVIE

IN gentlest worship has he bowed
  To Nature. Rescued from the crowd
And din of town and thoroughfare,
He turns him from all worldly care
Unto the sacred fastness of
The forests, and the peace and love
That breathes there prayer-like in the breeze
And coo of doves in dreamful trees—
Their tops in laps of sunshine laid,
Their lower boughs all slaked with shade.

With head uncovered has he stood,
Hearing the Spirit of the Wood—
Hearing aright the Master speak
In trill of bird, and warbling creek;
In lisp of reeds, or rainy sigh
Of grasses as the loon darts by—
Hearing aright the storm and lull,
And all earth's voices wonderful,—
Even this hail an unknown friend
Lifts will he hear and comprehend.

HER WAITING FACE

IN some strange place
 Of long-lost lands he finds her waiting
   face—
Comes marveling upon it, unaware,
Set moonwise in the midnight of her hair.

BLOOMS OF MAY

BUT yesterday! . . . .
O blooms of May,
And summer roses—Where-away?
O stars above,
And lips of love
And all the honeyed sweets thereof!

O lad and lass
And orchard pass,
And briered lane, and daisied grass!
O gleam and gloom,
And woodland bloom,
And breezy breaths of all perfume!—

No more for me
Or mine shall be
Thy raptures—save in memory,—
No more—no more—
Till through the Door
Of Glory gleam the days of yore.

A SONG OF THE ROAD

O I will walk with you, my lad, whichever
  way you fare,
You'll have me, too, the side o' you, with heart as
  light as air;
No care for where the road you take's a-leadin'—
  *any*where,—
It can but be a joyful ja'nt the whilst *you* journey
  there.
The road you take's the path o' love, an' that's the
  bridth o' two—
And I will walk with you, my lad—O I will walk
  with you.

  Ho! I will walk with you, my lad,
   Be weather black or blue
  Or roadsides frost or dew, my lad—
   O I will walk with you.

Ay, glad, my lad, I'll walk with you, whatever winds
  may blow,
Or summer blossoms stay our steps, or blinding
  drifts of snow;
The way that you set face and foot's the way that I
  will go,

94

And brave I'll be, abreast o' you, the Saints and
    Angels know!
With loyal hand in loyal hand, and one heart made
    o' two,
Through summer's gold, or winter's cold, it's I
    will walk with you.

      Sure, I will walk with you, my lad,
        As love ordains me to,—
      To Heaven's door, and through, my lad,
        O I will walk with you.

THE ENDURING

A MISTY memory—faint, far away
And vague and dim as childhood's long-lost
    day—
Forever haunts and holds me with a spell
Of awe and wonder indefinable:—
A grimy old engraving tacked upon
A shoe-shop wall.—An ancient temple, drawn
Of crumbling granite, sagging portico,
And gray, forbidding gateway, grim as woe;
And o'er the portal, cut in antique line,
The words—cut likewise in this brain of mine—
    "Wouldst have a friend?—Wouldst know what
        friend is best?
    Have GOD thy friend: He passeth all the rest."

Again the old shoemaker pounds and pounds
Resentfully, as the loud laugh resounds
And the coarse jest is bandied round the throng
That smokes about the smoldering stove; and long,
Tempestuous disputes arise, and then—
Even as all like discords—die again;

96

The while a barefoot boy more gravely heeds
The quaint old picture, and tiptoeing reads
There in the rainy gloom the legend o'er
The lowering portal of the old church door—
    "Wouldst have a friend?—Wouldst know what
        friend is best?
    Have GOD thy friend: He passeth all the rest."

So older—older—older, year by year,
The boy has grown, that now, an old man here,
He seems a part of Allegory, where
He stands before Life as the old print there—
Still awed, and marveling what light must be
Hid by the door that bars Futurity:—
Though, ever clearer than with eyes of youth,
He reads with his *old* eyes—and tears forsooth—
    "Wouldst have a friend?—Wouldst know what
        friend is best?
    Have GOD thy friend: He passeth all the rest."

A HUMBLE SINGER

A MODEST singer, with meek soul and
heart,
Sat, yearning that his art
Might but inspire and suffer him to sing
Even the simplest thing.

And as he sang thus humbly, came a Voice:—
"All mankind shall rejoice,
Hearing thy pure and simple melody
Sing on immortally."

THE NOBLEST SERVICE

DR. WYCKLIFFE SMITH, LATE SURGEON 161ST REGI-
MENT INDIANA VOLUNTEERS, DELPHI,
DECEMBER 29, 1899

IF all his mourning friends unselfishly
   Might speak, high over grief, in one accord,
What voice of joy were lifted to the Lord
For having lent our need such ministry
As this man's life has ever proved to be!
   Yea, even through battle-crash of gun and sword
   His steadfast step still found the pathway toward
The noblest service paid Humanity.
O ye to whose rich firesides he has brought
   A richer light! O watcher at the door
      Of the lone cabin! O kindred! Comrades!—
         all!
Since universal good he dreamed and wrought,
   Be brave, to pleasure him, as, on before,
      He leads us, answering Glory's highest call.

OLD MAN WHISKERY-WHEE-KUM-WHEEZE

OLD Man Whiskery-Whee-Kum-Wheeze
Lives 'way up in the leaves o' trees.
An' wunst I slipped up-stairs to play
In Aunty's room, while she 'uz away;
An' I clumbed up in her cushion-chair
An' ist peeked out o' the winder there;
An' there I saw—wite out in the trees—
Old Man Whiskery-Whee-Kum-Wheeze!

An' Old Man Whiskery-Whee-Kum-Wheeze
Would bow an' bow, with the leaves in the breeze,
An' waggle his whiskers an' raggledy hair,
An' bow to me in the winder there!
An' I'd peek out, an' he'd peek in
An' waggle his whiskers an' bow ag'in,
Ist like the leaves 'u'd wave in the breeze—
Old Man Whiskery-Whee-Kum-Wheeze!

An' Old Man Whiskery-Whee-Kum-Wheeze,
Seem-like, says to me: "See my bees
A-bringin' my dinner? An' see my cup
O' locus'-blossoms they've plum filled up?"

100

An' *"Um-yum, honey!"* wuz last he said,
An' waggled his whiskers an' bowed his head;
An' I yells, "Gimme some, won't you, please,
Old Man Whiskery-Whee-Kum-Wheeze?"

LITTLE-GIRL-TWO-LITTLE-GIRLS

I'M twins, I guess, 'cause my Ma say
  I'm two little girls. An' one o' me
    Is *Good* little girl; an' th' other 'n' she
    Is *Bad little girl as she can be!*
An' Ma say so, 'most ever' day.
An' she's the *funniest* Ma! 'Cause when
    My Doll won't mind, and I ist cry,
    W'y, nen my Ma she sob an' sigh,
    An' say, "Dear *Good* little girl, good-by!—
Bad little girl's comed here again!"

Last time 'at Ma act' thataway,
    I cried all to myse'f a while
    Out on the steps, an' nen I smile,
    An' git my Doll all fix' in style,
An' go in where Ma's at, an' say:
    "Morning to you, Mommy dear!
    Where's that Bad little girl wuz here?
    Bad little girl's goned clean away,
    An' Good little girl's comed back to stay."

THE PENALTY OF GENIUS

WHEN little 'Pollus Morton he's
  A-go' to speak a piece, w'y, nen
The Teacher smiles an' says 'at she's
  Most proud, of all her little men
An' women in her school—'cause 'Poll
He allus speaks the best of all.

An' nen she'll pat him on the cheek,
  An' hold her finger up at you
Before he speak'; an' *when* he speak'
  It's ist some piece *she* learn' him to!
'Cause he's her favor-ite. . . . An' she
Ain't pop'lar as she *ust* to be!

When 'Pollus Morton speaks, w'y, nen
  Ist all the other childern knows
They're smart as him an' smart-again!—
  Ef they *can't* speak an' got fine clo'es,
Their Parunts loves 'em more'n 'Poll-
Us Morton, Teacher, speech, an' all!

A PARENT REPRIMANDED

SOMETIMES I think 'at Parunts does
Things ist about as bad as *us*—
Wite 'fore our vurry eyes, at that!
Fer one time Pa he scold' my Ma
'Cause he can't find his hat;
An' she ist *cried,* she did! An' I
Says, "Ef you scold my Ma
Ever again an' make her cry,
W'y, you shan't *be* my Pa!"
An' nen he laugh' an' find his hat
Ist wite where Ma she said it's at!

IN FERVENT PRAISE OF PICNICS

PICNICS is fun 'at's purty hard to beat.
    I purt' nigh ruther go to them than *eat*.—
I purt' nigh ruther go to them than go
With our Char*lot*ty to the Trick-Dog Show!

THE HOME-VOYAGE

GENERAL HENRY W. LAWTON——FELL AT SAN MATEO,
DECEMBER 19, 1899. IN STATE, INDIAN-
APOLIS, FEBRUARY 6, 1900

BEAR with us, O Great Captain, if our pride
    Show equal measure with our grief's excess
  In greeting you in this your helplessness
To countermand our vanity or hide
Your stern displeasure that we thus had tried
    To praise you, knowing praise was your distress:
    But this home-coming swells our hearts no less—
Because for love of home you proudly died.
Lo! then, the cable, fathoms 'neath the keel
    That shapes your course, is eloquent of you;
    The old flag, too, at half-mast overhead—
We doubt not that its gale-kissed ripples feel
    A prouder sense of red and white and blue,—
    The stars—Ah, God, were *they* interpreted!

In strange lands were your latest honors won—
    In strange wilds, with strange dangers all beset;
    With rain, like tears, the face of day was wet,
As rang the ambushed foeman's fateful gun:

106

And as you felt your final duty done,
  We feel *that* glory thrills your spirit yet,—
  When at the front, in swiftest death, you met
The patriot's doom and best reward in one.
And so the tumult of that island war,
  At last, for you, is stilled forevermore—
    Its scenes of blood blend white as ocean foam
On your rapt vision as you sight afar
  The sails of peace, and from that alien shore
    The proud ship bears you on your voyage
      home.

Or rough or smooth the wave, or lowering day
  Or starlit sky—you hold, by native right,
  Your high tranquillity—the silent might
Of the true hero—so you led the way
To victory through stormiest battle-fray,
  Because your followers, high above the fight,
  Heard your soul's lightest whisper bid them smite
For God and man and space to kneel and pray.
And thus you cross the seas unto your own
  Beloved land, convoyed with honors meet,
    Saluted as your home's first heritage—
Nor salutation from your State alone,
  But *all* the States, gathered in mighty fleet,
    Dip colors as you move to anchorage.

TO THE QUIET OBSERVER

DEAR old friend of us all in need
    Who know the worth of a friend indeed,
How rejoiced are we all to learn
    Of your glad return.

We who have missed your voice so long—
Even as March might miss the song
Of the sugar-bird in the maples when
    They're tapped again.

Even as the memory of these
Blended sweets,—the sap of the trees
And the song of the birds, and the old camp too,
    We think of you.

Hail to you, then, with welcomes deep
As grateful hearts may laugh or weep!—
You give us not only the bird that sings,
    But all good things.

108

PROEM TO "HOME-FOLKS"

YOU Home-Folks:—Aid your grateful
        guest—
Bear with his pondering, wandering ways:
When idlest he is busiest,
    Being a dreamer of the days.

Humor his silent, absent moods—
    His restless quests along the shores
Of the old creek, wound through the woods,
    The haws, papaws, and sycamores:

The side-path home—the back-way past
    The old pump and the dipper there;
The afternoon of dreamy June—
    The old porch, and the rocking-chair.

Yea, bear with him a little space—
    His heart must smolder on a while
Ere yet it flames out in his face
    A wholly tearless smile.

OUR BOYHOOD HAUNTS

HO! I'm going back where
 We were youngsters.—Meet me there,
Dear old barefoot chum, and we
Will be as we used to be,—
Lawless rangers up and down
The old creek beyond the town—
Little sunburnt gods at play,
Just as in that far-away:—
Water nymphs, all unafraid,
Shall smile at us from the brink
Of the old mill-race and wade
Tow'rd us as we kneeling drink
At the spring our boyhood knew,
Pure and clear as morning-dew:
And, as we are rising there,
Doubly dow'r'd to hear and see,
We shall thus be made aware
Of an eery piping, heard
High above the happy bird
In the hazel: And then we,
Just across the creek, shall see
(Hah! the goaty rascal!) Pan

Hoof it o'er the sloping green,
Mad with his own melody,
Ay, and (bless the beasty man!)
Stamping from the grassy soil
Bruisèd scents of fleur-de-lis,
Boneset, mint, and pennyroyal.

UNCLE SIDNEY'S LOGIC

PA wunst he scold' an' says to me,—
    "Don't *play* so much, but try
To *study* more, and nen you'll be
    A great man, by an' by."
Nen Uncle Sidney says, "You let
    Him *be* a boy an' play.—
The greatest man on earth, I bet,
    'Ud trade with him to-day!"

HIS LOVE OF HOME

" AS love of native land," the old man said,
      "Er stars and stripes a-wavin' overhead,
Er nearest kith-and-kin, er daily bread,
A Hoosier's love is fer the old homestead."

TO "UNCLE REMUS"

WE love your dear old face and voice—
We're *all* Miss Sally's Little Boys,
Climbin' your knee,
In ecstasy,
Rejoicin' in your Creeturs' joys
And trickery.

The Lord who made the day and night,
He made the Black man and the White;
So, in like view,
We hold it true
That He hain't got no favor*ite*—
Onless it's you.

THE BALLADE OF THE COMING RAIN

WHEN the morning swoons in its highest heat,
  And the sunshine dims, and no dark shade
Streaks the dust of the dazzling street,
  And the long straw splits in the lemonade;
  When the circus lags in a sad parade,
And the drum throbs dull as a pulse of pain,
  And the breezeless flags hang limp and frayed—
O then is the time to look for rain.

When the man on the watering-cart bumps by,
  Trilling the air of an old fife-tune,
With a dull, soiled smile, and one shut eye,
  Lost in a dream of the afternoon;
  When the awning sags like a lank balloon,
And a thick sweat stands on the window-pane,
  And a five-cent fan is a priceless boon—
O then is the time to look for rain.

When the goldfish tank is a grimy gray,
  And the dummy stands at the clothing-store
With a cap pulled on in a rakish way,
  And a rubber-coat with the 'hind before;
  When the man in the barber chair flops o'er
And the chin he wags has a telltale stain,
  And the bootblack lurks at the open door—
O then is the time to look for rain.

115

TO THE JUDGE

A VOICE FROM THE INTERIOR OF OLD HOOP-POLE
TOWNSHIP

FRIEND of my earliest youth,
  Can't you arrange to come down
And visit a fellow out here in the woods—
  Out of the dust of the town?
Can't you forget you're a Judge
  And put by your dolorous frown
And tan your wan face in the smile of a friend—
  Can't you arrange to come down?

Can't you forget for a while
  The arguments prosy and drear,—
To lean at full-length in indefinite rest
  In the lap of the greenery here?
Can't you kick over "the Bench,"
  And "husk" yourself out of your gown
To dangle your legs where the fishing is good—
  Can't you arrange to come down?

Bah! for your office of State!
  And bah! for its technical lore!
What does our President, high in his chair,
  But wish himself low as before!

116

Pick between peasant and king,—
  Poke your bald head through a crown
Or shadow it here with the laurels of Spring!—
  Can't you arrange to come down?

"Judge it" out *here,* if you will,—
  The birds are in session by dawn;
You can draw, not *complaints,* but a sketch of the
    hill
  And a breath that your betters have drawn;
You can open your heart, like a case,
  To a jury of kine, white and brown,
And their verdict of "Moo" will just satisfy you!—
  Can't you arrange to come down?

Can't you arrange it, old Pard?—
  Pigeonhole Blackstone and Kent!—
Here we have "Breitmann," and Ward,
  Twain, Burdette, Nye, and content!
Can't you forget you're a Judge
  And put by your dolorous frown
And tan your wan face in the smile of a friend—
  Can't you arrange to come down?

A WHOLLY UNSCHOLASTIC OPINION

PLAIN hoss-sense in poetry-writin'
    Would jes' knock sentiment a-kitin'!
Mostly poets is all star-gazin'
And moanin' and groanin' and paraphrasin'!

A SHORT'NIN' BREAD SONG—PIECED OUT

BEHINE de hen-house, on my knees,
  Thought I hearn a chickin sneeze—
Sneezed so hard wi' de whoopin'-cough
I thought he'd sneeze his blame' head off.

CHORUS

Fotch dat dough fum the kitchin-shed—
Rake dem coals out hot an' red—
Putt on de oven an' putt on de led,—
Mammy's gwineter cook some short'nin' bread.

O I' got a house in Baltimo'—
Street-kyars run right by my do'—
Street-kyars run right by my gate,
Hit's git up soon an' set up late.

(CHORUS)

De raincrow hide in some ole tree
An' holler out, all hoarse, at me—
Sayes, "When I sing, de rain hit po'
So's you ain't 'bleedged to plow no mo'!"

(CHORUS)

119

Ole man Toad, on High-low Hill,
He steal my dram an' drink his fill,—
Heels in the path, an' toes in the grass—
Hit ain't de fus' time an' shain't be de las'!

(CHORUS)

When corn-plantin' done come roun',
Blackbird own de whole plowed-groun',—
Corn in de grain, as I've hearn said,
Dat's de blackbird's short'nin' bread.

(CHORUS)

De sweetes' chune what evah I heard
Is de sairanade o' de mockin'-bird;
Whilse de mou'nfullest an' de least I love
Is de Sund'y-song o' de ole woods-dove.

(CHORUS)

I nevah ain't know, outside o' school,
A smartah mare dan my ole mule,—
I holler "Wo," an' she go "gee,"
Des lak, de good Lord chast'nin' me.

(CHORUS)

Hit's no houn'-pup I taken to raise
Hain't nevah jes'ly airn' my praise:
De mo' cawn-pone I feed dat pup,
De mo' he des won't fattnin up.

(CHORUS)

I hangs a hoss-shoe ovah my head,
An' I keeps a' ole sieve under de bed,
So, quinchiquently, I sleep soun',
Wid no ole witches pester'n' roun'.

(CHORUS)

I jine de chu'ch las' Chuesday night,
But when Sis' Jane ain't treat me right
I 'low her chu'ch ain' none o' mine,
So I 'nounce to all I done on-jine.

(CHORUS)

THE UNHEARD

I

ONE in the musical throng
    Stood forth with his violin;
And warm was his welcome, and long
    The later applause and the din.—
He had uttered, with masterful skill,
    A melody hailed of men;
And his own blood leapt a-thrill,
      As they thundered again.

II

Another stood forth.—And a rose
    Bloomed in her hair—likewise
One at her tremulous throat—
    And a *rapture* bloomed in her eyes.
Tempests of cheers upon cheers,
    Praises to last a life long;
Roses in showers of tears—
      All for her song.

III

One sat apart and alone,
  Her lips clasped close and straight,
Uttering never a tone
  That the World might hear, elate—
Uttering never a low
  Murmurous verse nor a part
Of the veriest song—But O
  The song in her heart!

EQUITY—?

THE meanest man I ever saw
    Allus kep' inside o' the law;
And ten-times better fellers I've knowed
The blame' gran'-jury's sent over the road.

MOONSHINER'S SERENADE

THE night's blind-black, an' I 'low the stars's
 All skeered at that-air dog's bow-wows!
I sensed the woods-road, clumb the bars,
 An' arrove here, tromplin' over cows.
The mist hangs thick enough to cut,
 But there's her light a-glimmerin' through
The mornin'-glories, twisted shut—
 An' shorely there's her shadder too!

  Ho! hit's good night,
  My Beauty-Bright!
  The moon cain't match your can'le-light—
  Your can'le-light with you cain't shine,
  Lau-ree! Lady-love! tiptoe-fine!

Oomh! how them roses soaks the air!—
 Thess drenched with mist an' renched with
  dew!
They's a smell o' plums, too, 'round somewhere—
 An' I kin smell ripe apples, too.
Mix all them sweet things into one,—
 Yer roses, fruit, an' flower an' vine,
Yit I'll say, "No, I don't choose **none,**
 Ef I kin git that gal of mine!"

Ho! hit's good night,
My Beauty-Bright!
Primp a while, an' blow out the light—
Putt me in your prayers, an' then
I'll be twic't as good-again!

THE EDGE OF THE WIND

YE stars in ye skies seem twinkling
    In icicles of light,
And ye edge of ye wind cuts keener
    Than ever ye sword-edge might;
Ye footsteps crunch in ye courtway,
    And ye trough and ye cask go "ping!"—
Ye china cracks in ye pantry,
    And ye crickets cease to sing.

THE HIRED MAN'S FAITH IN CHILDREN

I BELIEVE *all* childern's good,
Ef they're only *understood,*—
Even *bad* ones, 'pears to me,
'S jes' as good as they kin be!

THE LOVELY HUSBAND

Oh a love-ly hus-band he was known, He loved his wife and her a-lone; She reaped the harvest he had sown; She ate the meat; he picked the bone. With mixed admirers ev-'ry size, She smiled on each with

THE LOVELY HUSBAND

out disguise; This love-ly hus-band closed his eyes Lest he might take her

by sur-prise. Trot! Run! Was-n't he a han-dy hub-by?

What Fun She could plot and plan! Not One

Oth - er such a dan - dy hub - by As this love - ly man!

130

II

He answered at her least command:
He fanned her, if she would be fanned;
He vanished when she willed it.—And
He always coughed behind his hand.
  She held him in such high esteem
  She let him dope her face with
    "Cream,"—
  He'd chink the wrinkles seam-by-seam,
  And call her "lovely as a dream!"

CHORUS

Hot
 Bun!
  Wasn't he a lovey-dovey?
What
 Fun
  She could plot and plan!
Not
 One
  Other such a dovey-lovey
  As this love-ly man!

III

Her lightest wishes he foreknew
And fell up-stairs to cater to:
He never failed to back from view,
Nor mispronounced *Don't* ( ) *you* "Doan
 chu."

He only sought to fill such space
As her friends left ;—he knew his place :—
He praised the form she could not lace.—
He praised her face before her face!

CHORUS

Shot
  Gun!
    Wasn't he a lovely fellow?
What
  Fun
    She could plot and plan!
Not
  One
    Lonesome little streak of yellow
     In this love-ly man!

THREE SEVERAL BIRDS

The Romancer, the Poet, and the Bookman

I

THE ROMANCER

THE Romancer's a nightingale,—
   The moon wanes dewy-dim
And all the stars grow faint and pale
   In listening to him.—
To him the plot least plausible
   Is of the most avail,—
He simply masters it because
   He takes it by the tale.

    O he's a nightingale,—
    His theme will never fail—
   It gains applause of all—because
    He takes it by the tale!

The Romancer's a nightingale:—
   His is the sweetest note—
The sweetest, woe-begonest wail
   Poured out of mortal throat:

So, glad or sad, he ever draws
  Our best godspeed and hail;
He highest lifts his theme—because
  He takes it by the tale.

     O he's a nightingale,—
     His theme will never fail—
It gains applause of all—because
     He takes it by the tale!

II

THE POET

The bobolink he sings a single song,
          Right along,—
And the robin sings another, all his own—
          One alone;
  And the whippoorwill, and bluebird,
  And the cockadoodle-doo-bird;—
But the mocking-bird he sings in every tone
          Ever known,
Or chirrup-note of merriment or moan.

  So the Poet he's the mocking-bird of men,—
  He steals his songs and sings them o'er again;
    And yet beyond believing
    They're the sweeter for his thieving.—
  So we'll howl for Mister Mocking-bird
    And have him out again!

It's mighty fond we are of bobolinks,
                    And chewinks;
And we dote on dinky robins, quite a few—
                    Yes, we do;
    And we love the dove, and bluebird,
    And the cockadoodle-doo-bird,—
But the mocking-bird's the bird for me and you,
                    Through and through,
Since he sings as everybody wants him to.

Ho! the Poet he's the mocking-bird of men,—
He steals his songs and sings them o'er again;
    And yet beyond believing
    They're the sweeter for his thieving.—
So we'll howl for Mister Mocking-bird
    And have him out again!

III

BOOKMAN'S CATCH

The Bookman he's a humming-bird—
    His feasts are honey-fine,—
            (With hi! hilloo!
            And clover-dew
        And roses lush and rare!)
His roses are the phrase and word
    Of olden tomes divine;
            (With hi! and ho!
            And pinks ablow
        And posies everywhere!)

The Bookman he's a humming-bird,—
  He steals from song to song—
He scents the ripest-blooming rhyme,
  And takes his heart along
And sacks all sweets of bursting verse
  And ballads, throng on throng.
      (With ho! and hey!
      And brook and brae,
      And brinks of shade and shine!)

A humming-bird the Bookman is—
  Though cumbrous, gray and grim,—
      (With hi! hilloo!
      And honey-dew
      And odors musty-rare!)
He bends him o'er that page of his
  As o'er the rose's rim
      (With hi! and ho!
      And pinks aglow
      And roses everywhere!)
Ay, he's the featest humming-bird,—
  On airiest of wings
He poises pendent o'er the poem
  That blossoms as it sings—
God friend him as he dips his beak
  In such delicious things!
      (With ho! and hey!
      And world away
      And only dreams for him!)

THE BED

I

"THOU, of all God's gifts the best,
    Blessèd Bed!" I muse, and rest
Thinking how it havened me
In my dazèd Infancy—
Ere mine eyes could bear the kind
Daylight through the window-blind,
Or my lips, in yearning quest,
Groping found the mother-breast,
Or mine utterance but owned
Minor sounds that sobbed and moaned.

II

Gracious Bed that nestled me
Even ere the mother's knee,—
Lulling me to slumber ere
Conscious of my treasure there—
Save the tiny palms that kept
Fondling, even as I slept,
That rare dual-wealth of mine,—
Softest pillow—sweetest wine!—
Gentlest cheer for mortal guest,
And of Love's fare lordliest.

137

III

By thy grace, O Bed, the first
Blooms of Boyhood-memories burst:—
Dreams of riches, swift withdrawn
As I, wakening, find the dawn
With its glad Spring-face once more
Glimmering on me as of yore:
Then the bluebird's limpid cry
Lulls me like a lullaby,
Till falls every failing sense
Back to sleep's sheer impotence.

IV

Or, a truant, home again,—
With the moonlight through the pane,
And the kiss that ends the prayer—
Then the footsteps down the stair;
And the close hush; and far click
Of the old clock; and the thick
Sweetness of the locust-bloom
Drugging all the enchanted room
Into darkness fathoms deep
As mine own pure childish sleep.

V

Gift and spell, O Bed, retell
Every lovely miracle—
Up from childhood's simplest dream
Unto manhood's pride supreme!—

Sacredness no words express,—
Lo, the young wife's fond caress
Of her first-born, while beside
Bends the husband, tearful-eyed,
Marveling of kiss and prayer
Which of these is holier there.

VI

Trace the vigils through the long,
Long nights, when the cricket's song
Stunned the sick man's fevered brain,
As he tossed and moaned in pain
Piteous—till thou, O Bed,
Smoothed the pillows for his head,
And thy soothest solace laid
Round him, and his fever weighed
Into slumber deep and cool,
And divinely merciful.

VII

Thus, O Bed, all gratefully
I would ever sing of thee—
Till the final sleep shall fall
O'er me, and the crickets call
In the grasses where at last
I am indolently cast
Like a play-worn boy at will.—
'Tis a Bed befriends me still—
Yea, and Bed, belike, the best,
Softest, safest, blessèdest.

HOME-FOLKS

HOME-FOLKS!—Well, that-air name, to me,
  Sounds jis the same as *poetry*—
That is, ef poetry is jis
As sweet as I've hearn tell it is!

Home-Folks—they're jis the same as *kin*—
All brung up, same as *we* have bin,
Without no overpowerin' sense
Of their oncommon consequence!

They've bin to school, but not to git
The habit fastened on 'em yit
So as to ever interfere
With *other* work 'at's waitin' here:

Home-Folks has crops to plant and plow,
Er lives in town and keeps a cow;
But whether country-jakes er town-,
They know when eggs is up er down!

La! can't you *spot* 'em—when you meet
'Em *anywheres*—in field er street?
And can't you see their faces, bright
As circus-day, heave into sight?

And can't you hear their "Howdy!" clear
As a brook's chuckle to the ear,
And allus find their laughin' eyes
As fresh and clear as morning skies?

And can't you—when they've gone away—
Jis feel 'em shakin' hands, all day?
And feel, too, you've bin higher raised
By sich a meetin'?—God be praised!

Oh, Home-Folks! you're the best of all
'At ranges this terreschul ball,—
But, north er south, er east er west,
It's home is where you're at your best.—

It's home—it's home your faces shine,
In-nunder your own fig and vine—
Your fambly and your neighbors 'bout
Ye, and the latch-string hangin' out.

. . . . . .

Home-Folks—*at home,*—I know o' one
Old feller now 'at hain't got none.—
Invite him—he may hold back some—
But *you* invite him, and he'll come.

AMERICA'S THANKSGIVING

1900

FATHER all bountiful, in mercy bear
With this our universal voice of prayer—
    The voice that needs must be
    Upraised in thanks to Thee,
O Father, from Thy children everywhere.

A multitudinous voice, wherein we fain
Wouldst have Thee hear no lightest sob of pain—
    No murmur of distress,
    Nor moan of loneliness,
Nor drip of tears, though soft as summer rain.

And, Father, give us first to comprehend,
No ill can come from Thee; lean Thou and lend
    Us clearer sight to see
    Our boundless debt to Thee,
Since all thy deeds are blessings, in the end.

And let us feel and know that, being Thine,
We are inheritors of heart divine,
    And hands endowed with skill,
    And strength to work Thy will,
And fashion to fulfilment Thy design.

142

So, let us thank Thee, with all self aside,
Nor any lingering taint of mortal pride;
      As here to Thee we dare
      Uplift our faltering prayer,
Lend it some fervor of the glorified.

We thank Thee that our land is loved of Thee
The blessed home of thrift and industry,
      With ever-open door
      Of welcome to the poor—
Thy shielding hand o'er all abidingly.

Ever thus we thank Thee for the wrong that grew
Into a right that heroes battled to,
      With brothers long estranged,
      Once more as brothers ranged
Beneath the red and white and starry blue.

Ay, thanks—though tremulous the thanks
      expressed—
Thanks for the battle at its worst, and best—
      For all the clanging fray
      Whose discord dies away
Into a pastoral-song of peace and rest.

TO EDMUND CLARENCE STEDMAN

THE AUTHORS' CLUB RECEPTION, NEW YORK,
DECEMBER 6, 1900

IT is a various tribute you command,
    O Poet-seer and World-sage in one!—
The scholar greets you; and the student; and
    The stoic—and his visionary son:
The painter, harvesting with quiet eye
    Your features; and the sculptor, dreaming, too,
A classic marble figure, lifted high
    Where Fame's immortal ones are waiting you.

The man of letters, with his wistful face;
    The grizzled scientist; the young A.B.;
The true historian, of force and grace;
    The orator, of pure simplicity;
The journalist—the editor, likewise;
    The young war-correspondent; and the old
War-seasoned general, with sagging eyes,
    And nerve and hand of steel, and heart of gold.

The serious humorist; the blithe divine;
    The lawyer, with that twinkling look he wears;
The bleak-faced man in the dramatic line;
    The social lion—and the bulls and bears;

These—these, and more, O favored guest of all,
    Have known your benefactions, and are led
To pay their worldly homage, and to call
    Down Heaven's blessings on your honored head.

Ideal, to the utmost plea of art—
    As real, to labor's most exacting need,—
Your dual services of soul and heart
    Enrich the world alike in dream and deed:
For you have brought to us, from out the mine
    Delved but by genius in scholastic soil,
The blended treasures of a wealth divine,—
    Your peerless gift of song—your life of toil.

WHEN WE FIRST PLAYED "SHOW"

WASN'T it a good time,
    Long Time Ago—
When we all were little tads
    And first played "Show"!—
When every newer day
    Wore as bright a glow
As the ones we laughed away—
    Long Time Ago!

Calf was in the back-lot;
    Clover in the red;
Bluebird in the pear tree;
    Pigeons on the shed;
Tom a-chargin' twenty pins
    At the barn; and Dan
Spraddled out just like "The
    'Injarubber'-Man!"

Me and Bub and Rusty,
    Eck and Dunk and Sid,
'Tumblin' on the sawdust
    Like the A-rabs did;

Jamesy on the slack-rope
　　In a wild retreat,
Grappling back, to start again—
　　When he chalked his feet!

Wasn't Eck a wonder,
　　In his stocking-tights?
Wasn't Dunk—his leaping lion—
　　Chief of all delights?
Yes, and wasn't "Little Mack"
　　Boss of all the Show,—
Both Old Clown and Candy-Butcher—
　　Long Time Ago!

Sid the Bareback-Rider;
　　And—oh-me-oh-*my!*—
Bub, the spruce Ring-Master,
　　Stepping round so spry!—
In his little waist-and-trousers
　　All made in one,
Was there a prouder youngster
　　Under the sun!

And NOW—who will tell me,—
　　Where are they all?
Dunk's a sanatorium doctor,
　　Up at Waterfall;
Sid's a city street-contractor;
　　Tom has fifty clerks;
And Jamesy he's the "Iron Magnate"
　　Of "The Hecla Works."

And Bub's old and bald now,
    Yet still he hangs on,—
Dan and Eck and "Little Mack,"
    Long, long gone!
But wasn't it a good time,
    Long Time Ago—
When we all were little tads
    And first played "Show"!

From a photograph taken when fifty-five years old

WILLIAM PINKNEY FISHBACK

SAY first he loved the dear home-hearts, and
   then
He loved his honest fellow citizen—
He loved and honored him, in any post
Of duty where he served mankind the most.

All that he asked of him in humblest need
Was but to find him striving to succeed;
All that he asked of him in highest place
Was justice to the lowliest of his race.

When he found these conditions, proved and tried,
He owned he marveled, but was satisfied—
Relaxed in vigilance enough to smile
And, with his own wit, flay himself a while.

Often he liked real anger—as, perchance,
The summer skies like storm-clouds and the glance
Of lightning—for the clearer, purer blue
Of heaven, and the greener old earth, too.

All easy things to do he did with care,
Knowing the very common danger there;
In noblest conquest of supreme debate
The facts are simple as the victory great.

149

That which had been a task to hardiest minds
To him was as a pleasure, such as finds
The captive-truant, doomed to read throughout
The one lone book he really cares about.

Study revived him: Howsoever dim
And deep the problem, 'twas a joy to him
To solve it wholly; and he seemed as one
Refreshed and rested as the work was done.

And he had gathered, from all wealth of lore
That time has written, such a treasure-store,
His mind held opulence—his speech the rare
Fair grace of sharing all his riches there—

Sharing with all, but with the greatest zest
Sharing with those who seemed the neediest;
The young he ever favored; and through these
Shall he live longest in men's memories.

A GOOD MAN

I

A GOOD man never dies—
    In worthy deed and prayer
And helpful hands, and honest eyes,
    If smiles or tears be there:
Who lives for you and me—
    Lives for the world he tries
To help—he lives eternally.
    A good man never dies.

II

Who lives to bravely take
    His share of toil and stress,
And, for his weaker fellows' sake,
    Makes every burden less,—
He may, at last, seem worn—
    Lie fallen—hands and eyes
Folded—yet, though we mourn and mourn,
    A good man never dies.

JOHN CLARK RIDPATH

TO the lorn ones who loved him first and best,
And knew his dear love at its tenderest,
We seem akin—we simplest friends who knew
His fellowship, of heart and spirit too:

We who have known the happy summertide
Of his ingenuous nature, glorified
With the inspiring smile that ever lit
The earnest face and kindly strength of it;

His presence, all-commanding, as his thought
Into unconscious eloquence was wrought
Until the utterance became a spell
That awed us as a spoken miracle.

Learning, to him was native—was, in truth,
The earliest playmate of his lisping youth,
Likewise throughout a life of toil and stress;
It was as laughter, health and happiness;

And so he played with it—joyed at its call—
Ran rioting with it, forgetting all
Delights of childhood, and of age and fame,—
A devotee of learning, still the same!

In fancy, even now we catch the glance
Of the rapt eye and radiant countenance,
As when his discourse, like a woodland's stream,
Flowed musically on from theme to theme:

The skies, the stars, the mountains and the sea,
He worshiped as their high divinity—
Nor did his reverent spirit find one thing
On earth too lowly for his worshiping.

The weed, the rose, the wildwood or the plain,
The teeming harvest, or the blighted grain,—
All—all were fashioned beautiful and good,
As the soul saw and senses understood.

Thus broadly based, his spacious faith and love
Enfolded all below as all above—
Nay, ev'n if overmuch he loved mankind,
He gave his love's vast largess as designed.

Therefore, in fondest, faithful service, he
Wrought ever bravely for humanity—
Stood, first of heroes for the Right allied—
Foes, even, grieving, when (for them) he died.

This was the man we loved—are loving yet,
And still shall love while longing eyes are wet
With selfish tears that well were brushed away,
Remembering his smile of yesterday.—

For, even as we knew him, smiling still,
Somewhere beyond all earthly ache or ill,
He waits with the old welcome—just as when
We met him smiling, we shall meet again.

HIS HEART OF CONSTANT YOUTH

And I never hear the drums beat
that I do not think of him.
    —MAJOR CHARLES L. HOLSTEIN

TURN through his life, each word and deed
    Now sacred as it is—
How helped and soothed we are to read
    A history like his!

To turn the years, in far review,
    And find him—as To-day—
In orchard-lands of bloom and dew
    Again a boy at play:

The jeweled grass—the sumptuous trees
    And flower and fragrance there,
With song of birds and drone of bees
    And Spring-time everywhere:

Turn any chapter that we will,
    Read any page, in sooth,
We find his glad heart owning still
    The freshness of his youth.

154

With such a heart of tender care
  He loved his own, and thus
His home was, to the loved ones there,
  A temple glorious.

And, ever youthful, still his love
  Enshrined, all manifold,
The people—all the poor thereof,
  The helpless and the old.

And little children—Ah! to them
  His love was as the sun
Wrought in a magic diadem
  That crowned them, every one.

And ever young his reverence for
  The laws: like morning-dew
He shone as counsel, orator,
  And clear logician, too.

And, as a boy, his gallant soul
  Made answer to the trill
Of battle-trumpet and the roll
  Of drums that echo still:

His comrades—as his country, dear—
  They knew, and ever knew
That buoyant, boyish love, sincere
  As truth itself is true:

He marched with them, in tireless tramp—
   Laughed, cheered and lifted up
The battle-chorus, and in camp
   Shared blanket, pipe and cup.

His comrades! . . . When you meet again,
   In anguish though you bow,
Remember how he loved you then,
   And how he loves you *now*.

THE PATHS OF PEACE

MAURICE THOMPSON—FEBRUARY 15, 1901

HE would have holiday—outworn, in sooth,
   Would turn again to seek the old release,—
The open fields—the loved haunts of his youth—
   The woods, the waters, and the paths of peace.

The rest—the recreation he would choose
   Be his abidingly! Long has he served
And greatly—ay, and greatly let us use
   Our grief, and yield him nobly as deserved.

Perchance—with subtler senses than our own
   And love exceeding ours—he listens thus
To ever nearer, clearer pipings blown
   From out the lost lands of Theocritus.

Or haply, he is beckoned from us here,
   By knight or yeoman of the bosky wood,
Or, chained in roses, haled a prisoner
   Before the blithe Immortal, Robin Hood.

157

Or, mayhap, Chaucer signals, and with him
   And his rare fellows he goes pilgriming;
Or Walton signs him, o'er the morning brim
   Of misty waters midst the dales of Spring.

Ho! wheresoe'er he goes, or whosoe'er
   He fares with, he has bravely earned the boon.
Be his the open, and the glory there
   Of April-buds, May-blooms and flowers of June!

Be his the glittering dawn, the twinkling dew,
   The breathless pool or gush of laughing streams—
Be his the triumph of the coming true
   Of all his loveliest dreams!

THE TRIBUTE OF HIS HOME

BENJAMIN HARRISON—INDIANAPOLIS, MARCH
14, 1901

BOWED, midst a universal grief that makes
   Columbia's self a stricken mourner, cast
In tears beneath the old Flag at half-mast,
A sense of glory rouses us and breaks
Like song upon our sorrowing and shakes
   The dew from our drenched eyes, that smile at
      last
   In childish pride—as though the great man passed
To his most high reward for our poor sakes.
Loved of all men—we muse,—yet ours he was—
   Choice of the Nation's mighty brotherhood—
      Her soldier, statesman, ruler.—Ay, but then,
We knew him—long before the world's applause
   And after—as a neighbor, kind and good,
      Our common friend and fellow citizen.

AMERICA

O Thou, America—Messiah of Nations!

I

IN the need that bows us thus,
    America!
Shape a mighty song for us—
    America!
Song to whelm a hundred years'
Roar of wars and rain of tears
'Neath a world's triumphant cheers:
    America! America!

II

Lift the trumpet to thy mouth,
    America!
East and West and North and South—
    America!
Call us round the dazzling shrine
Of the starry old ensign—
New baptized in blood of thine,
    America! America!

III

Dying eyes through pitying mists,
>   America!
See the Assassin's shackled wrists,
>   America!
Patient eyes that turn their sight
From all blackening crime and blight
Still toward Heaven's holy light—
>   America! America!

IV

High o'erlooking sea and land,
>   America!
Trustfully with outheld hand,
>   America!
Thou dost welcome all in quest
Of thy freedom, peace and rest—
Every exile is thy guest,
>   America! America!

V

Thine a universal love,
>   America!
Thine the cross and crown thereof,
>   America!
Aid us, then, to sing thy worth:
God hath builded, from thy birth,
The first nation of the earth—
>   **America! America!**

EVEN AS A CHILD

CANTON, SEPTEMBER 19, 1901

EVEN as a child to whom sad neighbors speak
　　In symbol, saying that his father "sleeps"—
Who feels their meaning, even as his cheek
　　Feels the first tear-drop as it stings and leaps—
Who keenly knows his loss, and yet denies
　　Its awful import—grieves unreconciled,
Moans, drowses—rouses, with new-drowning eyes—
　　　　Even as a child.

Even as a child; with empty, aimless hand
　　Clasped sudden to the heart all hope deserts—
With tears that blur all lights on sea or land—
　　The lip that quivers and the throat that hurts:
Even so, the Nation that has known his love
　　Is orphaned now; and, whelmed in anguish wild
Knows but its sorrow and the ache thereof,
　　　　Even as a child.

THE HOOSIER IN EXILE

THE Hoosier in Exile—a toast
  That by its very sound
Moves us, at first, to tears almost,
  And sympathy profound;
But musing for a little space,
  We lift the glass and smile,
And poise it with a royal grace—
  The Hoosier in Exile!

The Hoosier in Exile, forsooth!
  For though his steps may roam
The earth's remotest bounds, in truth
  His heart is ever home!
O loyal still to every tie
  Of native fields and streams,
His boyhood friends, and paths whereby
  He finds them in his dreams!

Though he may fare the thronging maze
  Of alien city streets,
His thoughts are set in grassy ways
  And woodlands' cool retreats;

163

Forever, clear and sweet above
    The traffic's roar and din,
In breezy groves he hears the dove,
    And is at peace within.

When newer friends and generous hands
    Advance him, he returns
Due gratefulness, yet, pausing, stands
    As one who strangely yearns
To pay still further thanks, but sighs
    To think he knows not where,
Till—like as life—with misty eyes
    He sees his mother there.

The Hoosier in Exile? Ah, well,
    Accept the phrase, but know
The Hoosier heart must ever dwell
    Where orchard blossoms grow
The whitest, apples reddest, and,
    In cornlands, mile on mile,
The old homesteads forever stand—
    "The Hoosier in Exile!"

THE QUEST OF THE FATHERS

WHAT were our Forefathers trying to find
    When they weighed anchor, that desperate
  hour
They turned from home, and the warning wind
  Sighed in the sails of the old Mayflower?
What sought they that could compensate
  Their hearts for the loved ones left behind—
The household group at the glowing grate?—
  What were our Forefathers trying to find?

What were they trying to find more dear
  Than their native land and its annals old,—
Its throne—its church—and its worldly cheer—
  Its princely state, and its hoarded gold?
What more dear than the mounds of green
  There o'er the brave sires, slumbering long?
What more fair than the rural scene—
  What more sweet than the throstle's song?

Faces pallid, but sternly set,
  Lips locked close, as in voiceless prayer,
And eyes with never a tear-drop wet—
  Even the tenderest woman's there!

But O the light from the soul within,
  As each spake each with a flashing mind—
As the lightning speaks to its kith and kin!
  What were our Forefathers trying to find?

Argonauts of a godless day—
  Seers of visions, and dreamers vain!
Their ship's foot set in a pathless way,—
  The fogs, the mists, and the blinding rain!—
When the gleam of sun, and moon and star
  Seemed lost so long they were half forgot—
When the fixed eyes found nor near nor far,
  And the night whelmed all, and the world was not.

And yet, befriended in some strange wise,
  They groped their way in the storm and stress
Through which—though their look found not the
      skies—
  The Lord's look found *them* ne'ertheless—
Found them, yea, in their piteous lot,
  As they in their faith from the first divined—
Found them, and favored them—too. But what—
  What were our Forefathers trying to find?

Numb and agasp, with the frost for breath,
  They came on a frozen shore, at last,
As bleak and drear as the coasts of death,—
  And yet their psalm o'er the wintry blast
Rang glad as though 'twere the chiming mirth
  Of jubilant children landing there—
Until o'er all of the icy earth
  The snows seemed warm, as they knelt in prayer.

For, lo! they were close on the trail they sought:—
  In the sacred soil of the rights of men
They marked where the Master-hand had wrought;
  And there they garnered and sowed again.—
Their land—then *ours,* as to-day it is,
  With its flag of heaven's own light designed,
And God's vast love o'er all. . . . And *this*
  Is what our Forefathers were trying to find.

TO THE MOTHER

THE mother-hands no further toil may know;
   The mother-eyes smile not on you and me;
The mother-heart is stilled, alas!—But O
   The mother-love abides eternally.

NEW YEAR'S NURSERY JINGLE

OF all the rhymes of all the climes
    Of where and when and how,
We best and most can boost and boast
    The Golden Age of NOW!

FOOL-YOUNGENS

ME an' Bert an' Minnie-Belle
Knows a joke, an' we won't tell!
No, we don't—'cause we don't know
Why we got to laughin' so;
But we got to laughin' so,
    We ist kep' a-laughin'.

Wind uz blowin' in the tree—
An' wuz only ist us three
Playin' there; an' ever' one
Ketched each other, like we done,
Squintin' up there at the sun
    Like we wuz a-laughin'.

Nothin' funny anyway;
But I laughed, an' so did they—
An' we all three laughed, an' nen
Squint' our eyes an' laugh' again:
Ner we didn't ist *p'ten'*—
    We wuz *shore-'nough* laughin'.

We ist laugh' an' laugh', tel Bert
Say he *can't* quit an' it hurt.
Nen I *howl,* an' Minnie-Belle

She tear up the grass a spell
An' ist stop her yeers an' *yell*
    Like she'd *die* a-laughin'.

Never sich fool-youngens yit!
Nothin' funny,—not a bit!—
But we laugh' so, tel we whoop'
Purt' nigh like we have the croup—
All so hoarse we'd wheeze an' whoop
    An' ist *choke* a-laughin',

A GUSTATORY ACHIEVEMENT

LAST Thanksgivin'-dinner we
  Et at Granny's house, an' she
Had—ist like she alluz does—
Most an' best pies ever wuz.

Canned *black*burry-pie an' *goose-*
Burry, squshin'-full o' juice;
An' *roz*burry—yes, an' plum—
Yes, an' *churry*-pie—*um-yum!*
Peach an' punkin, too, you bet.
Lawzy! I kin taste 'em yet!
Yes, an' *custard*-pie, an' *mince!*

    .   .   .   .   .   .

An'—I—*ain't*—et—no—pie—since!

BILLY AND HIS DRUM

HO! it's come, kids, come!
With a bim! bam! bum!
Here's little Billy bangin' on his
    big bass drum!
He's a-marchin' round the room,
With his feather-duster plume
A-noddin' an' a-bobbin' with his
    bim! bom! boom!

Looky, little Jane an' Jim!
Will you only look at him,
A-humpin' an' a-thumpin' with his
    bam! bom! bim!
Has the Day o' Judgment come
Er the New Mi-len-nee-um?
Er is it only Billy with his
    bim! bam! bum!

I'm a-comin'; yes, I am—
Jim an' Sis, an' Jane an' Sam!
We'll all march off with Billy an' his
    bom! bim! bam!

173

Come hur*raw*in' as you come,
Er they'll think you're deef-an'-dumb
Ef you don't hear little Billy an' his
    big bass drum!

A DIVERTED TRAGEDY

GRACIE wuz allus a *careless* tot;
   But Gracie dearly loved her doll,
   An' played wiv it on the winder-sill
'Way up-stairs, when she ought to *not,*
   An' her muvver *telled* her so an' all;
     But she won't *mind* what *she* say—till,
First thing she know, her dolly fall
Clean spang out o' the winder, plumb
Into the street! An' here Grace come
   Down-stairs, two at a time, ist wild
     An' a-screamin', "Oh, my child! my child!"

Jule wuz a-bringin' their basket o' clo'es
   Ist then into their hall down there,—
     An' she ist stop' when Gracie bawl,
   An' Jule she say "She ist declare
She's ist in time!" An' what you s'pose?
   She sets her basket down in the hall,
An' wite on top o' the snowy clo'es
   Wuz Gracie's dolly a-layin' there
     An' ist ain't bu'st ner hurt a-tall!
   Nen Gracie smiled—ist *sobbed* an' smiled—
     An' cried, "My child! my precious child!"

THOMAS THE PRETENDER

TOMMY'S alluz playin' jokes,
   An' actin' up, an' foolin' folks;
   An' wunst one time he creep
In Pa's big chair, he did, one night,
An' squint an' shut his eyes bofe tight,
   An' say, "Now I'm asleep."
An' nen we knowed, an' Ma know' too,
He *ain't* asleep no more'n you!

An' wunst he clumbed on our back-fence
An' flop his arms an' nen commence
   To crow, like he's a hen;
But when he falled off, like he done,
He didn't fool us childern none,
   Ner didn't *crow* again.
An' our Hired Man, as he come by,
Says, "Tom can't *crow,* but he kin *cry.*"

An' one time wunst Tom 'tend'-like he's
His Pa an' goin' to rob the bees;
   An', first he know—oh, dear!
They ist come swarmin' out o' there

An' sting him, an' stick in his hair—
   An' one got in his yeer!—
An' Uncle sigh an' say to Ma,
An' grease the welts, "Pore Pa! pore Pa!"

TO MY SISTER

A BELATED OFFERING FOR HER BIRTHDAY

THESE books you find three weeks be-
    hind
  Your honored anniversary
Make me, I fear, to here appear
  Mayhap a trifle cursory.—
Yet while the Muse must thus refuse
  The chords that fall caressfully,
She seems to stir the publisher
  And dealer quite successfully.

As to our *birthdays*—let 'em run
  Until they whir and whiz!
Read Robert Louis Stevenson,
  And hum these lines of his:—
"The eternal dawn, beyond a doubt,
  Shall break on hill and plain
And put all stars and candles out
  Ere we be young again."

178

THE SOLDIER

THE DEDICATION OF THE SOLDIERS' AND SAILORS'
MONUMENT, INDIANAPOLIS, MAY 15, 1902

THE Soldier!—meek the title, yet divine:
Therefore, with reverence, as with wild
acclaim,
We fain would honor in exalted line
The glorious lineage of the glorious name:
The Soldier.—Lo, he ever was and is,
Our Country's high custodian, by right
Of patriot blood that brims that heart of his
With fiercest love, yet honor infinite.

The Soldier—within whose inviolate care
The Nation takes repose,—her inmost fane
Of Freedom ever has its guardian there,
As have her forts and fleets on land and main:
The Heavenward Banner, as its ripples stream
In happy winds, or float in languid flow,
Through silken meshes ever sifts the gleam
Of sunshine on its Sentinel below.

The Soldier!—Why, the very utterance
  Is music—as of rallying bugles, blent
With blur of drums and cymbals and the chants
  Of battle-hymns that shake the continent!—
The thunder-chorus of a world is stirred
  To awful, universal jubilee,—
Yet ever through it, pure and sweet, are heard
  The prayers of Womanhood, and Infancy.

Even as a fateful tempest sudden loosed
  Upon our senses, so our thoughts are blown
Back where The Soldier battled, nor refused
  A grave all nameless in a clime unknown.—
The Soldier—though, perchance, worn, old and
      gray;
    The Soldier—though, perchance, the merest
      lad,—
The Soldier—though he gave his life away,
  Hearing the shout of "Victory," was glad;

Ay, glad and grateful, that in such a cause
  His veins were drained at Freedom's holy
      shrine—
Rechristening the land—as first it was,—
  His blood poured thus in sacramental sign
Of new baptism of the hallowed name
  "My Country"—now on every lip once more
And blest of God with still enduring fame.—
  This thought even then The Soldier gloried
    o'er.

The dying eyes upraised in rapture there,—
  As, haply, he remembered how a breeze
Once swept his boyish brow and tossed his hair,
  Under the fresh bloom of the orchard-trees—
When his heart hurried, in some wistful haste
  Of ecstasy, and his quick breath was wild
And balmy-sharp and chilly-sweet to taste,—
  And he towered godlike, though a trembling
    child!

Again, through luminous mists, he saw the skies'
  Far fields white-tented; and in gray and blue
And dazzling gold, he saw vast armies rise
  And fuse in fire—from which, in swiftest view,
The Old Flag soared, and friend and foe as one
  Blent in an instant's vivid mirage. . . . Then
The eyes closed smiling on the smiling sun
  That changed the seer to a child again.—

And, even so, The Soldier slept.—Our own!—
  The Soldier of our plaudits, flowers and
    tears,—
O this memorial of bronze and stone—
  His love shall outlast *this* a thousand years!
Yet, as the towering symbol bids us do,—
  With soul saluting, as salutes the hand,
We answer as The Soldier answered to
  The Captain's high command.

A CHRISTMAS GLEE

FEIGNED AS FROM ELIZABETHAN COMEDY

I

WITH a hey! and a hi! and a hey-ho glee!
    O a Christmas glass for a sweet-lipped lass
To kiss and pass, in her coquetry—
      So rare!
And the lads all flush save the right one there—
      So rare—so rare!
With a hey! and a hi! and a ho—oh!
The Christmas holly and the mistletoe!

II

With a hey! and a hi! and a hey-ho wile!
    As he lifts the cup and his wan face up,
Her eyes touch his with a tender smile—
      So rare!
Then his hands grasp out—and her own are there—
      So rare—so rare!
With a hey! and a hi! and a ho—oh!
The Christmas holly and the mistletoe!

182

CHORUS

With a hey! and a hi! and a hey-ho-ho!
The wind, the winter and the drifting snow!
With a hey! and a hi! and a ho—oh!
The Christmas holly and the mistletoe!

NO BOY KNOWS

THERE are many things that boys may
     know—
Why this and that are thus and so,—
Who made the world in the dark and lit
The great sun up to lighten it:
Boys know new things every day—
When they study, or when they play,—
When they idle, or sow and reap—
But no boy knows when he goes to sleep.

Boys who listen—or should, at least,—
May know that the round old earth rolls East;—
And know that the ice and the snow and the
     rain—
Ever repeating their parts again—
Are all just water the sunbeams first
Sip from the earth in their endless thirst,
And pour again till the low streams leap.—
But no boy knows when he goes to sleep.

A boy may know what a long, glad while
It has been to him since the dawn's first smile,
When forth he fared in the realm divine
Of brook-laced woodland and spun-sunshine;—

He may know each call of his truant mates,
And the paths they went,—and the pasture-gates
Of the 'cross-lots home through the dusk so
    deep.—
But no boy knows when he goes to sleep.

O I have followed me, o'er and o'er,
From the flagrant drowse on the parlor-floor,
To the pleading voice of the mother when
I even doubted I heard it then—
To the sense of a kiss, and a moonlit room,
And dewy odors of locust-bloom—
A sweet white cot—and a cricket's cheep.—
But no boy knows when he goes to sleep.

HIS PA'S ROMANCE

ALL 'at I ever want to be
Is ist to be a man like Pa
When he wuz young an' married Ma!
Uncle he telled us yisterdy
Ist all about it then—'cause they,
My Pa an' Ma, wuz bofe away
To 'tend P'tracted Meetin', where
My Pa an' Ma is allus there
When all the big "Revivals" is,
An' "Love-Feasts," too, an' "Class," an'
    "Prayer,"
An' when's "Comoonian Servicis."
An', yes, an' Uncle said to not
To never tell *them* ner let on
Like we knowed now ist how they got
First married. So—while they wuz gone—
Uncle he telled us ever'thing—
'Bout how my Pa wuz ist a pore
Farm-boy.—He says, I tell you *what,*
Your Pa *wuz* pore! But neighbers they
All liked him—all but one old man
An' his old wife that folks all say
Nobody liked, ner never can!

Yes, sir! an' Uncle purt' nigh swore
About the mean old man an' way
He treat' my Pa!—'cause he's a pore
Farm-hand—but prouder 'an a king—
An' ist work' on, he did, an' wore
His old patched clo'es, ist anyway,
So he saved up his wages—then
He ist worked on an 'saved some more,
An' ist worked on, ist night an' day—
Till, sir, he save' up nine er ten
Er hunnerd dollars! But he keep
All still about it, Uncle say—
But he ist thinks—an' thinks a heap!
Though what he wuz a-thinkin', Pa
He never tell' a soul but Ma—
(Then, course, you know, he wuzn't Pa,
An', course, you know, she wuzn't Ma—
They wuz ist sweethearts, course you know);
'Cause Ma wuz ist a girl, about
Sixteen; an' when my Pa he go
A-courtin' her, her Pa an' Ma—
The very first they find it out—
Wuz maddest folks you ever saw!
'Cause it wuz her old Ma an' Pa
'At hate' my Pa, an' toss their head,
An' ist raise Ned! An' her Pa said
He'd ruther see his daughter dead!
An' said she's ist a child!—an' so
Wuz Pa!—An' ef he wuz man-grown
An' only man on earth below,
His daughter shouldn't marry him

Ef he's a king an' on his throne!
Pa's chances then looked mighty slim
Fer certain, Uncle said. But he—
He never told a soul but her
What he wuz keepin' quiet fer.
Her folks ist lived a mile from where
He lived at—an' they drove past there
To git to town. An' ever' one
An' all the neighbers they liked her
An' showed it! But her folks—no, sir!—
Nobody liked her parunts none!
An' so when they shet down, you know,
On Pa—an' old man tell' him so—
Pa ist went back to work, an' she
Ist waited. An', sir! purty soon
Her folks they thought he's turned his eye
Some other way—'cause by-an'-by
They heard he'd *rented* the old place
He worked on. An' one afternoon
A neighber, that had bust' a trace,
He tell' the old man they wuz signs
Around the old place that the young
Man wuz a-fixin' up the old
Log cabin some, an' he had brung
New furnichur from town; an' told
How th' old house 'uz whitewashed clean
An' sweet wiv morning-glory vines
An' hollyhawks all 'round the door
An' winders—an' a bran'-new floor
In th' old porch—an' wite-new green-
An'-red pump in the old sweep-well!

'An', Uncle said, when he hear tell
O' all them things, the old man he
Ist grin' an' says, he "reckon' now
Some gal, er widder anyhow,
That silly boy he's coaxed at last
To marry him!" he says, says-ee,
"An' ef he has, 'so mote it be'!"
Then went back to the house to tell
His *wife* the news, as he went past
The smokehouse, an' then went on in
The kitchen, where his daughter she
Wuz washin', to tell *her,* an' grin
An' try to worry her a spell!
The mean old thing! But Uncle said
She ain't cry much—ist pull her old
Sunbonnet forrerds on her head—
So's old man he can't see her face
At all! An' when he s'pose he scold
An' jaw enough, he ist clear' out
An' think he's boss of all the place!

Then Uncle say, the first you know
They's go' to be a Circus-show
In town; an' old man think he'll take
His wife an' go. An' when she say
To take their daughter, too, *she* shake
Her head like she don't *want* to go;
An' when he sees she wants to stay,
The old man takes her, anyway!
An' so she went! But Uncle he
Said she looked mighty sweet that day,

Though she wuz pale as she could be,
A-speshully a-drivin' by
Wite where her beau lived at, you know;
But out the corner of his eye
The old man watch' her; but she throw
Her pairsol 'round so she can't see
The house at all! An' then she hear
Her Pa an' Ma a-talkin' low
An' kind o' laughin'-like; but she
Ist set there in the seat behind,
P'tendin' like she didn't mind.
An', Uncle say, when they got past
The young man's place, an' 'pearantly
He wuzn't home, but off an' gone
To town, the old man turned at last
An' talked back to his daughter there,
All pleasant-like, from then clean on
Till they got into town, an' where
The Circus wuz, an' on inside
O' that, an' through the crowd, on to
The very top seat in the tent
Wite next the band—a-bangin' through
A tune 'at bu'st his yeers in two!
An' there the old man scrouged an' tried
To make his wife set down, an' she
A-yellin'! But ist what she meant
He couldn't hear, ner couldn't see
Till she turned 'round an' pinted. Then
He turned an' looked—an' looked again! . . .
He ist saw neighbers ever'where—
But, sir, *his daughter* wuzn't there!

'An', Uncle says, he even saw
Her beau, you know, he hated so;
An' he wuz with some other girl.
An' then he heard the Clown "Haw-haw!"
An' saw the horses wheel an' whirl
Around the ring, an' heard the zipp
O' the Ringmaster's long slim whip—
But that whole Circus, Uncle said,
Wuz all inside the old man's head!

An' Uncle said, he didn't find
His daughter all that afternoon—
An' her Ma says she'll lose her mind
Ef they don't find her purty soon!
But, though they looked all day, an' stayed
There fer the night p'formance—not
No use at all!—they never laid
Their eyes on her. An' then they got
Their team out, an' the old man shook
His fist at all the town, an' then
Shook it up at the moon ag'in,
An' said his time 'ud come, some day!
An' jerked the lines an' driv away.

Uncle, he said, he s'pect, that night,
The old man's madder yet when they
Drive past the young man's place, an' hear
A fiddle there, an' see a light
Inside, an' shadders light an' gay
A-dancin' 'crosst the winder-blinds.
An' some young chaps outside yelled, "Say!
What 'pears to be the hurry—hey?"

But the old man ist whipped the lines
An' streaked past like a runaway!
An' now you'll be su'prised, I bet!—
I hardly ain't quit laughin' yet
When Uncle say, that jamboree
An' dance an' all—w'y, that's a sign
That any old man ort to see,
As plain as 8 and 1 makes 9,
That they's *a weddin'* wite inside
That very house he's whippin' so
To git apast!—An', sir! the bride
There's his own daughter! Yes, an' oh!
She's my Ma now—an' young man she
Got married, he's my Pa! *Whoop-ee!*
But Uncle say to not laugh all
The laughin' yet, but please save some
To kind o' spice up what's to come!

Then Uncle say, about next day
The neighbers they begin to call
An' wish 'em well, an' say how glad
An' proud an' tickled ever' way
Their friends all is—an' how they had
The lovin' prayers of ever' one
That had homes of their own! But none
Said nothin' 'bout the home that she
Had run away from! So she sighed
Sometimes—an' wunst she purt' nigh cried.

Well, Uncle say, her old Pa, he
Ist like to died, he wuz so mad!
An' her Ma, too! But by-an'-by
They cool down some.

An', 'bout a week,
She want to see her Ma so bad,
She think she'll haf to go! An' so
She coax him; an' he kiss her cheek
An' say, Lord bless her, *course* they'll go!
An', Uncle say, when they're bofe come
A-knockin' there at her old home—
W'y, first he know, the door it flew
Open, all quick, an' she's jerked in,
An', quicker still, the door's banged to
An' locked: an' crosst the winder-sill
The old man pokes a shotgun through
An' says to git! "You stold my child,"
He says; "an', now she's back, w'y, you
Clear out, this minute, er I'll kill
You! Yes, an' I 'ull kill her, too,
Ef you don't go!" An' then, all wild,
His young wife begs him please to go!
An' so he turn' an' walk'—all slow
An' pale as death, but awful still
An' ca'm—back to the gate, an' on
Into the road, where he had gone
So many times alone, you know!
An', Uncle say, a whipperwill
Holler so lonesome, as he go
On back to'rds home, he say he 'spec'
He ist 'ud like to wring its neck!
An' I ain't think he's goin' back
All by hisse'f—but Uncle say
That's what he does, an' it's a fac'!

An' 'pears-like he's goin' back to *stay*—
'Cause there he stick', ist thataway,
An' don't go nowheres any more,
Ner don't nobody ever see
Him set his foot outside the door—
Till 'bout five days, a boy loped down
The road, a-comin' past from town,
An' he called to him from the gate,
An' sent the old man word: He's thought
Things over now; an', while he hate
To lose his wife, he think she ought
To mind her Pa an' Ma an' do
Whatever *they* advise her to.
An' sends word, too, to come an' git
Her new things an' the furnichur
That he had special' bought fer her—
'Cause, now that they wuz goin' to quit,
She's free to ist have all of it;—
So, fer his love fer her, he say
To come an' git it, wite away.
An' *spang!* that very afternoon,
Here come her Ma—ist 'bout as soon
As old man could hitch up an' tell
Her "hurry back!" An' 'bout as quick
As she's drove there to where my Pa—
I mean to where her son-in-law—
Lives at, he meets her at the door
All smilin', though he's awful pale
An' trimbly—like he's ist been sick;
He take her in the house—An', 'fore
She knows it, they's a cellar-door

Shet on her, an' she hears the click
Of a' old rusty padlock! Then,
Uncle, he say, she kind o' stands
An' thinks—an' thinks—an' thinks ag'in—
An' mayby thinks of her own child
Locked up—like her! An' Uncle smiled,
An' I ist laughed an' clapped my hands!
An' there she stayed! An' she can cry
Ist all she want! an' yell an' kick
To ist her heart's content! an' try
To pry out wiv a quiltin'-stick!
But Uncle say he guess at last
She's 'bout give up, an' holler through
The door-crack fer to please to be
So kind an' good as send an' tell
The old man, like she want him to,
To come 'fore night, an' set her free,
Er—they wuz rats down there! An' yell
She did, till, Uncle say, it soured
The morning's milk in the back yard!
But all the answer reached her, where
She's skeered so in the dark down there,
Wuz ist a mutterin' that she heard,—
"I've sent him word!—I've sent him word!"
An' shore enough, as Uncle say,
He *has* "sent word!"

                Well, it's plum night
An' all the house is shet up tight—
Only one winder 'bout half-way
Raised up, you know; an' ain't no light

Inside the whole house, Uncle say.
Then, first you know, there where the team
Stands hitched yet, there the old man
    stands—
A' old tin lantern in his hands
An' monkey-wrench; an' he don't seem
To make things out, a-standin' there.
He comes on to the gate an' feels
An' fumbles fer the latch—then hears
A voice that chills him to the heels—
"You halt! an' stand right where you air!"
Then, sir! my—my—his son-in-law,
There at the winder wiv his gun,
He tell the old man what he's done:
"You hold *my* wife a prisoner—
An' *your* wife, drat ye! I've got *her!*
An' now, sir," Uncle say he say,
"You ist turn round an' climb wite in
That wagon, an' drive home ag'in
An' bring my wife back wite away,
An' we'll trade then—an' not before
Will I unlock my cellar-door—
Not fer your wife's sake ner your own,
But *my* wife's sake—an' hers alone!"
An', Uncle say, it don't sound like
It's so, but yet it is!—He say,
From wite then, somepin' seem' to strike
The old man's funny-bone some way;
An', minute more, that team o' his
Went tearin' down the road *k'whiz!*
An' in the same two-forty style

Come whizzin' back! An' oh, that-air
Sweet girl a-cryin' all the while,
Thinkin' about her Ma there, shet
In her own daughter's cellar, where—
Ist week or so *she's* kep' house there—
She hadn't time to clean it yet!
So when her Pa an' her they git
There—an' the young man grab' an' kiss
An' hug her, till she make him quit
An' ask him where her mother is.
An' then he smile' an' try to not;
Then slow-like find th' old padlock key,
An' blow a' oat-hull out of it,
An' then stoop down there where he's got
Her Ma locked up so keerfully—
An' where, wite there, he say he thought
It *ort* to been *the old man*—though
Uncle, he say, he reckon not—
When out she bounced, all tickled so
To taste fresh air ag'in an' find
Her folks wunst more, an' grab' her child
An' cry an' laugh, an' even go
An' hug the old man; an' he wind
Her in his arms, an' laugh, an' pat
Her back, an' say he's riconciled,
In such a happy scene as that,
To swap his daughter for her Ma,
An' have so smart a son-in-law
As *they* had! "Yes, an' he's my Pa!"
I laugh' an' yell', "Hooray-hooraw!"

TO JOEL CHANDLER HARRIS

YOU who to the rounded prime
  Of a life of toil and stress,
Still have kept the morning-time
  Of glad youth in heart and spirit,
  So your laugh, as children hear it,
Seems their own, no less,—
Take this book of childish rhyme—
  The Book of Joyous Children.

Their first happiness on earth
  Here is echoed—their first glee:
Rich, in sooth, the volume's worth—
  Not in classic lore, but rich in
  The child-sagas of the kitchen;—
Therefore, take from me
To your heart of childish mirth
  The Book of Joyous Children.

THE BOOK OF JOYOUS CHILDREN

BOUND and bordered in leaf-green,
    Edged with trellised buds and flowers
And glad Summer-gold, with clean
    White and purple morning-glories
    Such as suit the songs and stories
Of this book of ours,
Unrevised in text or scene,—
    The Book of Joyous Children.

Wild and breathless in their glee—
    Lawless rangers of all ways
Winding through lush greenery
    Of Elysian vales—the viny,
    Bowery groves of shady, shiny
Haunts of childish days.
Spread and read again with me
    The Book of Joyous Children.

What a whir of wings, and what
    Sudden drench of dews upon
The young brows, wreathed, all unsought,
    With the apple-blossom garlands

Of the poets of those far lands
  Whence all dreams are drawn
Set herein and soiling not
    The Book of Joyous Children.

In their blithe companionship
  Taste again, these pages through,
The hot honey on your lip
    Of the sun-smit wild strawberry,
    Or the chill tart of the cherry;
  Kneel, all glowing, to
The cool spring, and with it sip
    The Book of Joyous Children.

As their laughter needs no rule,
  So accept their language, pray.—
Touch it not with any tool:
    Surely we may understand it,—
    As the heart has parsed or scanned it
  Is a worthy way,
Though found not in any School
    The Book of Joyous Children.

Be a truant—know no place
  Of prison under heaven's rim!
Front the Father's smiling face—
    Smiling, that *you* smile the brighter
    For the heavy hearts made lighter,
  Since you smile with Him.
Take—and thank Him for His grace—
    The Book of Joyous Children.

ELMER BROWN

AWF'LEST boy in this-here town
Er anywheres is Elmer Brown!
He'll mock you—yes, an' strangers, too,
An' make a face an' yell at you,—
  "Here's the way *you* look!"*

Yes, an' wunst in School one day,
An' Teacher's lookin' wite that way,
He helt his slate, an' hide his head,
An' maked a face at *her,* an' said,—
  "Here's the way *you* look!"*

'An'-sir! when Rosie Wheeler smile
One morning at him 'crosst the aisle,
He twist his face all up, an' black
His nose wiv ink, an' whisper back,—
  "Here's the way *you* look!"*

Wunst when his Aunt's all dressed to call,
An' kiss him good-by in the hall,
An' latch the gate an' start away,
He holler out to her an' say,—
  "Here's the way *you* look!"*

An' when his Pa he read out loud
The speech he maked, an' feel so proud
It's in the paper—Elmer's Ma
She ketched him—wite behind his Pa,—
   "Here's the way *you* look!"

Nen when his Ma she slip an' take
Him in the other room an' shake
Him good! w'y, he don't care—no-*sir!*—
He ist look up an' laugh at her,—
   "Here's the way *you* look!"

THE RAMBO-TREE

WHEN Autumn shakes the rambo-tree—
    It's a long, sweet way across the orchard!—
The bird sings low as the bumblebee—
    It's a long, sweet way across the orchard!—
The poor shote-pig he says, says he:
"When Autumn shakes the rambo-tree
There's enough for you and enough for me."—
    It's a long, sweet way across the orchard.

For just two truant lads like we,
When Autumn shakes the rambo-tree
There's enough for you and enough for me—
    It's a long, sweet way across the orchard.

When Autumn shakes the rambo-tree—
    It's a long, sweet way across the orchard!—
The mole digs out to peep and see—
    It's a long, sweet way across the orchard!—
The dusk sags down, and the moon swings free,
There's a far, lorn call, "Pig-*gee!* Pig-*gee!*"
And two boys—glad enough for three.—
    It's a long, sweet way across the orchard.

For just two truant lads like we,
When Autumn shakes the rambo-tree
There's enough for you and enough for me—
It's a long, sweet way across the orchard.

FIND THE FAVORITE

OUR three cats is Maltese cats,
    An' they's two that's white,—
An' bofe of 'em's *deef*—an' that's
    'Cause their *eyes* ain't right.—

Uncle say that *Huxley* say
    Eyes of *white* Maltese—
When they don't match thataway—
    They're deef as you please!

Girls, they like our white cats best,
    'Cause they're white as snow,
Yes, an' look the stylishest—
    But they're deef, you know!

They don't know their names, an' don't
    Hear us when we call
"Come in, Nick an' Finn!"—they won't
    Come fer us at all!

But our *other* cat, *he* knows
    Mister Nick an' Finn,—
Mowg's *his* name,—an' when *he* goes
    Fer 'em, they come in!

Mowgli's *all* his name—the same
   Me an' Muvver took
Like the Wolf-Child's *other* name,
   In "The Jungul Book."

I bet Mowg's the smartest cat
   In the world!—*He's* not
White, but mousy-plush, with that
   Smoky gloss he's got!

All's got little bells to ring,
   Round their neck; but none
Only Mowg *knows* anything—
   He's the only one!

I ist 'spect sometimes he hate
   White cats' stupid ways:—
He won't hardly 'sociate
   With 'em, lots o' days!

Mowg wants in where *we* air,—well,
   He'll ist take his paw
An' ist ring an' ring his bell
   There till me er Ma

Er *some*body lets him in
   Nen an' shuts the door.—
An', when he wants out ag'in,
   Nen he'll ring some more.

Ort to hear our Katy tell!
　She sleeps 'way up-stairs;
An' last night she hear Mowg's bell
　Ringin' round *some*wheres. . . .

Trees grows by her winder.—So,
　She lean out an' see
Mowg up there, 'way out, you know,
　In the clingstone-tree;—

An'-sir! he ist *hint* an' *ring,*—
　Till she ketch an' plat
Them limbs;—nen he crawl an' spring
　In where Katy's at!

THE BOY PATRIOT

I WANT to be a Soldier!—
               A Soldier!—
               A Soldier!—
I want to be a Soldier, with a saber in my hand
Or a little carbine rifle, or a musket on my shoulder,
Or just a snare-drum, snarling in the middle of the
         band;
I want to hear, high overhead, The Old Flag flap
         her wings
While all the Army, following, in chorus cheers
         and sings;
               I want to hear the tramp and jar
                  Of patriots a million,
               As gaily dancing off to war
                  As dancing a cotillion.

I want to be a Soldier!—
               A Soldier!—
               A Soldier!—
I want to be a Soldier, with a saber in my hand
Or a little carbine rifle, or a musket on my shoulder,
Or just a snare-drum, snarling in the middle of
         the band.

I want to see the battle!—
　　　　The battle!—
　　　　　　The battle!—
I want to see the battle, and be in it to the end;—
I want to hear the cannon clear their throats and
　　　catch the prattle
Of all the pretty compliments the enemy can send!—
And then I know my wits will go,—and where I
　　　shouldn't be—
Well, there's the spot, in any fight, that you may
　　　search for me.
　　　　So, when our foes have had their fill,
　　　　　Though I'm among the dying,
　　　　To see The Old Flag flying still,
　　　　　I'll laugh to leave her flying!

I want to be a Soldier!—
　　　　A Soldier!—
　　　　　　A Soldier!—
I want to be a Soldier, with a saber in my hand
Or a little carbine rifle, or a musket on my shoulder,
Or just a snare-drum, snarling in the middle of
　　　the band.

EXTREMES

I

A LITTLE boy once played so loud
That the Thunder, up in a thunder-cloud,
Said, "Since *I* can't be heard, why, then
I'll never, never thunder again!"

II

And a little girl once kept so still
That she heard a fly on the window-sill
Whisper and say to a ladybird,—
"She's the stilliest child I ever heard."

His home on Lockerbie Street

INTELLECTUAL LIMITATIONS

PARUNTS knows lots more than us,
　　But they don't know *all* things,—
'Cause we ketch 'em, lots o' times,
　　Even on little small things.

One time Winnie ask' her Ma,
　　At the winder, sewin',
What's the wind a-doin' when
　　It's a-not a-*blowin'?*

Yes, an' 'Del', that very day,
　　When we're nearly froze out,
He ask' Uncle *where* it goes
　　When the fire goes out?

Nen *I* run to ask my Pa,
　　That way, somepin' funny;
But I can't say ist but "Say,"
When he turn to me an' say,
　　"Well, what is it, Honey?"

A MASQUE OF THE SEASONS

SCENE.—*A kitchen.*—*Group of Children, popping corn.*—*The Fairy Queen of the Seasons discovered in the smoke of the corn-popper.*—*Waving her wand, and, with eery, sharp, imperious ejaculations, addressing the bespelled auditors, who neither see nor hear her nor suspect her presence.*

QUEEN

SUMMER or Winter or Spring or Fall,—
Which do you like the best of all?

LITTLE JASPER

When I'm dressed warm as warm can be,
    And with boots, to go
    Through the deepest snow,
Winter-time is the time for me!

QUEEN

Summer or Winter or Spring or Fall,—
Which do you like the best of all?

212

LITTLE MILDRED

I like blossoms, and birds that sing;
    The grass and the dew,
    And the sunshine, too,—
So, best of all I like the Spring.

QUEEN

Summer or Winter or Spring or Fall,—
Which do you like the best of all?

LITTLE MANDEVILLE

O little friends, I most rejoice
    When I hear the drums
    As the Circus comes,—
So Summer-time's my special choice.

QUEEN

Summer or Winter or Spring or Fall,—
Which do you like the best of all?

LITTLE EDITH

Apples of ruby, and pears of gold,
    And grapes of blue
    That the bee stings through.—
Fall—it is all that my heart can hold!

QUEEN

Soh! my lovelings and pretty dears,
You've *each* a favorite, it appears,—
Summer and Winter and Spring and Fall.—
That's the reason I send them *all!*

LITTLE DICK AND THE CLOCK

WHEN Dicky was sick
　　In the night, and the clock,
As he listened, said "Tick-
　　Atty—tick-atty—tock!"
He said that *it* said,
　　Every time it said "Tick,"
It said "Sick," instead,
　　And he *heard* it say "Sick!"
And when it said "Tick-
　　Atty—tick-atty—tock,"
He said it said "Sick-
　　Atty—sick-atty—sock!"
And he tried to *see* then,
　　But the light was too dim,
Yet he *heard* it again—
　　And 'twas *talking* to him!
And then it said "Sick-
　　Atty—sick-atty—sick!
You poor little Dick-
　　Atty—Dick-atty—Dick!—
Have you got the hick-
　　Atties? Hi! send for Doc
To hurry up quick-

Atty—quick-atty—quock,
'And heat a hot brick-
  Atty—brick-atty—brock,
'And rickle-ty wrap it
'And clickle-ty clap it
  Against his cold feet-
    Al-ty—weep-aty—eepaty—
There he goes, slapit-
    Ty—slippaty—sleepaty!"

THE KATYDIDS

SOMETIMES I keep
  From going to sleep,
To hear the katydids "cheep-cheep!"
And think they say
Their prayers that way;
But *katydids* don't have to *pray!*

I listen when
They cheep again;
And so, I think, they're *singing* then!
But, no; I'm wrong,—
The sound's too long
And all-alike to be a song!

I think, "Well, there!
I do declare,
If it is neither song nor prayer,
It's *talk*—and quite
Too vain and light
For me to listen to all night!"

217

And so, I smile,
And think,—"Now I'll
Not listen for a little while!"—
Then, sweet and clear,
Next *"cheep"* I hear
'S a *kiss*. . . . Good morning,
    Mommy dear!

THE NOBLE OLD ELM

O BIG Old Tree, so tall an' fine,
  Where all us childern swings an' plays,
Though neighbers says you're on the line
  Between Pa's house an' Mr. Gray's,—
Us childern used to almost fuss,
  Old Tree, about you when we'd play.
We'd argy you belonged to *us,*
  An' them Gray-kids the other way!

Till *Elsie,* one time *she* wuz here
  An' playin' wiv us—Don't you mind,
Old Mister Tree?—an' purty near
  She scolded us the hardest kind
Fer quar'llin' 'bout you thataway,
  An' say *she'll* find—ef we'll keep still—
Whose tree you air *fer shore,* she say,
  An' settle it *fer good,* she will!

So all keep still: An' nen she gone
  An' pat the Old Tree, an' says she,—
"Whose *air* you, Tree?" an' nen let on
  Like she's a-list'nin' to the Tree,—
An' nen she say, "It's settled,—'cause
  The Old Tree says he's *all* our tree—
His *trunk* belongs to bofe your Pas,
  But *shade* belongs to you an' me."

EVENSONG

LAY away the story,—
  Though the theme is sweet,
There's a lack of something yet,
  Leaves it incomplete :—
There's a nameless yearning—
  Strangely undefined—
For a story sweeter still
  Than the written kind.

Therefore read no longer—
  I've no heart to hear
But just something you make up,
  O my mother dear.—
With your arms around me,
  Hold me, folded-eyed,—
Only let your voice go on—
  I'll be satisfied.

AN IMPROMPTU FAIRY-TALE

When I wuz ist a little bit o' weenty-teenty kid
I maked up a Fairy-tale, all by myse'f, I did:—

I

WUNST upon a time wunst
    They wuz a Fairy King,
An' ever'thing he have wuz *gold*—
His clo'es, an' *ever*'thing!
An' all the other Fairies
    In his goldun Palace-hall
Had to hump an' hustle—
    'Cause he was bosst of all!

II

He have a golden trumput,
    An' when he blow' on that,
It's a sign he want' his boots,
    Er his coat er hat:

221

They's a sign fer ever'thing,—
An' all the Fairies knowed
Ever' sign, an' come a-hoppin'
When the King blowed!

III

Wunst he blowed an' telled 'em all:
"Saddle up yer bees—
Fireflies is gittin' fat
An' sassy as you please!—
Guess we'll go a-huntin'!"
So they hunt' a little bit,
Till the King blowed "Supper-time,"
Nen they all quit.

IV

Nen they have a Banqut
In the Palace-hall,
An' ist et! an' et! an' et!
Nen they have a *Ball;*
An' when the *Queen* o' Fairyland
Come p'omenadin' through,
The King says an' halts her,—
"Guess I'll marry you!"

THE TWINS

WE'RE The Twins from Aunt
     Marinn's,
          Igo and Ago.
When Dad comes, the show begins!—
          Iram, coram, dago.

Dad he says he named us two
          Igo and Ago
For a poem he always knew,
          Iram, coram, dago.

Then he was a braw Scotchman—
          Igo and Ago
Now he's Scotch-Amer-i-can.
          Iram, coram, dago.

"Hey!" he cries, and pats his knee,
          "Igo and Ago,
My twin bairnies, ride wi' me—
          Iram, coram, dago!"

"Here," he laughs, "ye've each a leg,
　　Igo and Ago,
Gleg as Tam O'Shanter's 'Meg'!
　　Iram, coram, dago!"

Then we mount, with shrieks of mirth—
　　Igo and Ago,—
The two gladdest twins on earth!
　　Iram, coram, dago.

Wade and Silas-Walker cry,—
　　"Igo and Ago—
Annie's kissin' 'em 'good-by'!"—
　　Iram, coram, dago.

Aunty waves us fond farewells.—
　　"Igo and Ago,"
Granny pipes, "tak care yersels!"
　　Iram, coram, dago.

THE LITTLE LADY

O THE Little Lady's dainty
  As the picture in a book,
And her hands are creamy-whiter
  Than the water-lilies look;
Her laugh's the undrown'd music
  Of the maddest meadow-brook.—
Yet all in vain I praise The Little Lady!

Her eyes are blue and dewy
  As the glimmering Summer-dawn,—
Her face is like the eglantine
  Before the dew is gone;
And were that honied mouth of hers
  A bee's to feast upon,
He'd be a bee bewildered, Little Lady!

Her brow makes light look sallow;
  And the sunshine, I declare,
Is but a yellow jealousy
  Awakened by her hair—
For O the dazzling glint of it
  Nor sight nor soul can bear,—
So Love goes groping for The Little Lady.

And yet she's neither Nymph nor Fay,
    Nor yet of Angelkind :—
She's but a racing schoolgirl, with
    Her hair blown out behind
And tremblingly unbraided by
    The fingers of the Wind,
As it wildly swoops upon The Little Lady.

"COMPANY MANNERS"

WHEN Bess gave her Dollies a tea, said she,—
  "It's unpolite, when they's Company,
To say you've drinked *two* cups, you see,—
But say you've drinked *a couple* of tea."

THE GOOD, OLD-FASHIONED PEOPLE

WHEN we hear Uncle Sidney tell
    About the long-ago
An' old, old friends he loved so well
    When *he* was young—My-oh!—
Us childern all wish *we'd* 'a' bin
    A-livin' then with Uncle,—so
We could a-kind o' happened in
    On them old friends *he* used to know!—
      The good, old-fashioned people—
      The hale, hard-working people—
      The kindly country people
         'At Uncle used to know!

They was God's people, Uncle says,
    An' gloried in His name,
An' worked, without no selfishness,
. An' loved their neighbors same
As they was kin: An' when they biled
    Their tree-molasses, in the Spring,
Er butchered in the Fall, they smiled
    An' sheered with all jist ever'thing!—
      The good, old-fashioned people—
      The hale, hard-working people—
      The kindly country people
         'At Uncle used to know!

He tells about 'em, lots o' times,
   Till we'd all ruther hear
About 'em than the Nurs'ry Rhymes
   Er Fairies—mighty near!—
Only, sometimes, he stops so long
   An' then talks on so low an' slow,
It's purt' nigh sad as any song
    To listen to him talkin' so
      Of the good, old-fashioned people—
      The hale, hard-working people—
      The kindly country people
        'At Uncle used to know!

THE BEST TIMES

WHEN Old Folks they wuz young like us
  An' little as you an' me,—
Them wuz the best times ever wuz
  Er ever goin' ter be!

"HIK-TEE-DIK"

THE WAR-CRY OF BILLY AND BUDDY

WHEN two little boys—renowned but for
    noise—
Hik-tee-dik! Billy and Buddy!—
May hurt a whole school, and the head it employs,
    Hik-tee-dik! Billy and Buddy!
Such loud and hilarious pupils indeed
Need learning—and yet something further they
    need,
Though fond hearts that love them may sorrow and
    bleed.
    Hik-tee-dik! Billy and Buddy!

O the schoolmarm was cool, and in nowise a fool;
    Hik-tee-dik! Billy and Buddy!
And in ruling her ranks it was *her* rule to *rule;*
    Hik-tee-dik! Billy and Buddy!
So when these two pupils conspired, every day,
Some mad piece of mischief, with whoop and
    hoo-ray,
That hurt yet defied her,—how happy were they!—
    Hik-tee-dik! Billy and Buddy!

At the ring of the bell they'd rush in with a yell—
  Hik-tee-dik! Billy and Buddy!
And they'd bang the school-door till the plastering
    fell,
  Hik-tee-dik! Billy and Buddy!
They'd clinch as they came, and pretend not to see
As they knocked her desk over—then, *My!* and
    O-me!
How awfully sorry they'd both seem to be!
  Hik-tee-dik! Billy and Buddy!

This trick seemed so neat and so safe a conceit,—
  Hik-tee-dik! Billy and Buddy!—
They played it three times—though the third they
    were beat;
  Hik-tee-dik! Billy and Buddy!
For the teacher, she righted her desk—raised the lid
And folded and packed away each little kid—
Closed the incident so—yes, and locked it, she did—
  Hik-tee-dik! Billy and Buddy!

"OLD BOB WHITE"

OLD Bob White's a funny bird!—
Funniest you ever heard!—
    Hear him whistle,—"Old—Bob—*White!*"
You can hear him, clean from where
He's 'way 'crosst the wheat-field there,
Whistlin' like he didn't care—
                "Old—Bob—*White!*"

Whistles alluz ist the same—
So's we won't fergit his name!—
    Hear him say it?—"Old—Bob—*White!*"
There! he's whizzed off down the lane—
Gone back where his folks is stayin'—
Hear him?—There he goes again,—
                "Old—Bob—*White!*"

A SESSION WITH UNCLE SIDNEY

[1869]

I

ONE OF HIS ANIMAL STORIES

NOW, Tudens, you sit on *this* knee—and 'scuse
It having no side-saddle on;—and, Jeems,
You sit on *this*—and don't you wobble so
And chug my old shins with your coppertoes;—
And, all the rest of you, range round someway,—
Ride on the rockers and hang to the arms
Of our old-time split-bottom carryall!—
Do anything but *squabble* for a place,
Or push or shove or scrouge, or breathe *out loud,*
Or chew wet, or knead taffy in my beard!—
Do *anything* almost—act *anyway,*—
Only *keep still,* so I can hear myself
Trying to tell you "just one story more!"

One winter afternoon my father, with
A whistle to our dog, a shout to us—
His two boys—six and eight years old we were,—
Started off to the woods, a half a mile

From home, where he was chopping wood. We
    raced,
We slipped and slid; reaching, at last, the north
Side of Tharp's corn-field.—There we struck what
    seemed
To be a coon-track—so we all agreed:
And father, who was not a hunter, to
Our glad surprise, proposed we follow it.
The snow was quite five inches deep; and we,
Keen on the trail, were soon far in the woods.
Our old dog, "Ring," ran nosing the fresh track
With whimpering delight, far on ahead.
After following the trail more than a mile
To northward, through the thickest winter woods
We boys had ever seen,—all suddenly
He seemed to strike *another* trail; and then
Our joyful attention was drawn to
Old "Ring"—leaping to this side, then to that,
Of a big, hollow, old oak tree, which had
Been blown down by a storm some years before.
There—all at once—out leapt a lean old fox
From the black hollow of a big bent limb,—
Hey! how he scudded!—but with our old "Ring"
Sharp after him—and father after "Ring"—
We after father, near as we could hold.
And father noticed that the fox kept just
About four feet ahead of "Ring"—just *that*—
No farther, and no nearer! Then he said:—
"There are young foxes in that tree back there,
And the mother-fox is drawing 'Ring' and us
Away from their nest there!"

                    "Oh, le' 's go back!—
Do le' 's go back!" we little vandals cried,—
"Le' 's go back, quick, and find the little things—
Please, father!—Yes, and take 'em home for pets—
'Cause 'Ring' he'll kill the old fox anyway!"

So father turned, at last, and back we went.
And then he chopped a hole in the old tree
About ten feet along the limb from which
The old fox ran: and—Bless their little lives!—
There, in the hollow of the old tree-trunk—
There, on a bed of warm dry leaves and moss—
There, snug as any bug in any rug—
We found—one—two—three—four, and, yes-sir,
        five
Wee, weenty-teenty baby-foxes, with
Their eyes just barely opened.—*Cute?*—my-oh!—
The cutest—the most cunning little things
Two boys ever saw, in all their lives!—
"Raw weather for the little fellows *now!*"
Said father, as though talking to himself,—
"Raw weather, and no home *now!*"—And off came
His warm old "waumus"; and in that he wrapped
The helpless little fellows then, and held
Them soft and warm against him as he could,—
And home we happy children followed him.—

Old "Ring" did not reach home till nearly dusk:
The mother-fox had led him a long chase—
"Yes, and a *fool's* chase, too!" he seemed to say,

And looked ashamed to hear us *praising* him.
But, *mother*—well, we *could not* understand
Her acting as she did—and we so *pleased!*
I can see yet the look of pained surprise
And deep compassion of her troubled face
When father very gently laid his coat,
With the young foxes in it, on the hearth
Beside her, as she brightened up the fire.
She urged—for the old fox's sake and theirs—
That they be taken back to the old tree;
But father—for *our* wistful sakes, no doubt—
Said we would keep them, and would try our best
To raise them. And at once he set about
Building a snug home for the little things
Out of an old big bushel-basket, with
Its fractured handle and its stoven ribs:
So, lining and padding this all cozily,
He snuggled in its little tenants, and
Called in John Wesley Thomas, our hired man,
And gave him in full charge, with much advice
Regarding the just care and sustenance of
Young foxes.—"John," he said, "you feed 'em
    milk—
Warm milk, John Wesley! Yes, and *keep 'em by*
The stove—and keep your stove *a-roarin'*, too,
Both night and day!—And keep 'em *covered* up—
Not *smothered,* John, but snug and comfortable—
And now, John Wesley Thomas, first and last,—
You feed 'em *milk*—*fresh* milk—and always
    warm—

Say five or six or seven times a day—
Of course we'll grade that by the way they *thrive*."
But, for all sanguine hope, and care, as well,
The little fellows *did not* thrive at all.—
Indeed, with *all* our care and vigilance,
By the third day of their captivity
The last survivor of the fated five
Squeaked, like some battered little rubber-toy,
Jist clean wore out.—And that's jist what 'e wuz!
And—nights,—the cry of the mother-fox for her
    young
Was heard, with awe, for long weeks afterward.
And we boys, every night, would go to the door
And, peering out in the darkness, listening,
Could hear the poor fox in the black bleak woods
Still calling for her little ones in vain.
As, all mutely, we returned to the warm fireside,
Mother would say: "How would you like for *me*
To be out there, this dark night, in the cold woods,
Calling for *my* children?"

II

UNCLE BRIGHTENS UP—

UNCLE he says 'at 'way down in the sea
    Ever'thing's ist like it *used* to be:—
He says they's mermaids an' mermans, too,
An' little merchildern, like me an' you—
Little merboys, with tops an' balls,
An' little mergirls, with little merdolls.

III

A PET OF UNCLE SIDNEY'S

UNCLE Sidney's vurry proud
    Of little Leslie-Janey,
'Cause she's so smart an' goes to school
    Clean 'way in Pennsylvany!
She print' an' sent a postul-card
    To Uncle Sidney, telling
How glad he'll be to hear that she
    "Toock the onners in Speling."

IV

IN THE KINDERGARTEN OF NOBLE SONG

UNCLE he learns us to rhyme an' write
    An' all be poets an' all recite:
His little-est poet's his little-est niece,
An' this is her little-est poetry-piece.

V

SINGS A "WINKY-TOODEN" SONG—

O HERE'S a little rhyme for the Spring- or
    Summer-time—
    An' a-ho-winky-tooden-an'-a-ho!—
Just a little bit o' tune you can twitter, May or June,
    An' a-ho-winky-tooden-an'-a-ho!
It's a song that soars and sings,
As the birds that twang their wings
Or the katydids and things
    Thus and so, don't you know,
    An' a-ho-winky-tooden-an'-a-ho!

It's a song just broken loose, with no reason or ex-
     cuse—
  An' a-ho-winky-tooden-an'-a-ho!
You can sing along with it—or it matters not a bit—
  An' a-ho-winky-tooden-an'-a-ho!

It's a lovely little thing
That 'most any one could sing
With a ringle-dingle-ding,
  Soft and low, don't you know,
  An' a-ho-winky-tooden-an'-a-ho!

VI

AND ANOTHER OF OUR BETSY—

US childern's all so lonesome,
  We hardly want to *play*
Or skip or swing or anything,—
  'Cause Betsy she's away!
She's gone to see her people
  At her old home.—But then—
Oh! every child'll jist be wild
  When she's back here again!

CHORUS

Then it's whoopty-doopty dooden!—
  Whoopty-dooden then!
Oh! it's whoopty-doopty dooden,
  When Betsy's back again!

She's like a mother to us,
   And like a sister, too—
Oh! she's as sweet as things to eat
   When all the dinner's through!
And hey! to hear her laughin'!
   And ho! to hear her sing!—
To have her back is all we lack
   Of havin' *everything!*

CHORUS

Then it's whoopty-doopty dooden!—
   Whoopty-dooden then!
Oh! it's whoopty-doopty dooden,
   When Betsy's back again!

Oh! some may sail the northern lakes,
   And some to foreign lands,
And some may seek old Nameless Creek,
   Or India's golden sands;
Or some may go to Kokomo,
   And some to Mackinac,—
But I'll go down to Morgantown
   To fetch our Betsy back.

CHORUS

Then it's whoopty-doopty dooden!—
   Whoopty-dooden then!
Oh! it's whoopty-doopty dooden,
   When Betsy's back again!

VII

AND MAKES NURSERY RHYMES

I

THE DINERS IN THE KITCHEN

OUR dog Fred
Et the bread.

Our dog Dash
Et the hash.

Our dog Pete
Et the meat.

Our dog Davy
Et the gravy.

Our dog Toffy
Et the coffee.

Our dog Jake
Et the cake.

Our dog Trip
Et the dip.

And—the worst,
From the first,—

Our dog *Fido*
Et the pie-dough.

2

THE IMPERIOUS ANGLER

Miss Medairy Dory-Ann
Cast her line and caught a man,
But when he looked so pleased, alack!
She unhooked and plunked him back.—
"I never like to catch what I can,"
Said Miss Medairy Dory-Ann.

3

THE GATHERING OF THE CLANS

[*Voice from behind high board-fence.*]

"Where's the crowd that dares to go
Where I dare to lead?—you know!"

"Well, here's *one!*"
Shouts Ezry Dunn.

"Count me *two!*"
Yells Cootsy Drew.

"Here's yer *three!*"
Sings Babe Magee.

"Score me *four!*"
Roars Leech-hole Moore.

"Tally—*five!*"
Howls Jamesy Clive.

"I make *six!*"
Chirps Herbert Dix.

"Punctchul!—*seven!*"
Pipes Runt Replevin.

"Mark me *eight!*"
Grunts Mealbag Nate.

"I'm yet *nine!*"
Growls "Lud'rick" Stein.

"Hi! here's *ten!*"
Whoops Catfish Ben.

"And now we march, in daring line,
For the banks of Brandywine!"

4

"IT"

A WEE little worm in a hickory-nut
 Sang, happy as he could be,—
"O I live in the heart of the whole round world,
 And it all belongs to me!"

5

THE DARING PRINCE

A DARING prince, of the realm Rangg Dhune,
Once went up in a big balloon
That caught and stuck on the horns of the moon,
And he hung up there till next day noon—
When all at once he exclaimed, "Hoot-toot!"
And then came down in his parachute.

A SONG OF SINGING

SING! gangling lad, along the brink
  Of wild brook-ways of shoal and deep,
Where killdees dip, and cattle drink,
  And glinting little minnows leap!
Sing! slimpsy lass who trips above
  And sets the foot-log quivering!
Sing! bittern, bumblebee, and dove—
    Sing! Sing! Sing!

Sing as you will, O singers all
  Who sing because you *want* to sing!
Sing! peacock on the orchard wall,
  Or tree-toad by the trickling spring!
Sing! every bird on every bough—
  Sing! every living, loving thing—
Sing any song, and anyhow,
    But Sing! Sing! Sing!

246

THE JAYBIRD

THE Jaybird he's my favor*ite*
　　Of all the birds they is!
I think he's quite a stylish sight
　　In that blue suit of his:
An' when he 'lights an' shuts his wings,
　　His coat's a "cutaway"—
I guess it's only when he sings
　　You'd know he wuz a jay.

I like to watch him when he's lit
　　In top of any tree,
'Cause all birds git wite out of it
　　When *he* 'lights, an' they see
How proud he act', an' swell an' spread
　　His chest out more an' more,
An' raise the feathers on his head
　　Like it's cut pompadore!

A BEAR FAMILY

WUNZT, 'way West in Illinoise,
  Wuz two Bears an' their two boys:
An' the two boys' names, you know,
Wuz—like *ours* is,—Jim an' Jo;
An' their *parunts'* names wuz same's
All big grown-up people's names,—
Ist *Miz* Bear, the neighbors call
'Em, an' *Mister* Bear—'at's all.
Yes—an' Miz Bear scold him, too,
Ist like grown folks *shouldn't* do!
Wuz a grea'-big river there,
An', 'crosst that, 's a mountain where
Old Bear said some day he'd go,
Ef she don't quit scoldin' so!
So, one day when he been down
The river, fishin', 'most to town,
An' come back 'thout no fish a-tall,
An' Jim an' Jo they run an' bawl
An' tell their ma their pa hain't fetch'
No fish,—she scold again an' ketch
Her old broom up an' biff him, too.—
An' he ist cry, an' say, *"Boo-hoo!*
I *told* you what I'd do some day!"

An' he ist turned an' runned away
To where's the grea'-big river there,
An' ist *splunged* in an' swum to where
The mountain's at, 'way th' other side,
An' clumbed up there. An' Miz Bear *cried*—
An' little Jo an' little Jim—
Ist like their ma—bofe cried fer him!—
But he clumbed on, *clean out o' sight,*
He wuz so mad!—An' served 'em right!
Nen—when the Bear got 'way on top
The mountain, he heerd somepin' flop
Its wings—an' somepin' else he heerd
A-rattlin'-like.—An' he wuz *skeered,*
An' looked 'way up, an'—*Mercy sake!*
It wuz a' Eagul an' a SNAKE!
An'-sir! the Snake, he bite an' kill'
The Eagul, an' they bofe fall till
They strike the ground—*k'spang-k'spat!*
Wite where the Bear wuz standin' at!
An' when here come the Snake at *him,*
The Bear he think o' little Jim
An' Jo, he did—an' their ma, too,—
All safe at home; an' he ist flew
Back down the mountain—an' could hear
The old Snake rattlin', sharp an' clear,
Wite clos't behind!—An' Bear he's so
All tired out, by time, you know,
He git down to the river there,
He know' he can't *swim* back to where
His folks is at. But ist wite nen

He see a boat an' six big men
'At's been a-shootin' ducks: An' so
He skeered them out the boat, you know,
An' ist jumped in—an' Snake *he* tried
To jump in, too, but falled outside
Where all the water wuz; an' so
The Bear grabs one the things you row
The boat wiv an' ist whacks the head
Of the old Snake an' kills him dead!—
An' when he's killed him dead, w'y, nen
The old Snake's drownded dead again!
Nen Bear set in the boat an' bowed
His back an' rowed—an' rowed—an' rowed—
Till he's safe home—so tired he can't
Do nothin' but lay there an' pant
An' tell his childern, "Bresh my coat!"
An' tell his wife, "Go chain my boat!"
An' they're so glad he's back, they say
"They *knowed* he's comin' thataway
To ist su'prise the dear ones there!"
An' Jim an' Jo they dried his hair
An' pulled the burs out; an' their ma
She ist set there an' helt his paw
Till he wuz sound asleep, an' nen
She telled him she won't scold again—
    Never—never—never—
    Ferever an' ferever!

SOME SONGS AFTER MASTER-SINGERS

I

SONG

[w. s.]

WITH a hey! and a hi! and a hey-ho
rhyme!
O the shepherd lad
He is ne'er so glad
As when he pipes, in the blossom-time,
So rare!
While Kate picks by, yet looks not there.
So rare! so rare!
With a hey! and a hi! and a ho!
The grasses curdle where the daisies blow!

With a hey! and a hi! and a hey-ho vow!
Then he sips her face
At the sweetest place—
And ho! how white is the hawthorn now!—
So rare!—
And the daisied world rocks round them there.
So rare! so rare!
With a hey! and a hi! and a ho!
The grasses curdle where the daisies blow!

II

TO THE CHILD JULIA

[R. H.]

LITTLE Julia, since that we
   May not as our elders be,
Let us blithely fill the days
Of our youth with pleasant plays.
First we'll up at earliest dawn,
While as yet the dew is on
The sooth'd grasses and the pied
Blossomings of morningtide;
Next, with rinsèd cheeks that shine
As the enamel'd eglantine,
We will break our fast on bread
With both cream and honey spread;
Then, with many a challenge-call,
We will romp from house and hall,
Gipsying with the birds and bees
Of the green-tress'd garden trees.
In a bower of leaf and vine
Thou shalt be a lady fine
Held in duress by the great
Giant I shall personate.
Next, when many mimics more
Like to these we have played o'er,
We'll betake us home-along
Hand in hand at evensong.

III

THE DOLLY'S MOTHER

[w. w.]

A LITTLE maid, of summers four—
   Did you compute her years,—
And yet how infinitely more
   To me her age appears:

I mark the sweet child's serious air,
   At her unplayful play,—
The tiny doll she mothers there
   And lulls to sleep away,

Grows—'neath the grave similitude—
   An infant real, to me,
And *she* a saint of motherhood
   In hale maturity.

So, pausing in my lonely round,
   And all unseen of her,
I stand uncovered—her profound
   And abject worshiper.

IV

WIND OF THE SEA

[A. T.]

WIND of the Sea, come fill my sail—
Lend me the breath of a freshening
gale
And bear my port-worn ship away!
For O the greed of the tedious town—
The shutters up and the shutters down!
Wind of the Sea, sweep over the bay
And bear me away!—away!

Whither you bear me, Wind of the Sea,
Matters never the least to me:
Give me your fogs, with the sails adrip,
Or the weltering path thro' the starless
night—
On, somewhere, is a new daylight
And the cheery glint of another ship
As its colors dip and dip!

Wind of the Sea, sweep over the bay
And bear me away!—away!

V

SUBTLETY

[R. B.]

WHILST little Paul, convalescing, was staying
  Close indoors, and his boisterous classmates
    paying
Him visits, with fresh school-notes and
    surprises,—
With nettling pride they sprung the word "Athletic,"
With much advice and urgings sympathetic
Anent "athletic exercises." Wise as
Lad might look, quoth Paul: "I've pondered o'er
    that
'Athletic,' but I mean to take, before that,
  Downstairic and outdooric exercises."

VI

BORN TO THE PURPLE

[W. M.]

MOST-LIKE it was this kingly lad
  Spake out of the pure joy he had
In his child-heart of the wee maid
Whose eery beauty sudden laid
A spell upon him, and his words
Burst as a song of any bird's:—

A peerless Princess thou shalt be,
Through wit of love's rare sorcery:
To crown the crown of thy gold hair
Thou shalt have rubies, bleeding there
Their crimson splendor midst the marred
Pulp of great pearls, and afterward
Leaking in fainter ruddy stains
Adown thy neck-and-armlet-chains
Of turquoise, chrysoprase, and mad
Light-frenzied diamonds, dartling glad
Swift spirts of shine that interfuse
As though with lucent crystal dews
That glance and glitter like split rays
Of sunshine, born of burgeoning Mays
When the first bee tilts down the lip
Of the first blossom, and the drip
Of blended dew and honey heaves
Him blinded midst the underleaves.
For raiment, Fays shall weave for thee—
Out of the phosphor of the sea
And the frayed floss of starlight, spun
With counterwarp of the firm sun—
A vesture of such filmy sheen
As, through all ages, never queen
Therewith strove truly to make less
One fair line of her loveliness.
Thus gowned and crowned with gems and
      gold,
Thou shalt, through centuries untold,
Rule, ever young and ever fair,
As now thou rulest, smiling there.

CLIMATIC SORCERY

WHEN frost's all on our winder, an' the snow's
All out-o'-doors, our "Old-Kriss"-milkman
      goes
A-drivin' round, ist purt' nigh froze to death,
With his old white mustache froze full o' breath.

But when it's summer an' all warm ag'in,
He comes a-whistlin' an' a-drivin' in
Our alley, 'thout no coat on, ner ain't cold,
Ner his mustache ain't white, ner he ain't old.

THE TREASURE OF THE WISE MAN

O THE night was dark and the night was late,
   And the robbers came to rob him;
And they picked the locks of his palace-gate,
   The robbers that came to rob him—
They picked the locks of his palace-gate,
Seized his jewels and gems of state,
His coffers of gold and his priceless plate,—
   The robbers that came to rob him.

But loud laughed he in the morning red!—
   For of what had the robbers robbed him?—
Ho! hidden safe, as he slept in bed,
   When the robbers came to rob him,—
They robbed him not of a golden shred
Of the childish dreams in his wise old head—
"And they're welcome to all things else," he said,
   When the robbers came to rob him.

OLD GRANNY DUSK

OLD Granny Dusk, when the sun goes,
Here *she* comes into thish-yer town!
Out o' the wet black woods an' swamps
In she traipses an' trails an' tromps—
With her old sunbonnet all floppy an' brown,
An' her cluckety shoes, an' her old black gown,
Here *she* comes into thish-yer town!

Old Granny Dusk, when the bats begin
To flap around, comes a-trompin' in!
An' the katydids they rasp an' whir,
An' the lightnin'-bugs all blink at *her;*
An' the old Hop-toad turns in his thumbs,
An' the bunglin' June-bug booms an' bums,
An' the Bullfrog croaks, "O here *she* comes!"

Old Granny Dusk, though I'm 'feard o' you,
Shore-fer-certain I'm sorry, too:
'Cause you look as lonesome an' starved an' sad
As a mother 'at's lost ever' child she had.—
Yet never a child in thish-yer town
Clings at yer hand er yer old black gown,
Er kisses the face you're a-bendin' down.

FIRE AT NIGHT

FIRE! Fire! Ring! and ring!
Hear the old bell bang and ding!
Fire! Fire! 'way at night,—
Can't you hear?—I think you might!—
Can't hear them-air clangin' bells?—
W'y, *I* can't hear nothin' else!
Fire! Ain't you 'wake at last!—
Hear them horses poundin' past—
Hear that ladder-wagon grind
Round the corner!—and, behind,
Hear the hose-cart, turnin' short,
And the horses slip and snort,
As the engine's clank-and-jar
Jolts the whole street, near and **far.**
Fire! Fire! Fire! Fire!
Can't you h'ist that winder higher?
La! they've all got past like "scat!" . . .
Night's as black as my old hat—
And it's rainin', too, at that! . . .
Wonder where their old fire's at!

THE YOUNG OLD MAN

VOLUNTARY BY ARTLESS "LITTLE BROTHER"

MAMMA is a widow: There's only us three—
   Our pretty Mamma, little sister, and me:
And we've come to live in this new neighborhood
Where all seems so quiet, old-fashioned and good.
  Mamma sits and sews at the window, and I—
   I'm out at the gate when an old man goes by—
   Such a *lovely* old man,—though I can't tell you
      why,
    Unless it's his greeting,—"Good morning!
  Good morning! good morning!" the old man will
     say,—
"Fine bracing weather we're having to-day!—
     And how's little brother—
     And sister—and mother?—
     So dear to each other!—
      Good morning!"

The old man goes by, in his glossy high-hat,
And stripe-trousers creased, and all turned-up, at
     that,
And his glancing nose-glasses—and pleasantest eyes,
As he smiles on me, always in newer surprise:
  And though his mustache is as white as the snow,

He wears it waxed out and all pointed, you know,
And gloves, and high collar and bright, jaunty
      bow,
      And stylish umbrella.—"Good morning!
Good morning! good morning!" the old man will
      say,—
"Fine falling weather we're promised to-day!—
            And how's little brother—
            And sister—and mother?—
            So fond of each other!—
            Good morning!"

.   .   .   .

It's Christmas!—it's Christmas! and oh, but we're
      gay!
The postman's been here, and Ma says, "Run and
      play:—
You must leave your Mamma to herself for a
      while!"
And so sweet is her voice, and so tender her
      smile!—
      And she looks *so* pretty and happy and—Well!—
      She's just too delicious for language to tell!—
      So Sis hugs her *more*—and *I* answer the bell,—
            And there in the doorway—"Good morning!—
Good morning! good morning! good morning, I
      say!—
Fine Christmas weather we're having to-day!—
            And how's little brother—
            Dear sister—er, ruther—
            Why, here *is* your *mother* . . .
            Good morning!"

SOME CHRISTMAS YOUNGSTERS

I

THE STRENGTH OF THE WEAK

*L*AST Chris'mus, little Benny
　　Wuzn't sick so bad,—
Now he's had the worst spell
　　Ever yet he had.
Ever' Chris'mus-morning, though,
　　He'll p'tend as if
He's asleep—an' first you know
　　He's got your "Chris'mus-gif'"!

Pa he's good to *all* of us
　　All the time; but when,
Ever' time it's *Chris'mus,*
　　He's as good-again!—
'Sides our toys an' candy,
　　Ever' Chris'mus he
Gives us all a quarter,
　　Certain as can be!

Pa, this morning, tiptoe' in
  To make the fire, you know,
Long 'fore it's daylight,
  An' all's ice an' snow!—
An' Benny holler, *"Chris'mus-gif' !"*
  An' Pa jump an' say,
"You'll only git a *dollar* if
  You skeer me thataway!"

II

THE LITTLE QUESTIONER

BABE she's so always
    Wantin' more to hear
All about Santy Claus,
  An' says: "Mommy dear,
Where's Santy's *home* at
  When he ain't *away?*—
An' is they *Mizzuz* Santy Claus
  An' *little* folks—say?—
Chris'mus, Santy's always *here*—
  Don't *they* want him, too?
When it *ain't* Chris'mus
  What does he do?"

III

PARENTAL CHRISTMAS PRESENTS

PARUNTS don't git *toys* an' things,
  Like you'd think they *ruther*.—
Mighty funny Chris'mus-gif's
  Parunts gives each other !—
Pa give Ma a barrel o' flour,
  An' Ma she give to Pa
The nicest dinin'-table
  She know he ever saw !

TWILIGHT STORIES

NEITHER daylight, starlight, moonlight,
    But a sad-sweet term of some light
By the saintly name of Twilight.

The Grandma Twilight Stories!—Still,
    A childish listener, I hear
The katydid and whippoorwill,
    In deepening atmosphere
Of velvet dusk, blent with the low
    Soft music of the voice that sings
And tells me tales of long ago
    And old enchanted things. . . .

While far fails the last dim daylight,
And the fireflies in the Twilight
Drift about like flakes of starlight.

"GO READ YOUR BOOK!"

HOW many times that grim old phrase
Has silenced me, in childish days!—
   And *now*—as then it did—
The phantom admonition, clear
And dominant, rings,—and I hear,
   And do as I am bid.

"Go read your book!" my good old sire
Commanded, in affected ire,
   When I, with querying look
And speech, dared vex his studious mind
With idle words of any kind.—
   And so I read my book.

Though seldom, in that *wisest* age,
Did I discern on Wisdom's page
   More than the *task*: That led
At least to *thinking,* and at last
To reading less, and not so fast,
   And longing as I read.

And, lo! in gracious time, I grew
To love a book all through and through!—
   With yearning eyes I look

On any volume,—old, maybe,
Or new—'tis meat and drink to me.—
   And so I read my book.

Old dog's-eared Readers, scarred and inked
With schoolboy hatred, long extinct;—
   Old Histories that bored
Me worst of all the school;—old, worn
Arithmetics, frayed, ripped, and torn—
   Now Ye are all adored.

And likewise I revere and praise
My sire, as now, with vainest gaze
   And hearing, still I look
For the old face so grave yet dear—
Nay, still I *see,* and still I *hear!*
   And so I read my book.

Next even to my nearest kin,—
My wife—my children romping in
   From school to ride my knee,—
I love a book, and dispossess
My lap of it with loathfulness,
   For all their love of me.

For, grave or gay the book, it takes
Me as an equal—calms, or makes
   Me, laughing, overlook
My little self—forgetful all
Of being so exceeding small.
   And so I read my book.

WHEN UNCLE DOC WAS YOUNG

THOUGH Doctor Glen—the best of
    men—
  Is wrinkled, old, and gray,
He'll always smile and stop a while
    Where little children play:
And often then he tells us, when
    He was a youngster, too,
He was as glad and bad a lad
    As old folks ever knew!

As he walks down, no boy in town
    But sees him half a block,
And stops to shout a welcome out
    With "Here comes Uncle Doc!"
Then all the rest, they look their best
    As he lines up among
Us boys of ten—each thinking then
    When Uncle Doc was young.

We *run* to him!—Though grave and grim,
    With voice pitched high and thin,
He still reveals the joy he feels
    In all that *he* has been:

With heart too true, and honest, too,
   To ever *hide* a truth,
He frankly owns, in laughing tones,
   He was "a sorry youth!"—

When he was young, he says, he sung
   And howled his level-best;
He says he guyed, and sneaked, and lied,
   And wrecked the robin's nest.—
All this, and worse, will he rehearse,
   Then smooth his snowy locks
And look the saint he says he ain't. . . .
   Them eyes of Uncle Doc's!

He says, when he—like you and me—
   Was just too low and mean
To slap asleep, he used to weep
   To find his face was clean:
His hair, he said, was just too red
   To tell with mortal tongue—
"The Burning Shame" was his nickname
   When Uncle Doc was young.

THE LISPER

ELSIE MINGUS *lisps,* she does!
  She lives wite acrosst from us
In Miz. Ayers'uz house 'at she
Rents part to the Mingusuz.—
  Yes, an' Elsie plays wiv me.

Elsie lisps so, she can't say
Her own name, ist *anyway!*—
  She say *"Elthy"*—like they wuz
Feathers on her words, an' they
  Ist stick on her tongue like fuzz.

My! she's *purty,* though!—An' when
She *lisps,* w'y, she's purty *nen!*
  When she telled me, wunst, her doll
Wuz so "thweet," an' I p'ten'
  I lisp too,—she laugh'—'at's all!—

She don't never git mad none—
'Cause she know I'm ist in fun.—
  Elsie she ain't one bit sp'iled.—
Of all childerns—ever' one—
  She's the *ladylikest* child!—

271

My Ma *say* she is! One time
Elsie start to say the rhyme
   "Thing a thong o' thixpenth"—*Whee!*
I ist *yell!* An' Ma say I'm
   Unpolite as I can be!

Wunst I went wiv Ma to call
On Elsie's Ma, an' eat an' all;
   An' nen Elsie, when we've et,
An' we're playin' in the hall,
   Elsie say: It's etikett

Fer young gentlemens, like me,
Eatin' when they's *company,*
   Not to never ever crowd
Down their food, ner "thip their tea
   Ner thup thoop so awful loud!"

A MOTTO

THE *Brightest* Star's the *modestest,*
  And mor'n likely writes
His motto like the lightnin'-bug's—
  According To His Lights.

A SIMPLE RECIPE

TO be a wholly worthy man,
　　As you, my boy, would like to be,—
This is to show you how you can—
　　This simple recipe :—

Be honest—both in word and act,
　　Be strictly truthful through and through:
Fact can not fail.—You stick to fact,
　　And fact will stick to you.

Be clean—outside and in, and sweep
　　Both hearth and heart and hold them bright;
Wear snowy linen—aye, and keep
　　Your *conscience* snowy-white.

Do right, your utmost—good *must* come
　　To you who do your level-best—
Your very hopes will help you some,
　　And work will do the rest.

HER LONESOMENESS

WHEN little Elizabeth whispers
     Her morning-love to me,
Each word of the little lisper's,
    As she clambers on my knee—
Hugs me and whispers, "Mommy,
      Oh, I'm so glad it's day
      And the night's all gone away!"
How it does thrill and awe me,—
      "The night's all gone away!"

"Sometimes I wake, all listenin',"
     She sighs, "and all's so still!—
The moon and the stars half-glistenin'
     Over the window-sill:—
And I look where the gas's pale light
      Is all turned down in the hall—
      And you ain't here at all!—
And oh, how I wish it was daylight!
      —And you ain't here at all!

"And oh," she goes eerily whining
     And laughing, too, as she speaks,
"If only the sun kept shining
     For weeks and weeks and weeks!—

For the world's so dark, without you,
   And the moon's turned down so low—
   'Way in the night, you know,—
And I get so lonesome about you!—
   'Way in the night, you know!"

ALMOST BEYOND ENDURANCE

I AIN'T a-goin' to cry no more, no more!
  I'm got ear-ache, an' Ma can't make
      It quit a-tall;
      An' Carlo bite my rubber-ball
  An' puncture it; an' Sis she take
An' poke' my knife down through the stable-floor
      An' loozed it—blame it all!
But I ain't goin' to cry no more, no more!

An' Aunt Mame *wrote* she's comin', an' she *can't*—
  Folks is come *there!*—An' I don't care
      She *is* my Aunt!
      An' my eyes stings; an' I'm
  Ist coughin' all the time,
An' hurts me so; an' where my side's so sore
      Grampa felt where, an' he
      Says "Mayby it's *pleurasy!*"
But I ain't goin' to cry no more, no more!

An' I clumbed up an' nen falled off the fence,
  An' Herbert he ist laugh at me!
      An' my fi'-cents
It sticked in my tin bank, an' I ist tore
      Purt' nigh my thumbnail off, a-tryin' to git
      It out—nen *smash* it!—An' it's in there yit!
But I ain't goin' to cry no more, no more!

Oo! I'm so wickud!—An' my breath's so *hot*—
    Ist like I run an' don't res' none
But ist run on when I ought to not;
        Yes, an' my chin
      An' lips's all warpy, an' teeth's so fast,
      An' 's a place in my throat I can't swaller past—
        An' they all hurt so!—
        An' oh, my-oh!
    I'm a-startin' ag'in—
I'm a-*startin'* ag'in, but I *won't,* fer shore!—
I ist ain't goin' to cry no more, no more!

THE TOY-BALLOON

THEY wuz a Big Day wunst in town,
  An' little Jason's Pa
Buyed him a little toy-balloon,
  The first he ever saw.—
An' oh! but Jase wuz *more'n* proud,
  A-holdin' to the string
An' scrougin' through the grea'-big crowd,
  To hear the Glee Club sing.

The Glee Club it wuz goin' to sing
  In old Masonic Hall;
An' Speakin', it wuz in there, too,
  An' soldiers, folks an' all:
An' Jason's Pa he git a seat
  An' set down purty soon,
A-holdin' little Jase, an' him
  A-holdin' his balloon.

An' while the Speakin' 's startin' up
  An' ever'body still—
The first you know wuz little Jase
  A-yellin' fit to kill!—

279

Nen Jason's Pa jump on his seat
    An' grab up in the air,—
But little Jason's toy-balloon
    Wuz clean away from there!

An' Jase he yelled; an' Jase's Pa,
    Still lookin' up, clumb down—
While that-air little toy-balloon
    Went bumpin' roun' an' roun'
Ag'inst the ceilin', 'way up there
    Where ever'body saw,
An' *they* all yelled, an' *Jason* yelled,
    An' little Jason's Pa!

But when his Pa he packed him out
    A-screamin'—nen the crowd
Looked down an' hushed—till they looked up
    An' howled ag'in out loud;
An' nen the speaker, mad an' pale,
    Jist turned an' left the stand,
An' all j'ined in the Glee Club—"Hail,
    Columby, Happy Land!"

Cartoon by Hubbard

THE OLD DAYS

THE old days—the far days—
  The overdear and fair!—
The old days—the lost days—
  How lovely they were!
The old days of Morning,
  With the dew-drench on the flowers
And apple-buds and blossoms
  Of those old days of ours.

Then was the *real* gold
  Spendthrift Summer flung;
Then was the *real* song
  Bird or Poet sung!
There was never censure then,—
  Only honest praise—
And all things were worthy of it
  In the old days.

There bide the true friends—
  The first and the best;
There clings the green grass
  Close where they rest:
Would they were here? No;—
  Would we were there! . . .
The old days—the lost days—
  How lovely they were!

TO A POET ON HIS MARRIAGE

MADISON CAWEIN

EVER and ever, on and on,
   From winter dusk, to April dawn,
This old enchanted world we range
From night to light—from change to change
Or paths of burs or lily-bells,
We walk a world of miracles.

The morning evermore must be
A newer, purer mystery—
The dewy grasses, or the bloom
Of orchards, or the wood's perfume
Of wild sweet-williams, or the wet
Blent scent of loam and violet.

How wondrous all the ways we fare—
What marvels wait us, unaware! . . .
But yesterday, with eyes ablur
And heart that held no hope of Her,
You paced the lone path, but the true
That led to where she waited you.

LOCKERBIE FAIR

O THE Lockerbie Fair!—Have you heard of
its fame
And its fabulous riches, too rare for a name!—
The gold of the noon of the June-time refined
To the Orient-Night, till the eyes and the mind
Are dazed with the sights, in the earth and the air,
Of the opulent splendors of Lockerbie Fair.

What more fortunate fate might to mortal befall,
Midst the midsummer beauty and bloom of it all,
Than to glit with the moon o'er the rapturous scene
And twink with the stars as they laughingly lean
O'er the luminous revel and glamour and glare
Fused in one dazzling glory at Lockerbie Fair.

The Night, like a queen in her purple and lace,
With her diamonded brow, and imperious grace,
As she leads her fair votaries, train upon train,
A-dance thro' the feasts of this mystic domain
To the mandolin's twang, and the warble and blare
Of voice, flute and bugle at Lockerbie Fair.

All strange, ever-changing, enchanted delights
Found now in this newer Arabian Nights,—
Where each lovely maid is a Princess, and each
Lucky swain an Aladdin—all treasures in reach
Of the *"lamps"* and the *"rings"*—and with *Genii* to
    spare,
Simply waiting your orders, at Lockerbie Fair.

THE OLD MAN OF THE SEA

I'M The Old Man of the Sea—I am!—
  And this is my secret pride,
That I have a hundred shapes, all sham,
  And a hundred names beside:
They have named me "Habit," and "Way," forsooth,
  "Capricious," and "Fancy-free";—
But to you, O Youth, I confess the truth,—
  I'm The Old Man of the Sea.

I'm The Old Man of the Sea, yo-ho!
  So lift up a song with me,
As I sit on the throne of your shoulders, alone,
  I'm The Old Man of the Sea.

Crowned with the crown of your noblest thought,
  I'm The Old Man of the Sea:
I reign, rule, ruin, and palter not
  In my pitiless tyranny:
You, my lad, are my gay Sindbad,
  Frisking about, with me
High on the perch I have always had—
  I'm The Old Man of the Sea.

I'm The Old Man of the Sea, yo-ho!
  So lift up a song with me,
As I sit on the throne of your shoulders, alone,
  I'm The Old Man of the Sea.

Tricked in the guise of your best intent,
  I am your failures—all—
I am the victories you invent,
  And your high resolves that fall:
I am the vow you are breaking now
  As the wassail-bowl swings free
And the red guilt flushes your cheek and brow—
  I'm The Old Man of the Sea.

I'm The Old Man of the Sea, yo-ho!
  So lift up a song with me,
As I sit on the throne of your shoulders, alone,
  I'm The Old Man of the Sea.

I am your false dreams of success
  And your mythical future fame—
Your lifelong lies, and your soul's distress
  And your slowly-dying shame:
I'm the chattering half of your latest laugh,
  And your tongue's last perfidy—
Your doom, your tomb, and your epitaph . . .
  I'm The Old Man of the Sea.

I'm The Old Man of the Sea, yo-ho!
  So lift up a song with me,
As I sit on the throne of your shoulders, alone,
  I'm The Old Man of the Sea.

PROSE OR VERSE?

PROSE or Verse—or Verse or Prose?
   Ever thus the query goes,—
Which delight do we prefer—
Which the finer—daintier?

Each incites a zest that grows—
Prose or Verse—or Verse or Prose?—
Each a lotus-eater's spell
Wholly irresistible.

All that wit may fashion, free-
Voiced, or piped in melody,—
Prose or Verse—or Verse or Prose—
Which of these the mastery knows?

'Twere as wise to question, friend—
As of this alluring blend,—
The aroma or the rose?—
Prose or Verse—or Verse or Prose?

BILLY MILLER'S CIRCUS-SHOW

AT Billy Miller's Circus-Show—
   In their old stable where it's at—
The boys pays twenty pins to go,
   An' gits their money's-worth at that!—
'Cause Billy he can climb and chalk
His stockin'-feet an' purt' nigh walk
A tight-rope—yes, an' *ef* he fall
He'll ketch, an' "skin a cat"—'at's all!

He ain't afeard to swing and hang
   Ist by his legs!—an' mayby stop
An' yell "Look out!" an' nen—k-spang!—
   He'll let loose, upside-down, an' drop
Wite on his hands! An' nen he'll do
"Contortion-acts"—ist limber through
As "Injarubber Mens" 'at goes
With shore-fer-certain circus-shows!

At Billy Miller's Circus-Show
   He's got a circus-ring—an' they's
A dressin'-room,—so's he can go
   An' dress an' paint up when he plays

He's somepin' else ;—'cause sometimes he's
"Ringmaster"—bossin' like he please—
An' sometimes "Ephalunt"—er "Bare-
Back Rider," prancin' out o' there!

An' sometimes—an' the best of all!—
  He's "The Old Clown," an' got on clo'es
All stripud,—an' white hat, all tall
  An' peakud—like in shore-'nuff shows,—
An' got three-cornered red-marks, too,
On his white cheeks—ist like they do!—
An' you'd ist die, the way he sings
An' dances an' says funny things!

IT'S *GOT* TO BE

"WHEN it's *got* to be,"—like I always say,
    As I notice the years whiz past,
And know each day is a yesterday,
    When we size it up, at last,—
Same as I said when my boyhood went
    And I knowed *we* had to quit,—
"It's *got* to be, and it's *goin'* to be!"—
    So I said "Good-by" to *it*.

It's *got* to be, and it's *goin'* to be!
    So at least I always try
To kind o' say in a hearty way,—
    "Well, it's *got* to be. Good-by!"

The time just melts like a late, last snow,—
    When it's *got* to be, it melts!
But I aim to keep a cheerful mind,
    Ef I can't keep nothin' else!
I knowed, when I come to twenty-one,
    That I'd soon be twenty-two,—
So I waved one hand at the soft young man,
    And I said, "Good-by to *you!*"

It's *got* to be, and it's *goin'* to be!
  So at least I always try
To kind o' say, in a cheerful way,—
  "Well, it's *got* to be.—Good-by!"

They kep' a-goin', the years and years,
  Yet still I smiled and smiled,—
For I'd said "Good-by" to my single life,
  And now had a wife and child:
Mother and son and the father—one,—
  Till, last, on her bed of pain,
She jes' smiled up, like she always done,—
  And I said "Good-by" again.

It's *got* to be, and it's *goin'* to be!
  So at least I always try
To kind o' say, in a humble way,—
  "Well, it's *got* to be. Good-by!"

And then my boy—as he growed to be
  Almost a man in size,—
Was more than a pride and joy to me,
  With his mother's smilin' eyes.—
He gimme the slip, when the War broke out,
  And followed me. And I
Never knowed till the first fight's end . . .
  I found him, and then, . . . "Good-by."

It's *got* to be, and it's *goin'* to be!
  So at least I always try
To kind o' say, in a patient way,
  "Well, it's *got* to be. Good-by!"

I have said, "Good-by!—Good-by!—Good-by!"
  With my very best good will,
All through life from the first,—and I
  Am a cheerful old man still:
But it's *got* to end, and it's *goin'* to end!
  And this is the thing I'll do,—
With my last breath I will laugh, O Death,
  And say "Good-by" to *you!* . . .

It's *got* to be! And again I say,—
  When his old scythe circles high,
I'll laugh—of course, in the kindest way,—
  As I say "Good-by!—Good-by!"

CHRISTMAS SEASON

TO A FRIEND VISITING ENGLAND

THIS is a Christmas carol—
  A late one, it is true,—
But (dight in Truth's apparel)
  The best that we can do:—
        The best our Muse belated
        Thus offers, antedated,—
        E'en as the old waits waited
  We, waiting, sing for you.

So, haply, you may listen,
  As 'twere, with Fancy's ear,
And shape such songs of this-un
  As were worth worlds to hear,—
        Such anthemings ecstatic
        As scaled The Mermaid's attic
        In midnight's aromatic
  Of choicest Christmas cheer:

Such songs as Marlowe lifted,
  With throstle-throated Will
And rare Ben, as they shifted
  Their laughing voices till

The mirth, with music blended,
So oversweet ascended,
It well were never ended—
And, hark!—you hear it still! . . .

You hear it; aye, and love it!—
Beyond all voices dear—
Your master's!—none above it.—
So harken, and so hear!—
Your master's English.—Surely
No other rests so purely
On Fame, or more securely,—
O English of Shakespeare!

ART AND POETRY

TO HOMER C. DAVENPORT

"WESS," he says, and sort o' grins,
    "Art and Poetry is twins.
'F I could draw as you have drew,
Like to jes' swap pens with you."

THE CHILDREN OF THE CHILDLESS

THE Children of the Childless!—Yours—and
 mine.—
Yea, though we sit here in the pitying gaze
Of fathers and mothers whose fond fingers twine
Their children's locks of living gold, and praise
With warm, caressing palms, the head of brown,
Or crown
Of opulent auburn, with its amber floss
In all its splendor loosed and jostled down
Across
The mother-lap at prayer.—Yea, even when
These sweet petitioners are kissed, and then
Are kissed and kissed again—
The pursed mouths lifted with the worldlier prayer
That bed and oblivion spare
Them yet a little while
Beside their envied elders by the glow
Of the glad firelight; or wresting, as they go,
Some promise for the morrow, to beguile
Their long exile
Within the wild waste lands of dream and sleep.
Nay, nay, not even these most stably real
Of children are more loved than our ideal—

More tangible to the soul's touch and sight
Than *these—our* children by Divine birthright. . . .
These—these of ours, who soothe us, when we
     weep,
With tenderest ministries,
Or, flashing into smiling ecstasies,
Come dashing through our tears—ay, laughing leap
Into our empty arms, in Fate's despite,
And nestle to our hearts. O Heaven's delight!—
The children of the childless—even *these!*

HOOSIER SPRING-POETRY

WHEN ever'thing's a-goin' like she's got-
    a-goin' now,—
The maple-sap a-drippin', and the buds on ever'
    bough
A-sort o' reachin' up'ards all a-trimblin', ever' one,
Like 'bout a million Brownie-fists a-shakin' at the
    sun!
The childern wants 'heir shoes off 'fore their break-
    fast, and the Spring
Is here so good-and-plenty that the old hen has to
    sing!—
When things is goin' *thisaway,* w'y, that's the sign,
    you know,
That ever'thing's a-goin' like we like to see her go!

Oh, ever'thing's a-goin' like we like to see her go!
Old Winter's up and dusted, with his dratted frost
    and snow—
The ice is out the crick ag'in, the freeze is out the
    ground,
And you'll see faces thawin' too ef you'll jes' look
    around!—

The bluebird's landin' home ag'in, and glad to git
    the chance,
'Cause here's where he belongs at, that's a settled
    circumstance!
And him and mister robin now's a-chunin' fer the
    show.
Oh, ever'thing's a-goin' like we like to see her go!

The sun ain't jes' p'tendin' *now!*—The ba'm is in
    the breeze—
The trees'll soon be green as grass, and grass as
    green as trees;
The buds is all jes' *eechin'*, and the dogwood down
    the run
Is bound to bu'st out laughin' 'fore another week is
    done;
The bees is wakin', gap'y-like, and fumblin' fer their
    buzz,
A-thinkin' ever-wakefuler, of other days that wuz,—
When all the land wuz orchard-blooms and clover,
    don't you know. . . .
Oh, ever'thing's a-goin' like we like to see her go!

THE VOICE OF PEACE

INDEPENDENCE BELL: INDIANAPOLIS, NOVEMBER
17, 1904

THOUGH now forever still
    Your voice of jubilee—
We hear—we hear, and ever will,
    The Bell of Liberty!
Clear as the voice to them
    In that far night agone
Pealed from the heavens o'er Bethlehem,
    The voice of Peace peals on!

Stir all your memories up,
    O Independence Bell,
And pour from your inverted cup
    The song we love so well!
As you rang in the dawn
    Of Freedom—tolled the knell
Of Tyranny,—ring on—ring on—
    O Independence Bell!

300

Ring numb the wounds of wrong
  Unhealed in brain and breast;
With music like a slumber-song
  Lull tearful eyes to rest.—
Ring! Independence Bell!
  Ring on till worlds to be
Shall listen to the tale you tell
  Of Love and Liberty!

A DEFECTIVE SANTA CLAUS

Little Boy! Halloo!—halloo!
Can't you hear me calling you?—
Little Boy that used to be,
Come in here and play with me.

ALLUS when our Pa he's away
    Nen Uncle Sidney comes to stay
At our house here—so Ma an' me
An' Etty an' Lee-Bob won't be
Afeard ef anything at night
Might happen—like Ma says it might.
(Ef *Trip* wuz *big,* I bet you he
'Uz best watch-dog you ever see!)
An' so last winter—ist before
It's go' be Chris'mus-Day,—w'y, shore
Enough, Pa had to haf to go
To 'tend a lawsuit—"An' the snow
Ist right fer Santy Claus!" Pa said,
As he clumb in old Ayersuz sled,
An' said he's sorry *he* can't be
With us that night—"'Cause," he-says-ee,
"Old Santy *might* be comin' here—
This very night of all the year
I' got to be away!—so all

302

You kids must tell him—ef he call—
He's mighty welcome, an' yer Pa
He left his love with you an' Ma
An' Uncle Sid!" An' clucked, an' leant
Back, laughin'—an' away they went!
An' Uncle wave' his hands an' yells
"Yer old horse ort to have on bells!"
But Pa yell back an' laugh an' say
"I 'spect when *Santy* come this way
It's time enough fer sleighbells nen!"
An' holler back "Good-by!" again,
An' reach out with the driver's whip
An' cut behind an' drive back Trip.

An' so all day it snowed an' snowed!
An' Lee-Bob he ist watched the road,
In his high-chair; an' Etty she
'Ud play with Uncle Sid an' me—
Like she wuz he'ppin' fetch in wood
An' keepin' old fire goin' good,
Where Ma she wuz a-cookin' there
In kitchen, too, an' ever'where!
An' Uncle say, "'At's ist the way
Yer Ma's b'en workin', night an' day,
Sence she hain't big as Etty is
Er Lee-Bob in that chair o' his!"
Nen Ma she'd laugh 't what Uncle said,
An' smack an' smoove his old bald head
An' say "Clear out the way till I
Can keep that pot from b'ilin' dry!"
Nen Uncle, when she's gone back to

The kitchen, says, "We *ust* to do
Some cookin' in the *ashes.—Say,*
S'posin' we try some, thataway!"
An' nen he send us to tell Ma
Send two big 'taters in he saw
Pa's b'en a-keepin' 'cause they got
The premiun at the Fair! An' what
You think?—He rake a grea'-big hole
In the hot ashes, an' he roll
Them old big 'taters in the place
An' rake the coals back—an' his face
Ist swettin' so's he purt' nigh swear
'Cause it's so hot! An' when they're there
'Bout time 'at we fergit 'em, he
Ist rake 'em out again—an' *gee!*—
He bu'st 'em with his fist wite on
A' old stove-led, while Etty's gone
To git the salt, an' butter, too—
Ist like he said she haf to do,
No matter what *Ma* say! An' so
He salt an' butter 'em, an' blow
'Em cool enough fer us to eat—
An' *me-o-my!* they're hard to beat!
An' Trip 'ud ist lay there an' pant
Like he'd laugh *out loud,* but he can't.
Nen Uncle fill his pipe—an' we
'Ud he'p him light it—Sis an' me,—
But mostly little Lee-Bob, 'cause
"He's the best *Lighter* ever wuz!"
Like Uncle told him wunst when Lee-
Bob cried an' jerked the light from me,

He wuz so mad! So Uncle pat
An' pet him (Lee-Bob's ust to that—
'Cause he's the *little*-est, you know,
An' allus has b'en humored so!)
Nen Uncle gits the flat-arn out,
An', while he's tellin' us all 'bout
Old Chris'mus-times when *he's* a kid,
He ist cracked hickernuts, he did,
Till they's a crockful, mighty nigh!
An' when they're all done by an' by,
He raked the red coals out again
An' telled me, "Fetch that popcorn in,
An' old three-leggud skillut—an'
The *led* an' all now, little man,—
An' yer old Uncle here 'ull show
You how corn's popped, long years ago
When me an' Santy Claus wuz boys
On Pap's old place in Illinoise!—
An' your Pa, too, wuz chums, all through,
With Santy!—Wisht Pa'd be here, too!"
Nen Uncle sigh at Ma, an' she
Pat him again, an' say to me
An' Etty,—"You take warning fair!—
Don't talk too much, like Uncle there,
Ner don't fergit, like *him*, my dears,
That 'little pitchers has big ears!' "
But Uncle say to her, "Clear out!—
Yer brother knows what he's about.—
You git your Chris'mus-cookin' done
Er these pore childern won't have none!"
Nen Trip wake' up an' raise', an' nen

Turn roun' an' nen lay down again.
An' one time Uncle Sidney say,—
"When dogs is sleepin' thataway,
Like Trip, an' *whimpers,* it's a sign
He'll ketch *eight* rabbits—mayby *nine*—
Afore his fleas'll wake him—nen
He'll bite hisse'f to sleep again
An' *try* to dream he's go' ketch *ten.*"
An' when Ma's gone again back in
The kitchen, Uncle scratch his chin
An' say, "When Santy Claus an' Pa
An' me wuz little boys—an' Ma,
When she's 'bout big as Etty there;—
W'y,—'When we're *growed*—no matter *where,*'
Santy he cross' his heart an' say,—
'I'll come to see you, all, some day
When *you*' got childerns—all but me
An' pore old Sid!' " Nen Uncle he
Ist kind o' shade his eyes an' pour'
'Bout forty-'leven bushels more
O' popcorn out the skillut there
In Ma's new basket on the chair.
An' nen he telled us—an' talk' low,
"So Ma can't hear," he say:—"You know
Yer *Pa* know', when he drived away,
To-morry's go' be Chris'mus-*Day;*—
Well, nen *to-night,*" he whisper, "see?—
It's go' be Chris'mus-*Eve,*" says-ee,
"An', like yer Pa hint, when he went,
Old Santy Claus (now hush!) he's sent
Yer Pa a postul-card, an' write

He's shorely go' be here to-night. . . .
That's why yer Pa's so bored to be
Away to-night, when Santy he
Is go' be here, sleighbells an' all,
To make you kids a Chris'mus-call!"
An' we're so glad to know *fer shore*
He's comin', I roll on the floor—
An' here come Trip a-waller'n' roun'
An' purt' nigh knock the clo'eshorse down!—
An' Etty grab Lee-Bob an' prance
All roun' the room like it's a dance—
Till Ma she come an' march us nen
To dinner, where we're *still* again,
But *tickled* so we ist can't eat
But pie, an' ist the hot mincemeat
With raisins in.—But *Uncle* et,
An' *Ma.* An' there they set an' set
Till purt' nigh supper-time; nen we
Tell him he's got to fix the Tree
'Fore *Santy* gits here, like he said.
We go nen to the old woodshed—
All bundled up, through the deep snow—
"An' snowin' yet, *jee-rooshy-O!*"
Uncle he said, an' he'p us wade
Back where's the Chris'mus-Tree he's made
Out of a little jackoak-top
He git down at the sawmill-shop—
An' Trip 'ud run ahead, you know,
An' 'tend-like he 'uz *eatin'* snow—
When we all waddle back with it;
An' Uncle set it up—an' git

It wite in front the fireplace—'cause
He says "'Tain't *so* 'at Santy Claus
Comes down *all* chimblies,—least, to-night
He's comin' in *this* house all right—
By the front-door, as ort to be!—
We'll all be hid where we can *see!*"
Nen he look up, an' he see Ma
An' say, "It's ist too bad their *Pa*
Can't be here, so's to see the fun
The childern *will* have, ever' one!"

Well, *we!*—We hardly couldn't wait
Till it wuz dusk, an' dark an' late
Enough to light the lamp!—An' Lee-
Bob light a candle on the Tree—
"Ist *one*—'cause I'm 'The Lighter'!"—Nen
He clumb on Uncle's knee again
An' hug us *bofe;*—an' Etty git
Her little chist an' set on it
Wite clos't, while Uncle telled some more
'Bout Santy Claus, an' clo'es he wore
"All maked o' furs, an' trimmed as white
As cotton is, er snow at night!"
An' nen, all sudden-like, he say,—
"Hush! Listen there! Hain't that a sleigh
An' sleighbells jinglin'?" Trip go *"whooh!"*
Like *he* hear bells and *smell* 'em, too.
Nen we all listen. . . . An'-sir, shore
Enough, we hear bells—more an' more
A-jinglin' clos'ter—clos'ter still
Down the old crook-road roun' the hill.

'An' Uncle he jumps up, an' all
The chairs he jerks back by the wall
An' th'ows a' overcoat an' pair
O' winder-curtains over there
An' says, *"Hide quick, er you're too late!—*
Them bells is stoppin' at the gate!—
Git back o' them-'air chairs an' hide,
'Cause I hear Santy's voice outside!"
'An' *Bang! bang! bang!* we heerd the door—
Nen it flewed open, an' the floor
Blowed full o' snow—that's *first* we saw,
Till little Lee-Bob shriek' at Ma
"There's Santy Claus!—I know him by
His big white mufftash!"—an' ist cry
An' laugh an' *squeal* an' dance an' *yell*—
Till, when he quiet down a spell,
Old Santy bow an' th'ow a kiss
To him—an' one to me an' Sis—
'An' nen go *clos't* to Ma an' stoop
'An' kiss her—An' nen give a whoop
That *fainted* her!—'Cause when he bent
An' kiss her, he ist backed an' went
Wite 'g'inst the Chris'mus-Tree ist where
The candle's at Lee-Bob lit there!—
'An' set his white-fur belt afire—
'An' blaze streaked roun' his waist an' higher
Wite up his old white beard an' th'oat!—
Nen Uncle grabs th' old overcoat
'An' flops it over Santy's head,
'An' swing the door wide back an' said,
"Come out, old man!—an' *quick* about

It!—I've ist *got* to put you out!"
An' out he sprawled him in the snow—
"Now *roll!*" he says—"*Hi-roll-ee-O!*"—
An' Santy, sputter'n' "*Ouch! Gee-whiz!*"
Ist roll an' roll fer all they is!
An' Trip he's out there, too,—I know,
'Cause I could hear him yappin' so—
An' I heerd Santy, wunst er twic't,
Say, as he's rollin', "*Drat the fice't!*"
Nen Uncle come back in, an' shake
Ma up, an' say, "Fer mercy-sake!—
He hain't hurt none!" An' nen he said,—
"You youngsters h'ist up-stairs to bed!—
Here! kiss yer Ma 'Good night,' an' me,—
We'll he'p old Santy fix the Tree—
An' all yer whistles, horns an' drums
I'll he'p you toot when morning comes!"

.   .   .   .

It's long while 'fore we go to sleep,—
'Cause down-stairs, all-time somepin' keep
A-kind o' scufflin' roun' the floors—
An' openin' doors, an' *shettin'* doors—
An' could hear Trip a-whinin', too,
Like he don't know ist *what* to do—
An' tongs a-clankin' down *k'thump!*—
Nen some one squonkin' the old pump—
An' *Wooh!* how cold it soun' out there!—
I could ist *see* the pump-spout where
It's got ice chin-whiskers all wet
An' drippy—An' I see it yet!
An' nen, seem-like, I hear some mens

'A-talkin' out there by the fence,
An' one says, "Oh, 'bout twelve o'clock!"
"Nen," 'nother'n' says, "Here's to you, Doc!—
God bless us ever one!" An' nen
I heerd the old pump squonk again.
An' nen I say my prayer all through
Like Uncle Sidney learn' me to,—
"O Father mine, e'en as Thine own,
This child looks up to Thee alone:
Asleep or waking, give him still
His Elder Brother's wish and will."
An' that's the last I know . . . Till **Ma**
She's callin' us—an' so is *Pa*,—
He holler *"Chris'mus-gif'!"* an' say,—
"I'm got back home fer Chris'mus-Day!—
An' Uncle Sid's here, too—an' he
Is nibblin' 'roun' yer Chris'mus-Tree!"
Nen *Uncle* holler, "I suppose
Yer Pa's so proud he's froze his nose
He wants to turn it up at us,
'Cause *Santy* kick' up such a fuss—
Tetchin' hisse'f off same as ef
He wuz his own fireworks hisse'f!"

An' when we're down-stairs,—shore enough,
Pa's nose *is* froze, an' salve an' stuff
All on it—an' one hand's froze, too,
An' got a old yarn red-and-blue
Mitt on it—"An' he's froze some more
Acrost his chist, an' kind o' sore
All roun' his *dy*-fram," Uncle say.—

"But Pa he'd ort a-seen the way
Santy bear up last night when that-
Air fire break out, an' quicker'n *scat*
He's all a-blazin', an' them-'air
Gun-cotton whiskers that he wear
Ist *flashin'!*—till I burn a hole
In the snow with him, an' he roll
The front-yard dry as Chris'mus jokes
Old parents plays on little folks!
But, long's a smell o' tow er wool,
I kep' him rollin' *beautiful!*—
Till I wuz *shore* I *shorely* see
He's *squenched!* W'y, hadn't b'en fer *me*,
That old man might a-burnt clear down
Clean—plum'—level with the groun'!"
Nen Ma say, *"There,* Sid; that'll do!—
Breakfast is ready—*Chris'mus,* too.—
Your voice 'ud soun' best, sayin' *Grace*—
Say it." An' Uncle bow' his face
An' say so long a *Blessing* nen,
Trip bark' *two* times 'fore it's "A-men!"

WHAT LITTLE SAUL GOT, CHRISTMAS

US parents mostly thinks our own's
    The smartest childern out!
But Widder Shelton's little Saul
    Beats all I know about!
He's weakly-like—in p'int o' health,
    But strong in word and deed
And heart and head, and snap and spunk,
    And allus in the lead!

Comes honest by it, fer his Pa—
    Afore he passed away—
He was a leader—(Lord, I'd like
    To hear him preach to-day!)
He led his flock; he led in prayer
    Fer spread o' Peace—and when
Nothin' but War could spread it, he
    Was first to lead us then!

So little Saul has grit to take
    Things jes' as they occur;
And Sister Shelton's proud o' him
    As he is proud o' her!

313

And when she "got up"—jes' fer him
　And little playmates all—
A Chris'mus-tree—they ever'one
　Was there but little Saul.

Pore little chap was sick in bed
　Next room; and Doc was there,
And said the childern might file past,
　But go right back to where
The *tree* was, in the settin'-room.
　And Saul jes' laid and smiled—
Ner couldn't nod, ner wave his hand,
　It hurt so—Bless the child!

And so they left him there with Doc—
　And warm tear of his Ma's . . .
Then—suddent-like—high over all
　Their laughture and applause—
They heerd: "I don't care what you git
　On yer old Chris'mus-tree,
'Cause I'm got somepin' you all hain't—
　I'm got the pleurisy!"

GENERAL LEW WALLACE

FEBRUARY 15, 1905

NAY, Death, thou mightiest of all
  Dread conquerors—thou dreadest chief,—
Thy heavy hand can here but fall
  Light as the Autumn leaf:
As vainly, too, its weight is laid
  Upon the warrior's knightly sword;—
Still through the charge and cannonade
  It flashes for the Lord.

In forum—as in battle-field—
  His voice rang for the truth—the right—
Keyed with the shibboleth that pealed
  His Soul forth to the fight:
The inspiration of his pen
  Glowed as a star, and lit anew
The faces and the hearts of men
  Watching, the long night through.

A destiny ordained—divine
  It seemed to hosts of those who saw
His rise since youth and marked the line
  Of his ascent with awe:—

From the now-storied little town
    That gave him birth and worth, behold,
Unto this day of his renown,
    His sword and word of gold.

Serving the Land he loved so well—
    Hailed midsea or in foreign port,
Or in strange-bannered citadel
    Or Oriental Court,—
He—honored for his Nation's sake,
    And loved and honored for his own—
Hath seen his Flag in glory shake
    Above the Pagan Throne.

ON READING DR. HENRY VAN DYKE'S
VOLUME OF POEMS—MUSIC

MUSIC!—Yea, and the airs you play—
Out of the faintest Far-Away
And the sweetest, too; and the dearest Here,
With its quavering voice but its bravest cheer—
The prayer that aches to be all expressed—
The kiss of love at its tenderest:
Music—music, with glad heart-throbs
Within it; and music with tears and sobs
Shaking it, as the startled soul
Is shaken at shriek of the fife and roll
Of the drums;—then as suddenly lulled again
With the whisper and lisp of the summer rain:
Mist of melodies fragrance-fine—
The bird-song flicked from the eglantine
With the dews when the springing bramble
    throws
A rarer drench on its ripest rose,
And the wingèd song soars up and sinks
To the dove's dim coo by the river-brinks
Where the ripple's voice still laughs along
Its glittering path of light and song.
Music, O Poet, and all your own
By right of capture and that alone,—

For in it we hear the harmony
Born of the earth and the air and the sea,
And over and under it, and all through,
We catch the chime of The Anthem, too.

HER SMILE OF CHEER AND VOICE OF SONG

ANNA HARRIS RANDALL

SPRING fails, in all its bravery of brilliant gold
    and green,—
The sun, the grass, the leafing tree, and all the
        dazzling scene
    Of dewy morning—orchard blooms,
    And woodland blossoms and perfumes
    With bird-songs sown between.

Yea, since *she* smiles not any more, so every flowery
        thing
Fades, and the birds seem brooding o'er her silence
        as they sing—
    Her smile of cheer and voice of song
    Seemed so divinely to belong
    To ever-joyous Spring!

Nay, still she smiles.—Our eyes are blurred and see
        not through our tears:
And still her rapturous voice is heard, though not of
        mortal ears:—
    Now ever doth she smile and sing
    Where Heaven's unending Clime of Spring
    Reclaims those gifts of hers.

319

THINKIN' BACK

I'VE be'n thinkin' back, of late,
 S'prisin'!—And I'm here to state
I'm suspicious it's a sign
Of age, maybe, er decline
Of my faculties,—and yit
I'm not feelin' old a bit—
Any more than sixty-four
Ain't no young man any more!

Thinkin' back's a thing 'at grows
On a feller, I suppose—
Older 'at he gits, i jack,
More he keeps a-thinkin' back!
Old as old men git to be,
Er as middle-aged as me,
Folks'll find us, eye and mind
Fixed on what we've left behind—
Rehabilitatin'-like
Them old times we used to hike
Out barefooted fer the crick,
'Long 'bout Aprile first—to pick
Out some "warmest" place to go
In a-swimmin'—*Ooh! my-oh!*

Wonder now we hadn't died!
Grate horseradish on my hide
Jes' *a-thinkin'* how cold then
That-'ere worter must 'a' be'n!

Thinkin' back—W'y, goodness me!
I kin call their names and see
Every little tad I played
With, er fought, er was afraid
Of, and so made *him* the best
Friend I had of all the rest!
Thinkin' back, I even hear
Them a-callin', high and clear,
Up the crick-banks, where they seem
Still hid in there—like a dream—
And me still a-pantin' on
The green pathway they have gone!
Still they hide, by bend er ford—
Still they hide—but, thank the Lord
(Thinkin' back, as I have said),
I hear laughin' on ahead!

SIS RAPALYE

WHEN rainy-greener shoots the grass
        And blooms the cherry tree,
And children laugh by glittering brooks,
    Wild with the ecstasy
Of bursting Spring, with twittering bird
    And hum of honey-bee,—
"Sis Rapalye!" my spirit shouts . . .
    And she is here with me!

As laugh the children, so her laugh
    Haunts all the atmosphere;—
Her song is in the brook's refrain;
    Her glad eyes, flashing clear,
Are in the morning dews; her speech
    Is melody so dear,
The bluebird trills,—"Sis Rapalye!—
    I hear!—I hear!—I hear!"

Again in races, at "Recess,"
    I see her braided hair
Toss past me as I stay to lift
    Her straw hat, fallen there;
The school-bell sends a vibrant pang
    My heart can hardly bear.—
Yet still she leads—Sis Rapalye—
    And leads me everywhere!

Now I am old.—Yet she remains
   The selfsame child of ten.—
Gay, gallant little girl, to race
   On into Heaven then!
Yet gallant, gay Sis Rapalye—
   In blossom-time, and when
The trees and grasses beckon her—
   Comes back to us again.

And so, however long since youth
   Whose raptures wild and free
An old man's heart may claim no more,—
   With more than memory
I share the Spring's own joy that brings
   My boyhood back to me
With laughter, blossoms, singing birds
   And sweet Sis Rapalye.

TO BLISS CARMAN

HE is the morning's poet—
 The bard of mount and moor,
The minstrel fine of dewy shine,
 The dawning's troubadour:

The brother of the bluebird,
 'Mid blossoms, throng on throng,
Whose singing calls, o'er orchard walls,
 Seem glitterings of song.

He meets, with brow uncovered,
 The sunrise through the mist,
With raptured eyes that range the skies
 And seas of amethyst:

The brambled rose clings to him;
 The breezy wood receives
Him as the guest she loves the best
 And laughs through all her leaves:

Pan and his nymphs and dryads
 They hear, in breathless pause,
This earth-born wight lilt his delight,
 And envy him because . . . .

He is the morning's poet—
   The bard of mount and moor,
The minstrel fine of dewy shine,
   The dawning's troubadour.

A SONG O' CHEER

MY Grampa he's a-allus sayin',
    "Sing a song o' cheer!"—
And wunst I says "What kind *is* them?"
    He says,—"The kind to *hear*.—
'Cause they're the songs that *Nature* sings,
    In ever' bird that twitters!"
"Well, *whipperwills* and *doves*," says I,
    "Hain't over-cheery critters!"
"Then don't you sing like *them*," he says—
    "Ner *guinny-hens*, my dear—
Ner *peafowls* nuther (drat the boy!)
    You sing a song o' cheer!"
I can't sing nothin' anyhow;
    But, comin' home, to'rds night,
I kind o' sort o' kep' a-whistlin'
    "Old—Bob—White!"

CHILD'S CHRISTMAS CAROL

CHRIST used to be like you and me,
   When just a lad in Galilee,—
So when we pray, on Christmas Day,
He favors first the prayers we say:
Then waste no tear, but pray with cheer,
This gladdest day of all the year:

O Brother mine of birth Divine,
Upon this natal day of Thine
Bear with our stress of happiness
Nor count our reverence the less
Because with glee and jubilee
Our hearts go singing up to Thee.

I' GOT TO FACE MOTHER TO-DAY!

I' GOT to face Mother to-day, fer a fact!—
    I' got to face Mother to-day!
And jes' how I'll *dare* to, an' how she will act,
    Is more than a mortal can say!
But I' *got* to face her— I' *got* to! And so
Here's a' old father clean at the end of his row!

And Pink and Wade's gone to the farm fer her
        now—
    And I'm keepin' house fer 'em here—
Their purty, new house—and all paid fer!—But
        how
    Am *I* goin' to meet her, and clear
Uy *my* actchully he'ppin' 'em both to elope?—
('Cause Mother wuz set—and wuz no other hope!)

I don' think it's *Wade* she's so biased ag'in',
    But his *bizness,*—a railroadin' man
'At runs a switch-engine, day out and day in,
    And's got to make hay while he can,—
It's a *dangersome* job, I'll admit,—but see what
A fine-furnished home 'at he's already got!

And *Pink*—W'y, the girl wuz just pinin' away,—
    So what could her old father do,
When he found her, hid-like, in a loose load of hay,
    But jes' to drive on clean into
The aidge of the city, where—singular thing!—
Wade switched us away to the Squire, i jing!

Now—a-leavin' me here—they're driv off, with a
        cheer,
    On their weddin'-trip—which is to drive
Straight home and tell Mother, and tol her back
        here
    And surrender me, dead er alive!
So I'm waitin' here—not so blame' overly gay
As I *wuz,*—'cause I' got to face *Mother* to-day!

NAME US NO NAMES NO MORE

SING, oh, rarest of roundelays!—
   Sing the hilarity and delight
Of our childhood's gurgling, giggling days!
   When our eyes were as twinkling-keen and bright
   And our laughs as thick as the stars at night,
And our breasts volcanoes of pent hoo-rays!
   When we grouped together in secret mirth
   And sniggered at everything on earth—
But specially when strange visitors came
   And we learned, for instance, that their name
was Fishback—or Mothershead—or Philpott—
or Dalrymple—or Fullenwider—or Applewhite—
or Hunnicut—or Tubbs—or Oldshoe!
   " 'Oldshoe!'—jeminy-jee!" thinks we—
   "Hain't that a funny name!—tee-hee-hee!"

Barefoot racers from everywhere,
   We'd pelt in over the back-porch floor
For "the settin'-room," and cluster there
   Like a clot of bees round an apple-core,
   And sleeve our noses, and pinafore
Our smearcase-mouths, and slick our hair,
   And stare and listen, and try to look

Like "Agnes" does in the old school-book,—
Till at last we'd catch the visitor's name,—
Reddinhouse, Lippscomb, or Burlingame,—
or Winkler—or Smock—or Tutewiler—or
Daubenspeck—or Throckmorton—or Rubottom
—or Bixler—
   " 'Bixler!' jeminy-jee!" thinks we—
   "Hain't that a funny name!—tee-hee-hee!"

.   .   .   .

Peace!—Let be!—Fall away!—Fetch loose!—
We can't have fun as we had fun *then!*—
Shut up, Memory!—what's the use?—
   When the girls and boys of 8 and 10
   Are now—well, *matronly,* or *old men,*
And Time has (so to say) "cooked our goose"!
   But ah! if we only *could* have back
   The long-lost laughs that we now so lack
   And so vainly long for,—how—we—*could*
   Naturely wake up the neigh-ber-*hood,*
      over the still heterogenious names ever unroll-
      ing from the endless roster of orthographic
      actualities,—such names—for further instance
      of good faith—simply such names as Vander-
      lip—or Funkhouser—or Smoot—or Galbreath
      —or Frybarger—or Dinwiddie—or Bouslog—
      or Puterbaugh—or Longnecker—or Hartpence
      —or Wiggins—or Pangborn—or Bowersox—
"Bowersox"! Gee!—But alas! now we
Taste salt tears in our "tee-hee-hee"!

HENRY IRVING

OCTOBER 13, 1905

'TIS Art reclaims him! By those gifts of hers
    With which so nobly she endowed his mind,
He brought back Shakespeare, in quick grief and
    glee—
Tasting the world's salt tears and sweet applause,—
For, even as through his master's, so there ran
Through all his multitudinous characters
Kinship and love and honor of mankind.
So all mankind shall grace his memory
In musing proudly: Great as his genius was,
Great likewise was the man.

332

LINCOLN—THE BOY

O SIMPLE as the rhymes that tell
  The simplest tales of youth,
Or simple as a miracle
  Beside the simplest truth—
So simple seems the view we share
  With our Immortals, sheer
From Glory looking down to where
  They were as children here.

Or thus we know, nor doubt it not,
  The boy he must have been
Whose budding heart bloomed with the thought
  All men are kith and kin—
With love-light in his eyes and shade
  Of prescient tears:—Because
Only of such a boy were made
  The loving man he was.

NICHOLAS OBERTING

A hero of ancient mold is Nicholas Oberting, of Hardentown, Indiana, who, a few days ago, in saving three boys from being gored to death by his infuriated bull, performed a feat of daring comparable only with the valorous deeds of Roman gladiators. . . .

—INDIANAPOLIS STAR.

SING! O Voice of Valor, sing!—
Sing of Nicholas Oberting!
Giant of the strength of ten,
Yet the gentlest of all men.

He it was that loved the air,
And the green fields everywhere—
Loved the meadow slopes and rills,
And the cattle on the hills—
Loved all out-o'-doors, and took
Off his hat, with reverent look,
As the balmy winds of Spring
Waved the peach-bough, blossoming
At the orchard edge, where he
Paused to mark the minstrelsy
Of the daring first redbreast,
Whose lilt, at its loveliest,

Was not lovelier to hear
Than the laughter, ringing near,
Of child-voices—Truants,—three
Little stragglers, he could see,
Crossing the near pasture-land
Loiteringly, hand in hand,
Laughing as they came. . . . Until—
Sudden ran a sickening chill
Through the strong man's heart! . . . He heard
Scarce his own voice, afterward,
For the maddened, bellowing roar
Of the monster beast that bore
Down upon the lads. . . . Out rang
His quick warning.—Then he sprang
Forth to meet them, crying, *"Run!—*
Straight for me!—Come on!—Well done!"—
Praised them—cheered them.—*"Good! Hooray!*
Now, Red-top, you throw away
That cap! but don't"—And breathless hung
The sentence ;—for a root had flung
The youngster—stunned—prone on the ground . . .
Then—midst a trampling, thund'rous sound,
The bellowing beast, with his big bent head,
And great horns, white as his eyes were red!—
Charged for the lad, as he helpless lay . . .
There was a leap then ; and—they say
(For but one boy had swooned away)—
There was the *leap* and the *laugh* of *a Man* . . .
And the bravest war of the world began:
Pinned by the horns in the Hercules grip
Of his master—the slavering jaws adrip,

The foaming, steaming, sweltering, hot-
Mouthed monster raged and charged and fought,—
But ever the great strong hands were set
At their horny leverage, bloody-wet;
And ever steadier pressed the hold,
And ever the wild eyes wilder rolled
As the thick neck turned, and the great hulk grew
Like an o'er-fed engine, shuddering through—
Yet the thick neck turned—and turned—and
      turned—
Till the raw tongue shot from the throat and burned
The live air foul; and the beast lurched dead
Crunchingly.
             . . . And the youngster said
That the big man just lay there and cried—
He was so sorry and satisfied!

RABBIT

I S'POSE it takes a feller 'at's be'n
  Raised in a country-town, like me,
To *'preciate* rabbits! . . . Eight er ten
Bellerin' boys and two er three
Yelpin' dawgs all on the trail
O' one little pop-eyed cottontail!

'Bout the first good fall o' snow—
So's you kin track 'em, don't you know,
Where they've run,—and one by one
Hop 'em up and chase 'em down
And prod 'em out of a' old bresh-pile
Er a holler log they're a-hidin' roun',
Er, way en-nunder the ricked cord-wood
Er crosstie-stack by the railroad track
'Bout a mile
Out o' sight o' the whole ding town! . . .
Well! them's times 'at I call good!

Rabbits!—w'y, as my thoughts goes back
To them old boyhood days o' mine,
I kin sic him now and see "Old Jack"
A-plowin' snow in a rabbit-track

And a-pitchin' over him, head and heels,
Like a blame' hat-rack,
As the rabbit turns fer the timber-line
Down the County Ditch through the old corn-
    fields. . . .

Yes, and I'll say right here to you,
Rabbits that boys has *earnt,* like that—
Skinned and hung fer a night or two
On the old back-porch where the pump's done
    froze—
Then fried 'bout right, where your brekfust's at,
With hot brown gravy and shortenin' bread,—
Rabbits, like *them*—er I ort to 'a' said,
I s'pose,
Rabbits like *those*
Ain't so p'ticalar pore, I guess,
Fer *eatin'* purposes!

A SPRING SONG AND A LATER

SHE sang a song of May for me,
  Wherein once more I heard
The mirth of my glad infancy—
  The orchard's earliest bird—
The joyous breeze among the trees
  New-clad in leaf and bloom,
And there the happy honey-bees
  In dewy gleam and gloom.

So purely, sweetly on the sense
  Of heart and spirit fell
Her song of Spring, its influence—
  Still irresistible,—
Commands me here—with eyes ablur—
  To mate her bright refrain,
Though I but shed a rhyme for her
  As dim as Autumn rain.

OURS

LOUISVILLE, KENTUCKY, DECEMBER 8, 1906

READ AT A BANQUET IN HONOR OF HENRY WATTERSON
UPON HIS DEPARTURE FOR SPAIN

HERE where of old was heard
   The ringing, singing word
That orator and bard
    Alike set free
To soar, through heights profound,
Our land's remotest bound,
Till all is holy ground
    From sea to sea—

Here still, with voice and pen,
ONE cheers the hopes of men
And gives us faith again—
    This gifted one
We hold here as the guest
Most honored—loved the best—
Wisest and worthiest—
    Our Watterson.

340

His spirit is the Seer's—
For, though he sees and hears
Through human doubts and fears,
    His heart is one
With Earth's and the Divine—
With his home-hearts—and mine—
And the child's heart is thine,
    Our Watterson!

Give us to touch and praise
His worth in subtlest ways,
Lest even our fondest gaze
    He fain would shun—
Laugh, though a mist appears—
The glad wine salt with tears—
Laugh, as we drain it—"Here's
    Our Watterson!"

OLD INDIANY

INTENDED FOR A DINNER OF THE INDIANA
SOCIETY OF CHICAGO

OLD Indiany, 'course we know
   Is first, and best, and *most,* also,
Of *all* the States' whole forty-four :—
She's first in ever'thing, that's shore!—
And *best* in ever'way as yet
Made known to man ; and you kin bet
She's *most,* because she won't confess
She ever was, or will be, *less!*
And yet, fer all her proud array
Of sons, how many gits away!—
No doubt about her bein' *great*
But, fellers, she's a leaky State!
And them that boasts the most about
Her, them's the ones that's dribbled out.
Law! jes' to think of all you boys
'Way over here in Illinoise
A-celebratin', like ye air,
Old Indiany, 'way back there
In the dark ages, so to speak,
A-prayin' for ye once a week
And wonderin' what's a-keepin' you
From comin', like you ort to do.
You're all a-lookin' well, and like

You wasn't "sidin' up the pike,"
As the tramp-shoemaker said
When "he sacked the boss and shed
The blame town, to hunt fer one
Where they didn't work fer fun!"
Lookin' *extry* well, I'd say,
Your old home so fur away.—
Maybe, though, like the old jour.,
Fun hain't all yer workin' fer.
So you've found a job that pays
Better than in them old days
You was on The Weekly Press,
Heppin' run things, more er less;
Er a-learnin' telegraph-
Operatin', with a half-
Notion of the tinner's trade,
Er the dusty man's that laid
Out designs on marble and
Hacked out little lambs by hand,
And chewed finecut as he wrought,
"Shapin' from his bitter thought"
Some squshed mutterings to say,—
"Yes, hard work, and porer pay!"
Er you'd kind o' thought the far-
Gazin' kuss that owned a car
And took pictures in it, had
Jes' the snap you wanted—bad!
And you even wondered why
He kep' foolin' with his sky-
Light the same on shiny days
As when rainin'.   ('T leaked always.)

Wondered what strange things was hid
In there when he shet the door
And smelt like a burnt drug store
Next some orchard-trees, i swan!
With whole roasted apples on!
That's why Ade is, here of late,
Buyin' in the dear old state,—
So's to cut it up in plots
Of both town and country lots.

LONGFELLOW

1807—FEBRUARY 27—1907

O GENTLEST kinsman of Humanity!
  Thy love hath touched all hearts, even as thy
    Song
Hath touched all chords of music that belong
To the quavering heaven-strung harp of harmony:
Thou hast made man to feel and hear and see
  Divinely;—made the weak to be the strong;
  By thy melodious magic, changed the wrong
To changeless right—and joyed and wept as we.
Worlds listen, lulled and solaced at the spell
  That folds and holds us—soul and body, too,—
    As though thy songs, as loving arms in stress
Of sympathy and trust ineffable,
  Were thrown about us thus by one who knew
  Of common human need of kindliness.

WITH A CHILD-BOOK

TO MASTER PRESTON FROM HIS LONG INVISIBLE
PLAYMATE

THERE is LORE of more devices,
   And ROMANCE that more entices
Higher minds and higher prices;—
But, for "Giggle-boy" or "Cry-sis"
(With some sniffless interstices)
Here's a little tale suffices—
Sweet as oranges in slices
Slobbed in slues o' cream and ices,
Tanged with tingling, spangling spices.—
Ho! there's *no* tale half so nice as
This Old Tailor and his Mice is!

THE DOCTOR

He took the suffering human race,
  He read each wound, each weakness clear;
And struck his finger on the place,
  And said: "Thou ailest here, and here!"
                              —MATTHEW ARNOLD

WE may idealize the chief of men—
    Idealize the humblest citizen,—
Idealize the ruler in his chair—
The poor man, or the poorer millionaire;
Idealize the soldier—sailor—or
The simple man of peace—at war with war;—
The hero of the sword or fife-and-drum. . . .
Why not idealize the Doctor some?

The Doctor is, by principle, we know,
Opposed to sentiment. He veils all show
Of feeling, and is proudest when he hides
The sympathy which natively abides
Within the stoic precincts of a soul
Which owns strict duty as its first control,
And so must guard the ill, lest worse may
    come. . . .
Why not idealize the Doctor some?

He is the master of emotions—he
Is likewise certain of that mastery,—
Or dare he face contagion in its ire,
Or scathing fever in its leaping fire?
He needs must smile upon the ghastly face
That yearns up toward him in that warded
    place
Where even the Saint-like Sisters' lips grow
    dumb.
Why not idealize the Doctor some?

He wisely hides his heart from you and me—
He hath grown tearless, of necessity,—
He knows the sight is clearer, being blind;
He knows the cruel knife is very kind;
Ofttimes he must be pitiless, for thought
Of the remembered wife or child he sought
To save through kindness that was overcome.
Why not idealize the Doctor some?

Bear with him, trustful, in his darkest doubt
Of how the mystery of death comes out;
He knows—he knows,—ay, better yet than we,
That out of Time must dawn Eternity;
He knows his own compassion—what *he* would
Give in relief of all ills, if he could.—
We wait alike one Master: He will come.
Do we idealize the Doctor some?

ABE MARTIN

ABE MARTIN!—dad-burn his old picture!
P'tends he's a Brown County fixture—
A kind of a comical mixture
    Of hoss-sense and no sense at all!
His mouth, like his pipe, 's allus goin',
And his thoughts, like his whiskers, is flowin',
And what he don't know ain't wuth knowin'—
    From Genesis clean to baseball!

The artist, Kin Hubbard, 's so keerless
He draws Abe 'most eyeless and earless,
But he's never yet pictured him cheerless
    Er with fun 'at he tries to conceal,—
Whuther on to the fence er clean over
A-rootin' up ragweed er clover,
Skeert stiff at some "Rambler" er "Rover"
    Er newfangled automo*beel!*

It's a purty steep climate old Brown's in;
And the rains there his ducks nearly drowns in
The old man hisse'f wades his rounds in
    As ca'm and serene, mighty nigh

As the old handsaw-hawg, er the mottled
Milch cow, er the old rooster wattled
Like the mumps had him 'most so well throttled
    That it was a pleasure to die.

But best of 'em all's the fool-breaks 'at
Abe don't see at all, and yit makes 'at
Both me and you lays back and shakes at
    His comic, miraculous cracks
Which makes him—clean back of the power
Of genius itse'f in its flower—
This Notable Man of the Hour,
    Abe Martin, The Joker on Facts.

MORNING

BREATH of Morning—breath of May—
With your zest of yesterday
And crisp, balmy freshness, smite
Our old hearts with Youth's delight.

Tilt the cap of Boyhood—yea,
Where no "forelock" waves, to-day,—
Back, in breezy, cool excess,
Stroke it with the old caress.

Let us see as we have seen—
Where all paths are dewy-green,
And all human-kind are kin—
Let us be as we have been!

THE LOVELINESS

AH, what a long and loitering way
    And ever-lovely way, in truth,
We travel on from day to day
    Out of the realms of youth!

How eagerly we onward press
    The lovely path that lures us still
With ever-changing loveliness
    Of grassy vale and hill:

Of groves of May and morning-lands
    Dew-diamonded and gemmed with bloom;
With amber streams and golden sands
    And aisles of gleam and gloom;

Where lovely little Fairy-folk,
    In careless ambush, pipe and call
From tousled ferns 'neath elm and oak
    By shoal and waterfall:

Transparent even as the stream,
    The gnarlèd prison-tree reveals
Its lovely Dryad in a dream
    That scarce itself conceals;

The sudden redbird trips the sight
　And tricks the ear—or doubtless we
With happy palms had clapped the Sprite
　In new captivity.

On—on, through all the gathering years,
　Still gleams the loveliness, though seen
Through dusks of loss and mists of tears
　That vainly intervene.

Time stints us not of lovely things—
　Old Age hath still a treasure-store,—
The loveliness of songs and wings
　And voices on before.—

And—loveliness beyond all grace
　Of lovely words to say or sing,—
The loveliness of Hope's fair face
　Forever brightening.

A PARTING GUEST

WHAT delightful hosts are they—
    Life and Love!
Lingeringly I turn away,
    This late hour, yet glad enough
They have not withheld from me
    Their high hospitality.
So, with face lit with delight
    And all gratitude, I stay
    Yet to press their hands and say,
"Thanks.—So fine a time! Good night."

"OUT OF REACH"

YOU think them "out of reach," your dead?
   Nay, by my own dead, I deny
Your "out of reach."—Be comforted:
   'Tis not so far to die.

O by their dear remembered smiles
   And outheld hands and welcoming speech,
They wait for us, thousands of miles
   This side of "out of reach."

MY FOE

MY Foe? You name yourself, then,—I refuse
A term so dark to designate you by.
To me you are most kind and true; and I
Am grateful as the dust is for the dews
That brim the dusk, and falter, drip and ooze
From the dear darkness of the summer sky.
Vex not yourself for lack of moan or cry
Of mine. Not any harm, nor ache nor bruise
Could reach my soul through any stroke you fain
Might launch upon me,—it were as the lance
Even of the lightning did it leap to rend
A ray of sunshine—'twould recoil again.
So, blessing you, with pitying countenance,
I wave a hand to you, my helpless friend.

SOME IMITATIONS

I

POMONA

(Madison Cawein)

OH, the golden afternoon!—
   Like a ripened summer day
That had fallen oversoon
   In the weedy orchard-way—
As an apple, ripe in June.

He had left his fishrod leant
   O'er the footlog by the spring—
Clomb the hill-path's high ascent,
   Whence a voice, down showering,
Lured him, wondering as he went.

Not the voice of bee nor bird,
   Nay, nor voice of man nor child,
Nor the creek's shoal-alto heard
   Blent with warblings sweet and wild
Of the midstream, music-stirred.

'Twas a goddess! As the air
   Swirled to eddying silence, he
Glimpsed about him, half aware
   Of some subtle sorcery
Woven round him everywhere.

Suavest slopes of pleasaunce, sown
   With long lines of fruited trees
Weighed o'er grasses all unmown
   But by scythings of the breeze
In prone swaths that flashed and shone

Like silk locks of Faunus sleeked
   This, that way, and contrawise,
Through whose bredes ambrosial leaked
   Oily amber sheens and dyes,
Starred with petals purple-freaked.

Here the bellflower swayed and swung,
   Greenly belfried high amid
Thick leaves in whose covert sung
   Hermit-thrush, or katydid,
Or the glowworm nightly clung.

Here the damson, peach and pear;
   There the plum, in Tyrian tints,
Like great grapes in clusters rare;
   And the metal-heavy quince
Like a plummet dangled there.

'All ethereal, yet all
Most material,—a theme
Of some fabled festival—
Save the fair face of his dream
Smiling o'er the orchard wall.

II

THE PASSING OF A ZEPHYR

(*Sidney Lanier*)

UP from, and out of, and over the opulent woods
and the plains,
Lo! I leap nakedly loose, as the nudest of gods
might choose,
For to dash me away through the morning dews
And the rathe Spring rains—
Pat and pet the little green leaves of the trees and
the grass,
Till they seem to linger and cling, as I pass,
And are touched to delicate contemporaneous tears
of the rain and the dew,
That lure mine eyes to weeping likewise, and to
laughter, too:
For I am become as the balmiest, stormiest zephyr
of Spring,
With manifold beads of the marvelous dew and the
rain to string
On the bended strands of the blossoms, blown
And tossed and tousled and overthrown,

And shifted and whirled, and lifted unfurled
In the victory of the blossoming
Of the flags of the flowery world.
Yea, and behold! and a riotous zephyr, at last,
I subside; I abate; I pass by; I am past.
And the small, hoarse bass of the bumblebee
Is my requiem-psalm,
And I fling me down to a listless, loitering, long
    eternity
Of amiable calm.

III

EF UNCLE REMUS PLEASE TER 'SCUSEN ME

(*Joel Chandler Harris*)

D EY wunce wuz er time which I gwineter
    tell you 'bout it—
An' it's easy ter believe it sho'ly ez it is ter doubt
    it!—
So des you pick yer "ruthers" whilse I tell how ole
    Br'er Rabbit
Wunce know de time when he git de fightin' habit.
Co'se he ain't no bragger, des a-rippin' an' a-rarin'
An' a-darin' all de beestus an' a-des a-double-darin'
Sich ez Mr. Jonus Lion, er Sir Mr. Twister Tagger,
Er Sister Hisstopottomus, er A'nt Ferjinny Ja'gger!
Yit, des de same, he layin' low an' know he got de
    muscle
What sho' ter s'prise mos' any size what crowd 'im
    fer a tussle.—

EF UNCLE REMUS PLEASE TER 'SCUSEN ME.

DEY wunce wuz er time which I gwineter tell you 'bout it —
An' it's easy ter believe it sholy as it is ter doubt it!
So des you pick yer "ruthers" whilse I tell how ole Brer Rabbit
Wunce know de time when he git de fightin' habit.
Co'se he aint no bragger, des a-rippin' an' a-rarin'
An' a-darin' all de breetus an' a-des a double-darin'
Sich as Mr. Jonus Lion, er Sir Mr. Twister Tagger,
Er Sister Histopottoson, er Aint Ferjinny Jagger!
Yit, des de same, he layin' low an' know he got de muscle
What sho' ter 'sprise mos' any size what crowd 'im fer a tussle —
But speshully he 'spise de Dawg, an' sight er one des make 'im
Fergit hisse'f an' run 'em down an' grab 'em up an' shake 'em! —
An', mo' 'n dat, ef 'twa'nt fer de Dawg-law den agin it,
He'd des a-kilt off ev'y Dawg dats chasin' him dis minute!

[Yourz ever loyally, and lovingly,
  ] cJamesc [ ]

But speshully he 'spise de *Dawg,* an' sight er one
    des make 'im
Fergit hisse'f an' run 'em down an' grab 'em up an'
    shake 'em!—
An', mo' 'n dat, ef 'twuzn't fer de Dawg-law den
    ag'in' it,
He'd des a-kilt off ev'y Dawg dat's chasin' him dis
    minute!

IV

A RHYME FOR CHRISTMAS

IF *Browning* only were here,
   This yule-ish time o' the year—
This mule-ish time o' the year,
Stubbornly still refusing
To add to the rhymes we've been using
Since the first Christmas-glee
(One might say) chantingly
Rendered by rudest hinds
Of the pelt-clad shepherding kinds
Who didn't know Song from b-
U-double-l's-foot!—pah!—
(Haply the old Egyptian *ptah*—
Though I'd hardly wager a baw-
Bee—or a *bumble,* for that—
And that's flat!) . . .
But the thing that I want to get at
Is a rhyme for *Christmas*—
Nay! nay! nay! nay! not *isthmus*—
The t- and the h-sounds covertly are
Gnawing the nice auricular

Senses until one may hear them gnar—
And the terminal, too, for m*as* is m*us,*
So *that* will not do for us.
Try for it—sigh for it—cry for it—die for it!
O *but* if Browning were here to apply for it,
He'd rhyme you *Christmas—*
He'd make a *mist pass*
Over—something o' ruther—
Or find you the rhyme's very brother
In lovers that *kissed fast*
*To baffle the moon—*as he'd lose the *t*-final
In fas-t as it blended with *to* (mark the spinal
Elision—tip-clipt as exquisitely nicely
And hyper-exactingly sliced to precisely
The extremest technical need) : Or he'd *twist glass,*
Or he'd have a *kissed lass,*
Or shake 'neath our noses some great giant *fist-
     mass—*
No matter! If Robert were here, *he* could do it,
Though it took us till Christmas next year to see
     through it.

V

VAUDEVILLE SKITS

I

SERENADE AT THE CABIN

Oh, my little Sadie Sue, I's a-serenadin' you—
     Fer you's de onliest lady-love o' mine ;
De White Folk's dance done over, I has still a chune
     er two

Below your winder's mohnin'-glory-vine.
Your good ole mammy's gyarden is, fer shore, a
      ha'nted place,
   Dis midnight whilse I's cropin' 'mongst de bloom;
Yit de moon dah 'bove de chimbly ain' no fairer dan
      de face
   What's hidin' 'hind de curtain o' your room.

Chorus

Den wake, my colored blonde with eyes o' blue,
An' lips ez red ez roses renshed with dew;
     Yo' hair ez fair an' fine
     Ez de skeins o' June sunshine,
My little, light-complected Sadie Sue!

In de "Gran's" old dinin'-hall, playin' fer de White
      Folk's ball,
   I watch deir pick o' ladies ez dey glide,
An' says I, "My Sadie Sue she 'ud shorely best you
      all
   Ef she 'uz here a-waltzin' by my side!"
Den I laugh all to myse'f-like, ez I swipe de twangin'
      strings
   An' shet my eyes in sweetest dreams o' you,—
Fer you're my heart's own music dat forever beats
      an' sings—
   My soul's own serenade—my Sadie Sue!

Chorus

Den wake, my colored blonde with eyes o' blue,
An' lips ez red ez roses renshed with dew;
    Yo' hair ez fair an' fine
    Ez de skeins o' June sunshine,
My little, light-complected Sadie Sue!

2

CHUCK'S HOODOOS

Chuck's allus had de Hoodoos bad!—
    Do what he kin to lose 'em,
Dey track dat coon, by sun er moon,
    Des like dey cain't uxcuse 'im!
An' more he gyaurd 'em off, more hard
    Hit 'pear-like dat they press 'im—
De onliest luck dey 'low ole Chuck
    Is dis enough to 'stress 'im!

He taken care—no matter where
    He's walkin' 'long de street an'
See any ladder leanin' there,
    Er cross-eyed man he's meetin'—
Dat eye o' his ketch wher' dey is,
    An', quick as "scat," Chuck's hittin'
De curb outside, an' watch wile-eyed
    Fust lef'-han' place to spit in!

He' got toenails o' bats; an' snails
  Shet hot in deir shell-houses
Wid sealin'-wax; an' little backs
  O' turkles in his trouse's:
A moleskin-pu's'; an' possum's han'—
  Des ever' charm an' wonder—
An' barber-chair o' shore hosshair—
  An' hoss-shoe hangin' under!

"An' yit," says Chuck, "I got no luck:—
  De Hoodoos still a-bafflin'
Dis po' ole saint what knows he ain't—
  'Twix' shootin' craps an' rafflin'!
No overcoat—ner underwear,—
  Right on de aidge o' winter
I's up aginst de wust layout
  Dey's ever got me inter!"

THE ROSE-LADY

TO THE ROSES

I DREAM that you are kisses Allah sent
  In forms material, that all the earth
  May taste of you and guess of Heaven's worth,
Since it can waste such sweetness with content,—
Seeing you showered o'er the Battlement—
  By Angel-hands plucked ripe from lips of mirth
  And flung in lavish clusters, yet no dearth
Of rapture for the Anthem! . . . I have bent
  Above you, nestled in some low retreat,
Pressing your velvet mouths against the dust,
  And, ever nurturing this old conceit,
Have lifted up your lips in perfect trust
  Against my mouth, nor found them the less sweet
  For having kissed the dust beneath my feet.

A HOOSIER CALENDAR

JANUARY

BLEAK January! Cold as fate,
  And ever colder—ever keener—
Our very hair cut while we wait
  By winds that clip it ever cleaner:
Cold as a miser's buried gold,
  Or nether-deeps of old tradition—
Jeems January! you're a cold
      Proposition!

FEBRUARY

You, February,—seem to be
  Old January's understudy,
But play the part too vaudeville-y,—
  With wind too moist and snow too muddy—
You overfreeze and overthaw—
  Your "Hos'ler Jo"-like recitation
But hints that you're, at best, a raw
      Imitation.

MARCH

And, March, you've got no friends to spare—
  Warm friends, I mean—unless coal-dealers,
Or gas-well owners, pipin' where
  The piper's paid—above all spielers;

You are a month, too, of complex
　　Perversities beyond solution—
A sort o' "loveliest of your sex"
　　　　Institution!

APRIL

But, April, when you kind o' come
　　A-sa'nterin' down along our roadway,
The bars is down, and we're at home,
　　And you're as welcome as a show-day!
First thing we know, the sunshine falls
　　Spring-like, and drenches all Creation
With that-'ere ba'm the poets calls
　　　　"Inspiration."

MAY

And May!—It's warmin' jest to see
　　The crick thawed clear ag'in and dancin'—
'Pear-like it's tickled 'most as *me*
　　A-prancin' 'crosst it with my pants on!
And then to hear the bluebird whet
　　His old song up and lance it through you,
Clean through the boy's heart beatin' yet—
　　　　Hallylooya!

JUNE

June—'Ll, I jest git *doped* on June!—
　　The trees and grass all at their greenest—
The round earth swung 'twixt sun and moon,
　　Jest at its—so to say—serenest:—

In country,—stars and whipperwills;
  In town,—all night the boys invadin'
Leadin' citizens' winder-sills,
      Sair-a-nadin'.

JULY

Fish still a-bitin'—*some;* but 'most
  Too hot fer anything but layin'
Jest do-less like, and watchin' clos't
  The treetops and the squirrels playin'—
Their tail-tips switched 'bove knot and limb,
  But keepin' most in sequestration—
Leavin' a big part to the im-
      Magination.

AUGUST

Now when it's August—I can tell
  It by a hundred signs and over;—
They is a mixed ripe-apple-smell
  And mashed-down grass and musty clover;
Bees is as lazy 'most as me—
  Bee-bird eats 'em—gap's his wings out
So lazy 'at I don't think he
      Spits their stings out!

SEPTEMBER

September, you appeal to all,
  Both young and old, lordly and lowly;
You stuff the haymow, trough and stall,
  Till horse and cow's as roly-poly

As pigs is, slopped on buttermilk
    And brand, shipstuff and 'tater-peelin's—
And folks, too, feelin' fine as silk
        With all their feelin's!

OCTOBER

If I'd be'n asked for my advice,
    And thought the thing out, ca'm and sober—
Sizin' the months all once or twice,—
    I'd la'nch'd the year out with *October*. . . .
All Nature then jest veiled and dressed
    In weddin' gyarments, ornamented
With ripe-fruit-gems—and kissin' jest
        New-invented!

NOVEMBER

I'm 'feared November's hopes is few
    And far between!—Cold as a Monday-
Washday, er a lodge-man who
    You' got to pallbear for on Sunday;
Colder and colder every day—
    The fixed official time for sighin',—
A sinkin' state you jest can't stay
        In, or *die* in!

DECEMBER

December—why, of course we grin
    And bear it—shiverin' every minute,
Yet warm from time the month rolls in
    Till it skites out with Christmas in it;

And so, for all its coldest truths
  And chill, goose-pimpled imperfections,
It wads our lank old socks with Youth's
    Recollections.

THE LITTLE WOMAN

MY little woman, of you I sing
     With a fervor all divine,—
For I know the clasp of the hands that cling
     So closely here in mine.

Though the rosy palms I used to press
     Are faded and worn with care,
And tremulous is the old caress
     That nestles in my hair,—

Your heart to me is a changeless page;
     I have read it bit by bit,
From the dawn of love to the dusk of age,—
     And the tale is Holy Writ.

Fold your eyes,—for the twilight bends
     As a mother o'er her child—
Even as when, in the long-lost Then,
     You bent o'er ours and smiled. . . .

(Nay, but I spoke all unaware!
     See! I am kneeling, too,
And with mine, dear, is the rose's prayer,
     With a blur of tears and dew.)

But O little woman, I often grieve,
   As I think of the vanished years
And trace the course of the cares that leave
   Your features dim with tears:

I often grieve, for the frowns I wore
   When the world seemed all untrue,—
When my hard, proud heart was sick and
     sore
   And would not come to you!

I often grieve, as I hold your hand—
   As I hold your hand to-night,—
That it takes so long to understand
   The lesson of love aright!

But sing the song that I taught you once,
   Dear little woman, as *then*
Away far back in the golden months:—
   Sing me the song again!

For, as under the stars we loved of yore
   When the nights of love were long,
Your poor, pale lips grow glad once more
   And I kiss them into song:—

My little woman's hands are fair
   As even the moonflowers be
When fairies creep in their depths and sleep
   Till the sun leaps out o' the sea.

And O her eyes, they are spheres of light—
So brighter than stars are they,
The brightest day is the darkest night
When my little woman's away.

For my little woman has ever a tear
And a sigh when I am sad;
And I have a thousand smiles for her
When my little woman is glad.

But my little woman is strong and brave,
For all of her tears and sighs,
Her stanch little heart knows how to behave
Whenever the storms arise.

My little woman, of you I sing
With a fervor all divine,—
For I know the clasp of the hands that cling
So closely here in mine.

WHAT TITLE?

WHAT title best befits the man
    We hold our first American?
Or Statesman; Soldier; Hero; Chief,
Whose Country is his first belief:
Or sanest, safest Leader; or
True Patriot; or Orator,
Heard still at Inspiration's height,
Because he speaks for truth and right;
Or shall his people be content
With Our Republic's President,
Or trust his ringing worth to live
In song as Chief Executive?
Nay—his the simplest name—though set
Upon him like a coronet,—
God names our first American
The highest, noblest name—The MAN.

YOU MAY NOT REMEMBER

In the deep grave's charmèd chamber,
Lying tranced in breathless slumber,
You may haply not remember.

YOU may not remember whether
  It was Spring or Summer weather;
But *I* know—we two together
  At the dim end of the day—
How the fireflies in the twilight
  Drifted by like flakes of starlight,
    Till o'er floods of flashing moonlight
    They were wave-like swept away.

You may not remember any
Word of mine of all the many
Poured out for you there, though then a
  Soul inspirèd spake my love;—
But *I* knew—and still review it,
  All my passion, as with awe it
    Welled in speech as from a poet
    Gifted of the gods above.

Sleeping here, this hour I grieve in,
You may not remember even
Any kiss I still believe in,
    Or caress of ecstasy,—

May not even *dream*—O can't you?—
  That I kneel here—weep here—want you—
    Feign me in your grave, to haunt you,
      Since you come not back to me!

Vain! ah, vain is all my yearning
As the West's last embers burning
Into ashes, slowly turning
    Ever to a denser gray!—
While the fireflies in the twilight
  Drift about like flakes of starlight,
    Till o'er wastes of wannest moonlight
    They are wave-like swept away.

THE REST

V. K.—NATURALIST

HE rests at last, as on the mother-breast
The playworn child at evening lies at rest,—
For he, a buoyant child, in veriest truth,
Has looked on life with eyes of changeless youth:—
Has loved our green old earth here from the hour
Of his first memory of bud and flower—
Of morning's grassy lawns and dewy trees
And orchard-blossoms, singing birds and bees:

When all the world about him was a land
Elysian, with the mother near at hand:
With steadfast gaze of wonder and delight
He marked the miracles of day and night:—
Beheld the kingly sun, in dazzling reign
By day; and, with her glittering, glimmering train
Of stars, he saw the queenly moon possess
Her throne in midmost midnight's mightiness.

All living least of things he ever knew
Of mother Earth's he was a brother to:
The lone rose by the brook—or, under, where
The swaying water-lilies anchored there;

378

His love dipped even to the glossy things
That walked the waters and forgot their wings
In sheer insanity of some delight
Known but to that ecstatic parasite.

It was enough, thus childishly to sense
All works—since worthy of Omnipotence—
As worshipful: Therefor, as any child,
He knelt in tenderness of tears, or smiled
His gratefulness, as to a playmate glad
To share His pleasures with a poorer lad.
And so he lived: And so he *died?*—Ah, no,
We'll not believe that till he tells us so.

WE MUST BELIEVE

Lord, I believe: help Thou mine unbelief.

I

WE must believe—
   Being from birth endowed with love and
       trust—
Born unto loving;—and how simply just
That love—that faith!—even in the blossom-face
The babe drops dreamward in its resting-place,
Intuitively conscious of the sure
Awakening to rapture ever pure
And sweet and saintly as the mother's own
Or the awed father's, as his arms are thrown
O'er wife and child, to round about them weave
   And wind and bind them as one harvest-sheaf
Of love—to cleave to, and *forever* cleave. . . .
        Lord, I believe:
           Help Thou mine unbelief.

II

We must believe—
Impelled since infancy to seek some clear
Fulfilment, still withheld all seekers here;—
For never have we seen perfection nor
The glory we are ever seeking for:
But we *have* seen—all mortal souls as one—
Have seen its *promise,* in the morning sun—

380

Its blest assurance, in the stars of night;—
The ever-dawning of the dark to light;—
The tears down-falling from all eyes that grieve—
  The eyes uplifting from all deeps of grief,
Yearning for what at last we shall receive. . . .
         Lord, I believe:
                Help Thou mine unbelief.

III

We must believe:
For still all unappeased our hunger goes,
From life's first waking, to its last repose:
The briefest life of any babe, or man
Outwearing even the allotted span,
Is each a life unfinished—incomplete:
For these, then, of th' outworn, or unworn feet
Denied one toddling step—O there must be
Some fair, green, flowery pathway endlessly
Winding through lands Elysian! Lord, receive
  And lead each as Thine Own Child—even the
       Chief
Of us who didst Immortal life achieve. . . .
         Lord, I believe:
                Help Thou mine unbelief.

THE HIRED MAN'S DOG-STORY

Twa dogs that were na thrang at hame
Forgather'd ance upon a time.
—BURNS

DOGS, I contend, is jes' about
   Nigh human—git 'em studied out.
I hold, like us, they've got their own
Reasonin' powers 'at's theirs alone—
Same as their tricks and habits too,
Provin', by lots o' things they do,
That instinct's not the only thing
That dogs is governed by, i jing!—
And I'll say furder, on that line,
   And prove it, that they's dogs a-plenty
Will show intelligence as fine
   As ary ten men out o' twenty!

Jevver investigate the way
Sheep-killin' dogs goes at it—hey?
Well, you dig up the facts and you
Will find, first thing, they's always *two*
Dogs goes together on that spree
O' blood and puore dog-deviltry!
And, then, they always go at night—

Mind ye, it's never in daylight,
When folks is up and wide awake,—
No self-respectin' dogs'll make
Mistakes o' judgment on that score,—
And I've knowed fifty head or more
O' slaughtered sheep found in the lot,
Next morning the old farmer got
His folks up and went out to feed,—
And every livin' soul agreed
That all night long they never heerd
The bark o' dog ner bleat o' skeered
And racin', tromplin' flock o' sheep
   A-skallyhootin' roun' the pastur',
To rouse 'em from their peaceful sleep
   To that heart-renderin' disaster!

Well, now, they's actchul evidence
In all these facts set forth; and hence
When, by like facts, it has been foun'
That these two dogs—colloguin' roun'
At night as thick as thieves—*by day*
Don't go together anyway,
And, 'pearantly, hain't never met
Each other; and the facts is set
On record furder, that these smart
Old pards in crime lives miles apart—
Which is a trick o' theirs, to throw
Off all suspicion, don't you know!—
One's a *town*-dog—belongin' to
Some good man, maybe—er to you!—
And one's a *country*-dog, er *"jay,"*

As you nickname us thataway.
Well, now!—these is the facts I' got
(And, mind ye, these *is* facts—not
        guesses)
To argy on, concernin' what
    Fine reasonin' powers dogs p'sesses.

My idy is,—the dog lives in
The *town,* we'll say, runs up ag'in
The *country*-dog, some Saturday,
Under a' old farm-wagon, say,
Down at the Court-house hitchin'-rack.—
Both lifts the bristles on their back
And show their teeth and growl as though
They meant it pleasant-like and low,
In case the fight hangs fire.   And they
Both wag then in a friendly way,
The town-dog sayin':—"Seems to me,
Last Dimocratic jubilee,
I seen you here in town somewhere?"
The country-dog says:— "Right you air!—
And right here's where you seen me, too,
Under this wagon, watchin' *you!*"
"Yes," says the town-dog,—"and I thought
We'd *both* bear watchin', like as not."
And as he yawns and looks away,
The country-dog says, "What's your lay?"
The town-dog whets his feet a spell
And yawns ag'in, and then says,—"Well,
Before I answer that—Ain't you

'A Mill Crick dog, a mile er two
From old Chape Clayton's stock-farm—say?"
"Who *told* you?" says the jay-dog—"hey?"
And looks up, real su'prised. *"I guessed,"*
The town-dog says—*"You* tell the rest,—
How's old Chape's mutton, anyhow?—
How many of 'em's ready now—
How many of 'em's ripe enough fer use,
And how's the hot, red, rosy juice?"
"'Mm!" says the country-dog, "I think
I sort o' see a little blink
O' what you mean." And then he stops
And turns and looks up street and lops
His old wet tongue out, and says he,
Lickin' his lips, all slobbery,
"Ad-drat my melts! you're jes' my man!—
I'll trust you, 'cause I know I can!"
And then he says, "I'll tell you jes'
How things is, and Chape's carelessness
About his sheep,—fer instance, say,
To-morry Chapes'll all be 'way
To Sund'y-meetin'—and ag'in
At night." "At night? That lets us in!—
'Better the day' "—the town-dog says—
" 'Better the deed.' We'll pray; Lord, yes!—
May the outpourin' grace be shed
Abroad, and all hearts comforted
Accordin' to their lights!" says he,
"And that, of course, means you and me."
And then they both snarled, low and quiet—

Swore where they'd meet.   And both stood
    by it!
Jes' half-past eight on Sund'y night,
Them two dogs meets,—the *town*-dog, light
O' foot, though five mile' he had spanned
O' field, beech-wood and bottom-land.
But, as books says,—we draw a veil
Over this chapter of the tale! . . .
Yit when them two infernal, mean,
Low, orn'ry whelps has left the scene
O' carnage—chased and putt to death
The last pore sheep,—they've yit got breath
Enough to laugh and joke about
The fun they've had, while they sneak out
The woods-way fer the old crick where
They both plunge in and wash their hair
And rench their bloody mouths, and grin,
As each one skulks off home ag'in—
Jes' innardly too proud and glad
    To keep theirselves from kind o' struttin',
Thinkin' about the fun they'd had—
    When their blame wizzens needed cuttin'!

Dogs is deliber't.—They can bide
Their time till s'picions all has died.
The country-dog don't 'pear to care
Fer town no more,—he's off somewhere
When the folks whistles, as they head
The team t'ards town.   As I jes' said,—
Dogs is deliber't, don't forgit!

So this-here dog he's got the grit
To jes' deprive hisse'f o' town
For 'bout three weeks. But time rolls
    roun'! . . .
Same as they *first* met:—Saturday—
Same Court-house—hitch-rack—and same
    way
The team wuz hitched—same wagon where
The same *jay*-dog growls under there
When same *town*-dog comes loafin' by,
With the most innocentest eye
And giner'l meek and lowly style,
As though he'd never cracked a smile
In all his mortal days!—And both
Them dogs is strangers, you'd take oath!—
    Both keeps a-lookin' sharp, to see
If folks is watchin'—jes' the way
They acted that first Saturday
    They talked so confidentchully.
"Well"—says the town-dog, in a low
And careless tone—"Well, whatch you
    know?"
"*'Know?'*" says the country-dog—"Lots
    more
Than some smart people knows—that's
    shore!"
And then, in his dog-language, he
Explains how slick he had to be
When some suspicious folks come roun'
A-tryin' to track and run him down—
    Like *he'd* had anything to do

With killin' over fifty head
O' sheep! "Jes' think!—and *me*"—he said,
  "And me as innocent as *you,*
That very hour, five mile' away
In this town like you air to-day!"
"Ah!" says the town-dog, "there's the beauty
  O' bein' *prepared* for what may be,
And *washin'* when you've done your duty!—
  No stain o' blood on you er me
  Ner wool in *our* teeth!—*Then,*" says he,
"When wicked man has wronged us so,
  We ort to learn to be forgivin'—
Half the world, of course, don't know
  How the other gits its livin'!"

PERVERSITY

YOU have more'n likely noticed,
    When you *didn't* when you *could,*
That jes' the thing you *didn't* do
    Was jes' the thing you *should.*

HER POET-BROTHER

OH! what ef little childerns all
   Wuz big as parunts is!
Nen I'd join pa's Masonic Hall
   An' wear gold things like his!
An' you'd "receive," like ma, an' be
   My "hostuss"—An', gee-whizz!
We'd *alluz* have ice-cream, ef we
   Wuz big as parunts is!

Wiv all the money mens is got—
   We'd buy a *Store* wiv that,—
Ist candy, pies an' cakes, an' not
   No *drygoods*—'cept a hat-
An'-plume fer *you*—an' "plug" fer me,
   An' clothes like *ma's* an' *his,*
'At on'y ist fit *us*—ef we
   Wuz big as parunts is!

An'—ef *we* had a little boy
   An' girl like me an' you,—
Our Store'd keep ever' kind o' toy
   They'd ever want us to!—

We'd hire "Old Kriss" to 'tend to be
  The boss of all the biz
An' ist *"charge"* ever'thing—ef we
  Wuz big as parunts is!

GRAMPA'S CHOICE

FIRST and best of earthly joys,
    I like little girls and boys:
Which of all do I like best?
Why, the one that's happiest.

A LITTLE LAME BOY'S VIEWS

ON 'Scursion-days—an' Shows—an' Fairs—
They ain't no bad folks anywheres!—
On street-cars—same as *you*—
Seems like *some*body allus sees
I'm lame, an' takes me on their knees,
  An' holds my crutches, too—
An' asts me what's my name, an' pays
My fare theirse'f—On all Big Days!

The mob all *scrowdges* you an' makes
Enough o' bluffs, fer goodness-sakes!
  But none of 'em *ain't* mad—
They're only *lettin' on.*—*I* know;—
An' I can tell you *why* it's so:
  They're all of 'em too *glad*—
They're *ever' one,* jes' glad as *me*
To be there, er they *wouldn't* be!

The man that sells the tickets snoops
My "one-er" in, but sort o' stoops
  An' grins out at me—then
Looks mean an' business-like an' sucks

His big mustache at me an' chucks
    Too much change out again.—
He's a *smooth citizen,* an' yit
He don't fool *me* one little bit!

An' then, *inside*—fer all the jam—
Folks, seems-like, all knows who I am,
    An' tips me nods an' winks;
An' even country-folks has made
Me he'p eat pie an' marmalade,
    With bottled milk fer "drinks"!—
Folks *all's* so good to me that I—
Sometimes—I nearly purt' near' *cry.*

An' all the *kids,* high-toned er pore,
Seems better than they wuz before,
    An' wants to kind o' "stand
In" with a feller—see him through
The *free* lay-out an' *sideshows,* too,
    An' do the bloomin' "grand"!
On 'Scursion-days—an' Shows an' Fairs—
They ain't no bad folks anywheres!

A VERY TALL BOY

THE ONE LONE LIMERICK OF UNCLE SIDNEY'S

SOME credulous chroniclers tell us
Of a very tall youngster named Ellis,
    Whose Pa said, "Ma-ri-er,
    If Bubb grows much higher,
He'll have to be trained up a trellis."

THE RAGGEDY MAN ON CHILDREN

CHILDERN—take 'em as they run—
You kin *bet* on, ev'ry one!—
Treat 'em right and reco'nize
Human souls is all one size.

Jevver think?—the world's best men
Wears the same souls they had when
They run barefoot—'way back where
All these little children air.

Heerd a boy, not long ago,
Say his parents *sassed* him so,
He'd *correct* 'em, ef he could,—
Then be good ef *they'd* be good.

'LIZABUTH-ANN ON BAKIN'-DAY

OUR Hired Girl, when it's bakin'-day
      She's out o' patience allus,
An' tells us "Hike *outdoors* an' play,
An' when the cookies's done," she'll say,
   "Land sake! she'll come an' call us!"
An' when the little doughbowl's all
Ist heapin'-full, she'll come an' call—
   Nen say, "She ruther take a switchin'
Than have a pack o' pesky childern
   Trackin' round the kitchen!"

GOLDIE GOODWIN

MY old Uncle Sidney *he* says it's a sign
   All over the Worl', an' ten times out of nine,
He can tell by the *name* of a child ef the same
Is a good er bad youngun—ist knows by their
    name!—
So he says, "It's the vurry best sign in the Worl'
That *Goldie Goodwin* is a good little girl,"—
An' says, "First she's *gold*—then she's *good*—an'
    behold,
Good's 'bout 'leventy-*hunnerd* times *better* than
    gold!"

SYMPTOMS

I'M not a-workin' now!—
   I'm jes' a-layin' round
A-lettin' *other* people plow.—
   I'm cumberin' the ground! . . .
I jes' don't *keer!*—I've done my sheer
   O' sweatin'!—Anyhow,
In this dad-blasted weather here,
   I'm not a-workin' *now!*

The corn and wheat and all
   Is doin' well enough!—
They' got clean on from now tel Fall
   To show what kind o' stuff
'At's in their *own* dad-burn backbone;
   So, while the Scriptur's 'low
Man ort to reap as he have sown—
   I'm not a-workin' now!

The grass en-nunder these-
   Here ellums 'long "Old Blue,"
And shadders o' the sugar-trees,
   Beats farmin' quite a few!
As feller says,—I ruther guess
   I'll make my comp'ny bow
And *snooze* a few hours—more er less.—
   I'm not a-workin' now!

BUB SAYS

THE moon in the sky is a custard-pie,
　An' the clouds is the cream pour'd o'er it,
An' all o' the glittering stars in the sky
　Is the powdered sugar for it.

．　．　．　．　．　．　．

Johnts—he's proudest boy in town—
'Cause his Mommy she cut down
His Pa's pants fer Johnts—an' there
Is 'nuff left fer *'nother* pair!

．　．　．　．　．　．　．

One time, when her Ma was gone,
Little Elsie she put on
All her Ma's fine clothes—an' black
Grow-grain-silk, an' sealskin-sack;
Nen while she wuz flouncin' out
In the hall an' round about,
Some one knocked, an' Elsie she
Clean forgot an' run to see

400

Who's there at the door—an' saw
Mighty quick at wuz her Ma.
But ef she ain't saw at all,
She'd a-knowed her parasol!

. . . .

Gran'pas an' Gran'mas is funniest folks!—
Don't be jolly, ner tell no jokes,
Tell o' the weather an' frost an' snow
O' that cold New Year's o' long ago;
An' then they sigh at each other an' cough
An' talk about suddently droppin' off.

THE POOR STUDENT

WITH song elate we celebrate
  The struggling Student wight,
Who seeketh still to pack his pate
  With treasures erudite;
Who keepeth guard and watch and ward
  O'er every hour of day,
Nor less to slight the hours of night,
  He watchful is alway.

Though poor in pence, a wealth of sense
  He storeth in excess—
With poverty in opulence,
  His needs wax never less.
His goods are few,—a shelf or two
  Of classics, and a chair—
A banjo—with a bird's-eye view
  Of back-lots everywhere.

In midnight gloom, shut in his room,
  His vigils he protracts,
E'en to the morning's hectic bloom,
  Accumulating facts:

402

And yet, despite or wrong or right,
   He nurtureth a ban,—
He hath the stanchless appetite
   Of any hirèd man.

On Jason's fleece and storied Greece
   He feeds his hungry mind;
Then stuffs himself like a valise
   With "eats" of any kind:
With kings he feigns he feasts, and drains
   The wines of ages gone—
Then husks a herring's cold remains
   And turns the hydrant on.

In Trojan mail he fronts the gale
   Of ancient battle-rout,
When, 'las the hour! his pipe must fail,
   And his last "snipe" smush out—
Nor pauses he, unless it be
   To quote some cryptic scroll
And poise a sardine pensively
   O'er his immortal soul.

UNCLE SIDNEY'S RHYMES

LITTLE Rapacity Greed was a glutton:
   He'd eat any meat, from goose-livers to
      mutton;
All fowl, flesh, or sausage with all savors through
      it—
You never saw sausage stuffed as *he* could do it!
His nice mamma owned, "O he eats as none other
Than animal kind"; and his bright little brother
Sighed, pained to admit a phrase non-eulogistic,
"Rap eats like a—pardon me—Cannibalistic."
"He eats—like a *boor*," said his sister—"a shameless
Plebeian, in sooth, of an ancestry nameless!"
"He eats," moaned his father, despairingly placid
And hopeless,—"he eats like—he eats like an acid!"

"BLUE-MONDAY" AT THE SHOE SHOP.

IN THE EARLY SEVENTIES

OH, if we had a rich boss
    Who liked to have us rest,
With a dime's lift for a benchmate
    Financially distressed,—
A boss that's been a "jour." himself
    And ain't forgot the pain
Of restin' one day in the week,
    Then back to work againe!

Chorus

Ho, it's hard times together,
    We've had 'em, you and I,
In all kinds of weather,
    Let it be wet or dry;
But I'm bound to earn my livelihood
    Or lay me down and die!

Poverty compels me
    To face the snow and sleet,—
For pore wife and children
    Must have a crust to eat.—

The sad wail of hunger
    It would drive me insane,
If it wasn't for Blue-Monday
    When I git to work againe!

Chorus

Ho, it's hard times together,
    We've had 'em, you and I,
In all kinds of weather,
    Let it be wet or dry;
But I'm bound to earn my livelihood
    Or lay me down and die!

Then it's stoke up the stove, Boss,
    And drive off the damps:
Cut out me tops, Boss,
    And lend me your clamps;—
Pass us your tobacky
    Till I give me pipe a start. . . .
Lor', Boss! how we love ye
    For your warm kynd heart!

Chorus

Ho, it's hard times together,
    We've had 'em, you and I,
In all kinds of weather,
    Let it be wet or dry;
But I'm bound to earn my livelihood
    Or lay me down and die!

THE THOUGHTS OF YOUTH

THE BOYS'

THE lisping maid,
   In shine and shade
Half elfin and half human,
   We love as such—
   Yet twice as much
Will she be loved as woman.

THE GIRLS'

   The boy we see,
   Of two or three—
Or even as a baby,
   We love to kiss
   For what he is,
Yet more for what he may be.

O. HENRY

WRITTEN IN THE CHARACTER OF SHERRARD PLUMMER

O. HENRY, Afrite-chef of all delight!—
    Of all delectables conglomerate
That stay the starved brain and rejuvenate
The mental man. Th' esthetic appetite—
So long anhungered that its "in'ards" fight
    And growl gutwise,—its pangs thou dost
      abate
 And all so amiably alleviate,
Joy pats its belly as a hobo might
Who haply hath attained a cherry pie
   With no burnt bottom in it, ner no seeds—
     Nothin' but crispest crust, and thickness
      fit,
 And squshin'-juicy, and jes' mighty nigh
   Too dratted drippin'-sweet fer human needs,
     But fer the sosh of milk that goes with it.

408

WILLIAM McKINLEY

CANTON, OHIO, SEPTEMBER 30, 1907

HE said: "It is God's way:
　　His will, not ours be done."
And o'er our land a shadow lay
　　That darkened all the sun.
The voice of jubilee
　　That gladdened all the air,
Fell sudden to a quavering key
　　Of suppliance and prayer.

He was our chief—our guide—
　　Sprung of our common Earth,
From youth's long struggle proved and
　　　　tried
　　To manhood's highest worth:
Through toil, he knew all needs
　　Of all his toiling kind—
The favored striver who succeeds—
　　The one who falls behind.

The boy's young faith he still
　　Retained through years mature—
The faith to labor, hand and will,
　　Nor doubt the harvest sure—

409

The harvest of man's love—
　　A nation's joy that swells
To heights of Song, or deeps whereof
　　But sacred silence tells.

To him his Country seemed
　　Even as a Mother, where
He rested—slept; and once he dreamed—
　　As on her bosom there—
And thrilled to hear, within
　　That dream of her, the call
Of bugles and the clang and din
　　Of war. . . . And o'er it all

His rapt eyes caught the bright
　　Old Banner, winging wild
And beck'ning him, as to the fight . . .
　　When—even as a child—
He wakened—And the dream
　　Was real! And he leapt
As led the proud Flag through a gleam
　　Of tears the Mother wept.

His was a tender hand—
　　Even as a woman's is—
And yet as fixed, in Right's command,
　　As this bronze hand of his:
This was the Soldier brave—
　　This was the Victor fair—
This is the Hero Heaven gave
　　To glory here—and There.

"MOTHER"

I'M gittin' old—I know,—
It seems so long ago—
　　So long sence John was here!
He went so young!—our Jim
'S as old now 'most as him,—
　　Close on to thirty year'!

I know I'm gittin' old—
I know it by the *cold*,
　　From time 'at first frost flies.—
Seems like—sence John was here—
Winters is more severe;
　　And winter I de-spise!

And yet it seems, some days,
John's here, with his odd ways . . .
　　Comes soon-like from the corn-
Field, callin' "Mother" at
Me—like he called me that
　　Even 'fore Jim was *born!*

411

When Jim come—La! how good
Was all the neighborhood!—
    And Doctor!—when I heerd
Him joke John, kind o' low,
And say: Yes, folks could go—
    PA needn't be afeard!

When Jim come,—John says-'e—
A-bendin' over me
    And baby in the bed—
And jes' us three,—says-'e
"Our little family!"
    And that was all he said ⁞ ▪ ▪

And cried jes' like a child!—
Kissed me again, and smiled,—
    'Cause I was cryin' too.
And here I am *again*
A-cryin', same as then—
    Yet happy through and through!

The old home's most in mind
And joys long left behind . . ⁞
    Jim's little h'istin' crawl
Acrost the floor to where
John set a-rockin' there . ⁞ ⁞
    (I'm *gittin' old*—That's all!)]

I'm gittin' old—no doubt—
    (*Healthy* as all git-out!)—
    But, strangest thing I do,—

I cry so *easy* now—
I cry jes' anyhow
    The fool-tears wants me to!

But Jim *he* won't be told
'*At* "Mother" 's gittin' old! . . .
    Hugged me, he did, and smiled
This morning, and bragged *"shore"*
He loved me even more
    Than when he was a child!

That's *his* way; but ef *John*
Was here now, lookin' on,
    He'd shorely know and see:
"But, 'Mother,' " s'pect he'd say,
"S'pose you *air* gittin' gray,
    You're younger yet than *me!*"

I'm gittin' old,—because
Our young days, like they was,
    Keeps comin' back—so clear,
'At little Jim, once more,
Comes h'istin' crost the floor
    Fer John's old rockin'-cheer!

    ÷   .   °   .   .   ÷   .

O *beautiful!*—to be
A-gittin' old, like me! . . .
    Hey, Jim! Come in now, Jim!
Your supper's ready, dear!
(How more, every year,
    He looks and acts like *him!*)

THE BOYS OF THE OLD GLEE CLUB

YOU-FOLKS rickollect, I know—
'Tain't so *very* long ago—
Th' Old Glee Club—was got up here
'Bout first term Grant tuk the Cheer
Fer President four year—and then
Riz—and tuk the thing again!
Politics was runnin' high,
And the *Soldiers* mighty nigh
Swep' the Country—'bout on par
With their rickord through the War.
Glee Club, mainly, Soldiers, too—
Most the Boys had wore the blue,—
So their singin' had the swing—
Kind o' sort o' Shiloh-ring,
Don't you know, 'at kind o' got
Clean *inside* a man and shot
Telegrams o' joy dee-vine
Up and down his mortal spine!

They was jest *boys* then, all young—
And 'bout lively as they sung!
Now they hain't young any more—
('Less the ones 'at's gone before
'S got their youth back, glad and free
'N' keerless as they used to be!)
Burgess Brown's old friends all 'low
He is 'most as lively now,
And as full o' music, too,
As when Old Glee Club was new!
And *John Blake,* you mind, 'at had
The near-sightedness so bad,
When he sung by note, the rest
Read 'em fer him, er he *guessed*
How they run—and *sung* 'em, too,
Clair and sweet as honey-dew!
Harry Adams's here—and he's
Jollyin' ever' man he sees
'At complains o' gittin' gray
Er a-*age*in' anyway.
Harry he jest *thrives* on fun—
"Troubles?" *he* says,—"Nary one!—
Got gran'-children I can play
And keep young with, night and day!"
Then there's *Ozzy Weaver*—he's
Kickin', lively as you please,—
'N' *Dearie Macy.*—Called 'em then
"The Cherubs." Sung "We are two Men
O' th' Olden Time." Well! their duets
Was jest sweet as violets!
And *Dan Ransdell*—he's still here—

Not jest in the *town,* but near
Enough, you bet, to allus come
Prompt' on time to vote at home!
Dan he's be'n in Washington
Sence he went with Harrison. . . .
And *John Slauson*—(Boys called John
"Sloppy Weather.")—he went on
Once to Washington; and Dan
Intertained him:—Ever' man,
From the President, to all
Other big-guns Dan could haul
In posish 'ud have to shake
Hands with John fer old times' sake.
And to hear *John,* when he got
Home again, w'y, you'd 'a' caught
His own sperit and dry fun
And mis-*chieve*-y-ousness 'at run
Through his talk of all he see:—
"Ruther pokey there, fer *me,*"
John says,—"though, of course, I met
Mostly jest the *Cabinet*
Members; and the President
He'd drop round: and then we went
Incogg fer a quiet walk—
Er sometimes jest set and talk
'Bout old times back here—and how
All *you*-boys was doin' now,
And Old Glee Club songs; and then
He'd say, 'f he *could,* once again,
Jest hear *us*—'once more,' says he,—

'I'd shed Washington, D. C.,
And jest fall in ranks with you
And march home, a-singin', too!' "
And *Bob Geiger—Now* lives down
At Atlanty,—but this town
'S got Bob's *heart*—a permanent
And time-honored resident.
Then there's *Mahlon Butler*—still
Lookin' like he allus will!
"How you feelin'?" s'I, last time
I see Mahlon: 'N' *he* says, "I'm
'Feelin'?' " says, "so peert and gay
'F I's *hitched up* I'd run away!"
He says, "Course I'm *bald* a bit,
But not 'nough to *brag* on it
Like *Dave Wallace* does," he says,
"With his *two* shamefacetedness!"
(Dave jest laughs and lifts his "dice"
At the joke, and blushes—twice.)
And *Ed. Thompson,* he's gone on—
They's a whole quartette 'at's gone—
Yes, a whole quartette, and *more,*
Has crossed on the Other Shore. . . .
Sabold and *Doc Wood'ard's* gone—
'N' *Ward;* and—last,—*Will Tarkington.*—
Ward 'at made an Irish bull
Actchully jest beautiful!—
" 'Big-nose Ben,' " says Ward, "I s'pose,
Makes an eyesore of his nose!"
And *Will Tarkington*—Ef *he*

Ever had an *inemy,*
The Good Bein's plans has be'n
Tampered with!—because all men,
Women and childern—ever' one—
Loved to love Will Tarkington!

The last time I heerd 'em *all*
Was at Tomilsonian Hall,
As I rickollect—and *know,*—
Must be'n fifteen year' ago!—
Big Mass Meetin'—*thousands* here. . . .
Old Dick Thompson in the Cheer
On the stage—and three er four
Other "Silver-Tongues" er more! . . .
Mind Ben Harrison?—Clean, rich,
Ringin' voice—" 'bout concert-pitch,"
Tarkington *he* called it, and
Said its music 'clipsed the band
And Glee Club both rolled in one!—
('Course you all knowed *Harrison!*)
Yes, and Old Flag, streamin' clean
From the high arch 'bove the scene
And each side the Speaker's stand.—
And a *Brass,* and *Sheepskin* Band,
('Twixt the speeches 'at was made)
'At cut loose and banged and played—
S'pose, to have the *noise* all through
So's th' crowd could listen to
Some *real* music!—Then Th' Old Glee
Club marched out to victory!—

And sich singin'!—Boys was jest
At their very level-best! . . .
My! to *hear* 'em!—From old "Red-
White-and-Blue," to "Uncle Ned"!—
From "The Sword of Bunker Hill,"
To "Billy Magee-Magaw"!—And—still
The more they sung, the more, you know,
The crowd jest *wouldn't* let 'em go!—
Till they reached the final notch
O' glory with old "Larboard Watch"!
Well! *that* song's a song my soul
Jest swings off in, past control!—
Allus did and allus will
Lift me clair of earthly ill
And interrogance and doubt
O' what the good Lord's workin' out
Anyway er *anyhow!* . . .
Shet my eyes and hear it *now!*—
Till, at night, that ship and sea
And wet waves jest wallers me
Into that same sad yet glad
Certainty *the Sailor* had
When waked to his watch and ward
By th' lone whisper of the Lord—
Heerd high 'bove the hoarsest roar
O' any storm on sea er shore!

Time's be'n clockin' on, you know!
Sabold, who was first to go,
Died back East, in ninety-three,
At his old home, Albany:

Ward was next to leave us—Died
New York. . . . How we've laughed and
    cried
Both together at them two
Friends and comards tried and true!—
Ner they wasn't, when they died,
Parted long—'most side-by-side
They went singin', you might say,
Till their voices died away
Kind o' into a duet
O' silence they're rehearsin' yet.

Old Glee Club's be'n meetin' less
And less frequenter, I guess,
Sence so many's had to go—
And the rest all miss 'em so!
Still they's calls they' got to make,
Fer old reputation's sake,
So to speak; but, 'course, they all
Can't jest answer *ever'* call—
'Ceptin' Christmas-times, er when
Charity calls on 'em then;
And—not *chargin'* anything—
W'y, the Boys's jest *got* to sing! . . .
Campaign work, and jubilees
To wake up the primaries;
Loyal Legions—G. A. R.'s—
Big Reunions—Stripes-and-Stars
Fer Schoolhouses ever'where—
And Church-doin's, here and there—
And Me-morial Meetin's, when

Our War-Gov'ner lives again!
Yes, and Decoration Days—
Martial music—prayers and praise
Fer the Boys 'at marched away
So's *we'd* have a place to stay! . . .
Little childern, 'mongst the flowers,
Learnin' 'bout this Land of Ours,
And the price these Soldiers paid,
Gethered in their last parade. . . .
O that sweetest, saddest sound!—
"Tenting on the old Campground." . . .
The Old Glee Club—singin' so
Quaverin'-like and soft and low,
Ever' listener in the crowd
Sings in *whispers*—but, *out 'loud,*
Sings as ef he didn't keer—
Not fer *nothin'!* . . . Ketch me here
Whilse I'm honest, and I'll say
God's way is the only way! . . .
So I' allus felt, i jing!
Ever' time the Boys 'ud sing
'Bout "A Thousand Years, my Own
Columbia!"—er "The Joys we've Known"—
"Hear dem Bells"—er "Hi-lo, Hail!"—
I have felt God must prevail—
Jest like ever boy 'at's gone
Of 'em all, whilse he was on
Deck here with us, seemed to be
Livin', laughin' proof, to *me,*
Of Eternal Life—No more
Will than *them all,* gone before! . . .

Can't I—many-a-time—jest see
Them *all,* like they *used* to be!—
Tarkington, fer instance, clean
Outside o' the man you *seen,*
Singin'—till not only you
Heerd his voice but *felt* it, **too,**
In back of the bench you set
In—And 'most can feel it yet!
Yes, and Will's the last o' five
Now that's dead—yet still *alive,*
True as Holy Writ's own word
Has be'n spoke and man has heerd!
Them was left when Will went on
Has met once sence he was gone—
Met jest once—but not to sing
Ner to practise anything.—
Facts is, they jest didn't know
Why they *was* a-meetin' so;—
But *John Brush* he had it done
And invited ever' one
Of 'em he could find, to call
At his office, "Music Hall,"
Four o'clock—one Saturd'y
Afternoon.—And this was three
Er four weeks, mind, sence the **day**
We had laid poor Will away.
Mahlon Butler he come past
My shop, and I dropped my last
And went with him, wonder'n', too,
What new *joke* Brush had in view;—

But, when all got there, and one-
By-one was give' a seat, and none
O' Brush's *twinkles* seemed in sight,
'N' he looked *biz* all right, all right,—
We saw—when he'd locked the door—
What *some* of us, years before,
Had seen, and long sence fergot—
(*Seen* but not *heerd,* like as not.)—
How Brush, once when Admiral Brown
'S back here in his old home-town
And flags ever'wheres—and Old
Glee Club tellin' George to "Hold
The Fort!" and "We" would "make 'em flee
By land and sea," et cetery,—
How Brush had got the Boys to sing
A song in that-there very thing
Was on the table there to-day—
Some kind o' *'phone,* you know.—But *say!*
When John touched it off, and we
Heerd it singin'—No-sir-ee!—
Not the *machine* a-singin'—No,—
Th' *Old Glee Club* o' long ago! . . .
There was *Sabold's* voice again—
'N' *Ward's;*—and, sweet as summer-rain,
With glad boy-laughture's trills and runs,
Ed. Thompson's voice and *Tarkington's!* . . .
And *ah,* to *hear* them, through the storm
Of joy that swayed each listener's form—
Seeming to call, with hail and cheer,
From Heaven's high seas down to us here :—

"But who can speak the joy he feels
While o'er the foam his vessel reels,
And his tired eyelids slumbering fall,
He rouses at the welcome call
Of 'Larboard Watch, Ahoy!'"
.   .   .   .   .   .   And *O*
To *hear* them—same as long ago—
The listeners whispered, still as death,
With trembling lips and broken breath,
As with one voice—and eyes all wet,—
"GOD!—*God!—Thank God, they're singing*
    yet!"

THE LITTLE MAN IN THE TINSHOP.

2

WHEN I was a little boy, long ago,
And spoke of the theatre as "the Show",
The first one that I went to see —
Mother's brother it was took me
(My Uncle, of course — though he seemed to be
Only a boy — I loved him so!)
And oh, how pleasant he made it all!
And the things he knew that I should know! —
Of the stage, and "the drop", and the frescoed wall —
The balcony, and "the baldhead row"
The orchestra, with its melody,
And the lilt and jingle and jubilee
Of "The Little Man in the Tinshop!"

"MONA MACHREE"

Mona Machree, I'm the wanderin' creature now,
Over the sea;
Slave of no lass, but a lover of Nature now,
Careless and free.
—T. A. DALY

MONA MACHREE! och, the sootherin' flow
of it,
      Soft as the sea,
Yet, in under the mild, moves the wild undertow
of it
      Tuggin' at me,
Until both the head and the heart o' me's fightin'
For breath, night a death all so grandly invitin'
That—barrin' your own livin' yet—I'd delight in,
  Drowned in the deeps of this billowy song to you
Sung by a lover your beauty has banned,
Not alone from your love but his dear native land,
Whilst the kiss of his lips, and touch of his hand,
  And his song—all belong to you,
      Mona Machree!

SONG DISCORDANT

I WANT to say it, and I will:—
    You are as sour as you are sweet,
And sweeter than the daffodil
    That blossoms at your feet.—
You are as plain as you are fair;
    And though I hate, I love you still,
And so—*confound* you, darling! *There!*—
    I want to say it, and I will!

I want to ask it, and I do
    Demand of you a perfect trust,—
But love me as I want you to—
    You must, you minx!—you must!
You blight and bless me, till I swear
    And pray—chaotic even as you.—
I curse—Nay, dear,—I *kiss* you. *There!*—
    I want to, and I do!

LARRY NOOLAN'S NEW YEAR

BE-GORRIE, aI wor sorry
    When the Ould Year died:
An' aI says, "aI'll shtart to-morry,
    Like aI've always thried—
        aI'll give yes all fair warnin'
        aI'll be shtartin' in the mornin'
        From the wakeness aI was born in—
            When the Ould Year died."

The year forninsht the pasht wan,
    When the Ould Year died,
Says aI, "This is the lasht wan
    aI'll be filled—wid pride."
        So says aI til Miss McCarty
        aI wor meetin' at the party,
        "Lave us both be drinkin' hearty!"
            When the Ould Year died.

So we dined an' wined together,
    When the Ould Year died,
An' agreed on health an' weather,
    An' the whule wurrld wide,
        An' says aI,—"aI'm thinkin' very
        Much it's you aI'd like to marry."
        "Then," says she, "why don't you, Larry?"
            When the Ould Year died.

LISPING IN NUMBERS

W E' got a' Uncle writes poetry-rhymes
Fer me an' Eddie to *speak,* sometimes,—
'Cause *he's* a *poet*—an' he gits *paid*
Fer poetry-writin',—'cause that's his *trade.*
An' Eddie says he's goin' to try
To be a poet, too, by an' by
When he's a man!—an' I 'spect he is,
'Cause on his slate wunst he print' this
An' call it

"The Squirl and the Funy Litel Girl"

> *"A litel girl*
> *Whose name wuz Perl*
> *Went to the woods to play.*
> *The day wuz brite,*
> *An' her hart wuz lite*
> *As she galy skiped a way.*
>
> *"A queer litel chatter,*
> *A soft litel patter,*
> *She herd in the top of a tree:*
> *The surprizd litel Perl*
> *Saw a qute litel squirl,*
> *As cuning as cuning cud be.*

428

"She twisted her curl,
As she looked at the squirl,
An' playfully told it 'good day!'
She calld it 'Bunny'—
Wuzent that funy?
An' it noded an' bounded a way."

Ma read it, an' says "she's *awful proud,"*—
An' Pa says "Splen'id!" an' laugh' out loud;
But Uncle says, "You can talk as you please,
It's a purty good little poetry-piece!"

BENJAMIN HARRISON

ON THE UNVEILING OF HIS MONUMENT AT INDIAN-
APOLIS—OCTOBER 27, 1908

AS tangible a form in History
   The Spirit of this man stands forth as here
He towers in deathless sculpture, high and
      clear
Against the bright sky of his destiny.
Sprung of our oldest, noblest ancestry,
   His pride of birth, as lofty as sincere,
   Held kith and kin, as Country, ever dear—
Such was his sacred faith in you and me.
Thus, natively, from youth his work was one
   Unselfish service in behalf of all—
      Home, friends, and sharers of his toil and
         stress;
Ay, loving all men and despising none,
   And swift to answer every righteous call,
      His life was one long deed of worthiness.

The voice of Duty's faintest whisper found
   Him as alert as at her battle-cry—
   Whot awful War's battalions thundered by,
High o'er the havoc still he heard the sound

Of mothers' prayers and pleadings all around;
  And ever the despairing sob and sigh
  Of stricken wives and orphan children's cry.
Made all our Land thrice consecrated ground.
So ran his "Forward!" and so swept his sword—
    On!—on!—till from the fire-and-cloud once more
    Our proud Flag lifted in the glad sunlight
As though the very Ensign of the Lord
  Unfurled in token that the strike was o'er,
    And victory—as ever—with the right.

LEE O. HARRIS

CHRISTMAS DAY—1909

O SAY not he is dead,
 The friend we honored so;
Lift up a grateful voice instead
 And say: He lives, we know—
We know it by the light
 Of his enduring love
Of honor, valor, truth and right,
 And man, and God above.

Remember how he drew
 The child-heart to his own,
And taught the parable anew,
 And reaped as he had sown;
Remember with what cheer
 He filled the little lives,
And stayed the sob and dried the tear
 With mirth that still survives.

All duties to his kind
 It was his joy to fill;
With nature gentle and refined,
 Yet dauntless soul and will,

He met the trying need
  Of every troublous call,
Yet high and clear and glad indeed
  He sung above it all.

Ay, listen! Still we hear
  The patriot song, the lay
Of love, the woodland note so dear—
  These will not die away.
Then say not he is dead,
  The friend we honor so,
But lift a grateful voice instead,
  And say: He lives, we know.

TO BENJ. S. PARKER

YOU sang the song of rare delight
    " 'Tis morning and the days are long"—
A morning fresh and fair and bright
    As ever dawned in happy song;
A radiant air, and here and there
    Were singing birds on sprays of bloom,
And dewy splendors everywhere,
    And heavenly breaths of rose perfume—
All rapturous things were in the song
" 'Tis morning and the days are long."

O singer of the song divine,
    Though now you turn your face away
With never word for me or mine
    Nor smile forever and a day,
We guess your meaning, and rejoice
    In what has come to you—the meed
Beyond the search of mortal voice
    And only in the song indeed—
With you forever, as the song,
" 'Tis morning and the days are long."

THE HIGHEST GOOD

TO attain the highest good
  Of true man and womanhood,
Simply do your honest best—
God with joy will do the rest.

MY CONSCIENCE

SOMETIMES my Conscience says, says
    he,
"Don't you know me?"
And I, says I, skeered through and through,
"Of course I do.
You air a nice chap ever' way,
I'm here to say!
You make me cry—you make me pray,
And all them good things thataway—
That is, at *night*. Where do you stay
Durin' the day?"

And then my Conscience says, onc't more,
"You know me—shore?"
"Oh, yes," says I, a-trimblin' faint,
"You're jes' a saint!
Your ways is all so holy-right,
I love you better ever' night
You come around,—tel' plum daylight,
When you air out o' sight!"

And then my Conscience sort o' grits
His teeth, and spits
On his two hands and grabs, of course,
Some old remorse,
And beats me with the big butt-end
O' *that* thing—tel my clostest friend
'Ud hardly know me. "Now," says he,
"Be keerful as you'd orto be
And *allus* think o' me!"

NOTES

NOTES

p. 1   "THEM OLD CHEERY WORDS"

Printed in *The Century Magazine,* December, 1896; published in HOME-FOLKS—1900, SONGS OF HOME—1910.

p. 5   A DUBIOUS "OLD KRISS"

Printed in *The Ladies' Home Journal,* December, 1896; published in BOOK OF JOYOUS CHILDREN—1902.

p. 8   YOUR HEIGHT IS OURS

This poem to Richard Henry Stoddard was written for the banquet given in his honor by The Authors' Club in New York City, March 25, 1897; printed in *The Critic,* April 3, 1897; published in HOME-FOLKS—1900, THE LOCKERBIE BOOK—1911. Richard Henry Stoddard [1825-1903] was a distinguished journalist, poet, critic and editor.

p. 9   HYMN EXULTANT

Written for Easter, April 18, 1897; published in HOME-FOLKS—1900, THE LOCKERBIE BOOK—1911.

p. 10   "O LIFE! O BEYOND!"

Printed in *The Arena,* June, 1897; published in HOME-FOLKS—1900, THE LOCKERBIE BOOK—1911.

The title is taken from a favorite quotation to be found in Mrs. Browning's *A Rhapsody of Life's Progress:*—

O Life, O Beyond,
Thou art strange, thou art sweet!

p. 12 OUR QUEER OLD WORLD

Printed in *McClure's Magazine,* August, 1897; published in HOME-FOLKS—1900, SONGS O' CHEER —1905.

p. 14 ON A YOUTHFUL PORTRAIT OF STEVENSON

Written about September, 1897; printed with the portrait described in *Scribner's Magazine,* December, 1897; published in HOME-FOLKS—1900, THE LOCKERBIE BOOK—1911. In a letter to Miss Clara E. Laughlin, dated October 28, 1897, Mr. Riley tells of an incident associated with the poem :—

I've a youthful photograph of our beloved Robert Louis Stevenson,—and I wrote some maunderings to it—nay, to the lovely man himself—sent picture and lines to a magazine and publishing house,—and they wrote to say portrait and verses would appear in their Christmas magazine, and enclosed a great corpulent check which I had not dreamed of in such connection—so returned it, coyly saying even if I had intended the lines for money, their check was in vast excess of their worth,—but if, in lieu of such sordid compensation, Robert Louis Stevenson's publishers were to send me a set of his books, it would seem to me about all the recompense I could bear.—Well, now here's where only a poet can humor and account for the doings of Divinity: —As I stepped out into the golden morning-edge of my very *recentest birthday,* Robert Louis Stevenson was blithely seeing to it that his books were being then and there delivered into my hands by the expressman who looked and acted just for the world as though *he were* delivering the package to me.—Even made me sign something to that effect, I think!

See *To Robert Louis Stevenson,* Vol. III, p. 406.

p. 15 RUBÁIYÁT OF DOC SIFERS

Printed in *The Century Magazine,* November
and December, 1897; published in RUBÁIYÁT OF DOC
SIFERS—1897. Dr. Franklin W. Hays, to whom the
poem in book form is dedicated and to whom the
proem is addressed, was Mr. Riley's warm personal
friend, as well as physician. They became acquainted at Greenfield in the early days, and both of
them knew the wholesome, old-fashioned characters
who inspired the composite of Doc Sifers.

After writing the poem entitled *Doc Sifers* (Vol.
III, p. 416) Mr. Riley found that he had developed
a congenial subject which would not let him rest,
and so, out of pure love for the character, added
from time to time a quatrain in the same verse-form
and spirit. These stanzas were written on plain
white cards, two quatrains on a card, and tossed
aside in a haphazard fashion, and though no particular incident was ever left unfinished, or phase of
character left half developed, the poem was not made
a continuous story. This method was analogous to
the style of the *Rubáiyát,* in which there was no special continuity of plan. Though the writing of the
poem was similar in method to the *Rubáiyát of
Omar Khayyam,* its spirit offers a sharp contrast.
In fact, Mr. Riley's poem is an indirect reply to the
epicurean pessimism and cynicism of the other
poem, presenting "a picture of a wholesome, helpful,
industrious man,—a doctor with hale faith in God
and man, in contrast to the old Persian's utterly
hopeless doctrine." Doc Sifers is the embodiment
of altruism and unselfishness, and the incarnation of
a cheerful philosophy. Mr. Riley loves the character as devotedly as an old friend.

Mr. Riley's impressions of the *Rubáiyát of Omar
Khayyam* were contained in a letter dated August

25, 1880, and addressed to Mrs. John M. Judah, who had just loaned him her copy of the poem :—

> I owe you many thanks for the privilege given me for the careful reading of this remarkable poem of Khayyam's. As a poem, I think it wonderfully fine in many particulars —only, its logic lures one further and further from the old childish faith, which to possess again, in all its purity, would make me want to die at once while I could—without the vaguest doubt of immortality.

[Here followed the poem *At Sea*, Vol. II, p. 253.]

XLVIII: Daniel Boone [1735-1820] was a celebrated Kentucky pioneer. Mungo Park [1771-1806] was the great African traveler who explored the Niger. In 1799, he wrote *Travels in the Interior of Africa*. Adam Poe was a noted Indiana fighter and associate of Daniel Boone.

p. 55   WHERE THE CHILDREN USED TO PLAY

Printed in *The Indianapolis Journal*, November 14, 1897, with the title, *An Old-Home Song*, and subtitle, *Written for Music;* published in Afterwhiles (not in first edition)—1898, Farm-Rhymes—1901, The Lockerbie Book—1911, Knee Deep in June and Other Poems—1912. "Mother" is the wife.

p. 57   MR. FOLEY'S CHRISTMAS

Printed in *The Interior*, December, 1897; published in Home-Folks—1900. The introductory quotation is from O'Reilly's *The Cry of the Dreamer*, stanza 3, ll. 3-4.

p. 60   TO SANTA CLAUS

Printed in *The Arena*, December 1897, with the title, *Santa Claus;* published in Afterwhiles (not in first edition)—1898, THE LOCKERBIE BOOK— 1911.

p. 62   CHRISTMAS ALONG THE WIRES

Printed in a supplement to *The Chicago Tribune,* December 19, 1897, with the title, *Christmas Times Along the Wires;* published in HOME-FOLKS—1900.
p. 63, l. 12: Ben Custer's Band was a popular organization hailing from Centerville, Indiana.

p. 72   TO THE BOY WITH A COUNTRY

Written in March, 1898, for Dan Wallingford, age seven, who was a national boy hero at the time, voicing the indignant patriotism aroused through the destruction of the battleship Maine in Havana Harbor. Distressed by the disaster, he sent all his savings, amounting to forty-eight cents, to the Secretary of the Navy with this letter:—

> I have been wanting to do something for
> my country
> I think now is the time
> So I send you all the pennies
> I have to help build a new ship
> Dan Wallingford
> 7 years old

Secretary Long replied with fitting appreciation, and the entire country thrilled with the story of the little boy's patriotic spirit.

p. 73   AT CROWN HILL

Written at the death of Hiram King Curtis, March 19, 1898; printed in *The Indianapolis Journal,* May 26, 1901, with the title, *At Home,* published in HOME-FOLKS—1900, THE LOCKERBIE

BOOK—1911. Mr. Curtis [1823-1898], for several years principal of the public schools at Kokomo, Peru and Logansport, Indiana, was the father of John J. Curtis of The Bobbs-Merrill Publishing Company, in whose office he met Mr. Riley frequently and formed a cordial friendship with him.

p. 75   SNOW IN THE AIR

Written prior to May, 1898, at which time it was included in a volume of collected poems called THE GOLDEN YEAR as *Envoy;* published in THE LOCKERBIE BOOK—1911, with the same title.

p. 76   THE NAME OF OLD GLORY

An early version of this poem was given by Mr. Riley at a banquet of The Indianapolis Literary Club, May 18, 1898; during the summer it was revised and was printed in *The Atlantic Monthly,* December, 1898; published in HOME-FOLKS—1900, THE LOCKERBIE BOOK—1911. In *The Atlantic Monthly,* just following the title were the words: *"When, why, and by whom, was our flag, The Stars and Stripes, first called 'Old Glory'? Daily query to Press."* On February 23, 1903, when the State of Indiana presented a sword to Admiral Taylor, who commanded the battleship Indiana in the engagement off Santiago, Mr. Riley read the poem with this introductory tribute to the flag:—

It may seem a late day in which to attempt a tribute to our glorious old flag, the stars and stripes: but that it is an ever newer glory in our eyes and an ever dearer rapture to our hearts. The coming generations of its patriot followers, high and low, can but lift to it continuous voices of applause and benediction. Master orators may eulogize it till no further thrill of speech seems left with which to fitly glorify it, or poets may sing its praises till their song seems one with the music of the ripples of the breezes in its silken folds; but no tribute-voice of forum, harp or clarion may well hold mute the one all-universal voice that breaks, with cheers and tears, at every newer sight of our Nation's hallowed emblem—the old flag. Over its brave heroes and defenders, since "the shot heard round the world," it has been a panoply, a shelter and a shield, and yet how proudly have the embattled hosts gone down that they might lift it to securer heights. Its wavering shade has fallen on the weary marcher softly as the shadow of the maple at his father's door. He has heard its flutterings, like light laughter, in the lull of noonday battle; and, worn with agony, above the surgeon's tent, that all is well. Yea, and in death the sacred banner has enfolded him, even as a mother's fond caress. Ho, but the Lord's own victory in which he shares; the land he loved restored, inviolate, to kinsmen, comrades and oncoming patriot thousands yet to be—the broad old land of freedom firm under foot once more—the old flag overhead! And what inspiring symbol must this banner be to its like brave defenders who go down to sea in ships. One of these— a hapless prisoner for a while—says this of the old flag:— "There's an odd thing about that flag when you meet it on the high seas and the wind is blowing hard, namely, that of all flags I know, it is the most alive; when the wind blows, the most eager and keen, with the stripes flowing and darting, and the stars seeming to dance with the joy of excitement. So that there is none better to go into battle, or come down the street when the fifes are piping ahead; but if you want something to signify peace and quiet, you would be as well off with not such bristling stars and fewer stripes, for the stars will leap and the stripes show their energy whenever the wind blows." And with righteous pride it is recorded that upon the sea—borne on the throbbing bosom of the gale and baptized with the salt sea spray—this beloved flag of ours was first christened by the name of Old Glory.

p. 79   ONE WITH A SONG

Dated June 24, 1898; printed in *The Indianapolis Journal*, June 25, 1898, with the title, *Frank L. Stanton;* published in HOME-FOLKS—1900, THE

LOCKERBIE BOOK—1911. Between Mr. Riley and
Mr. Frank Lebby Stanton, of *The Atlanta Constitu-
tion,* there has long been a hearty friendship. The
latter has dedicated two of his happiest poems to
Mr. Riley, *A Dream of June* and *James Whitcomb
Riley.*

The following cordial verses (undated) were also
addressed to Mr. Stanton by Mr. Riley:—

TO FRANK L. STANTON

I

O singer of the South,
Singing on through drip or drouth,
With the very bees a-murmur round the honey of your
mouth,
Sweeter song or sweeter word
Never woodland ever heard—
Simply, Stanton, Master Songster,
Bard of Nature, you're a bird!

II

So from out the Northland stirred
May another bird be heard—
The chirrup of the merest wren beside the mocking-bird!
But la! no matter whether
It is wet or shiny weather,
We'll hop up on the selfsame bough and chirp, and sing
together.

p. 81   INDIANA

Published in AFTERWHILES (not in first edition)
—1898, THE LOCKERBIE BOOK—1911.

p. 82   CHRISTMAS AFTERTHOUGHT

Published in RHYMES OF CHILDHOOD (not in
first edition)—1898.

p. 83 THE CHRISTMAS LONG AGO

Published in RHYMES OF CHILDHOOD (not in first edition)—1898.

p. 84 EXCEEDING ALL

Published in RHYMES OF CHILDHOOD (not in first edition)—1898, SONGS O' CHEER—1905, THE LOCKERBIE BOOK—1911.

p. 85 CLAUDE MATTHEWS

Printed in *The Indianapolis Journal*, August 30, 1898; hitherto unpublished in book form. Claude Matthews, born in Bath County, Kentucky, December 14, 1845, died at Lafayette, Indiana, August 28, 1898. He married a daughter of Governor James Whitcomb, after whom Mr. Riley was named. In 1892 he became governor of Indiana.

p. 86 THE SERMON OF THE ROSE

Printed in *The Atlantic Monthly*, September, 1898; published in LOVE-LYRICS—1899, HOME-FOLKS—1900, THE LOCKERBIE BOOK—1911.

p. 88 THE ONWARD TRAIL

Written just following the death of Myron W. Reed, at Denver, January 30, 1899, and printed in *The Indianapolis Journal*, January 31, 1899; published in HOME-FOLKS—1900, THE LOCKERBIE BOOK—1911. Myron Reed, born in Brookfield, Vermont, July 24, 1836, was a well-known preacher.

He was one of Mr. Riley's most intimate friends, and accompanied him and W. P. Fishback on a visit to England in 1891. Mrs. May W. Donnan, of Indianapolis, said in *The Indianapolis Journal,* February 13, 1899:—

All who knew Mr. Reed will appreciate the naming of this poem, all who loved him will seize upon its suggestiveness. Many of us think of Mr. Reed as a scout, one who courted the unfamiliar, who loved to explore, who sought not old, tried, beaten paths, but new, untrodden ways. He had the keen eye, the quick ear, the unerring instinct of the Indian. There was an elemental force in him overbalancing rules and doctrines; there was a strain of the primitive, the simple, that opposed the artificial and acquired. He abhorred ceremony, merely as such; he loved freedom of thought, liberty of action, genuineness and spontaneity. There was no air of superiority or patronage in Mr. Reed's preaching, no assumption of righteousness, no pretense of spiritual authority. His listeners felt the oneness with themselves, his sympathy with their failures. They felt he, too, lost the way sometimes, that for him the trail was occasionally obscured, but there are many to whom it is a comfort to know that he had to try as hard as they to keep the good path. What a heart of affliction he had! What a hand to help! Who in Indianapolis does not remember the sermons delivered after the Johnstown disaster, the Lawrenceburg flood, the death of Garfield? Who has forgotten the talks given at the annual meetings of the Charity Association, and the plea for hearts alive to the suffering about us? Who has forgotten the address on Burns, with its call for loving judgment? Who does not remember how God was always pictured as a tender, loving Father? Mr. Reed believed God viewed sin "with other, larger eyes than ours," and he told us not to be afraid. His was the beautiful gospel of hope, as strenuous as that of Browning. His was the flag of courage, never dipping in the face of fear. And his, too, was the doctrine of cheerfulness. He continually echoed Mr. Riley's "When a man's jest glad plum through, God's pleased with him, same as you." A trail is not a made road; it is a line of march indicated by marks, now well defined, now faint, often deviating and uncertain, yet true in the main. He who first travels it with only faith to guide merits our love and gratitude. In his footsteps we may confidently place our own.

p. 90 TO LESLEY

Written for Lesley Payne, the poet's little niece; printed in *The Indianapolis Journal,* February 19, 1899; hitherto unpublished in book form. Compare Burns' *"O Saw Ye Bonnie Lesley."*

p. 91 THE NATURALIST

Dated Indianapolis, March 4, 1899; printed in *The Hesperian Tree, An Annual of the Ohio Valley* —1900, with the subtitle, *Oliver Davie, on Reading His "Reveries and Recollections"*; published in HOME-FOLKS—1900, THE LOCKERBIE BOOK—1911.

Oliver Davie [1856-1911], of Columbus, Ohio, was a naturalist, bookman, and author. Robert G. Ingersoll called his *Reveries and Recollections of a Naturalist* [1898] "one of the finest tributes to nature ever penned." Mr. Riley knew Mr. Davie by correspondence.

p. 92 HER WAITING FACE

Published in LOVE-LYRICS—1899. The fourth line also appears in *The Flying Islands of the Night* [Vol. I, p. 304, last line].

p. 93 BLOOMS OF MAY

Published in LOVE-LYRICS—1899.

p. 94 A SONG OF THE ROAD

Printed in *Lippincott's Magazine,* July, 1899; published in HOME-FOLKS—1900, SONGS O' CHEER —1905, THE LOCKERBIE BOOK—1911.

p. 96   THE ENDURING

Printed in *Scribner's Magazine,* July, 1899; published in HOME-FOLKS—1900, THE LOCKERBIE
BOOK—1911. This poem is a memory of the old
shoe-shop at Greenfield and its quaint English pro-
prietor, Tom Snow, as he was familiarly called, who
was an interesting character in the early days at
Greenfield. His place was much frequented by the
boys of the town because he was a fascinating talker.
He was chiefly interested in establishing the first li-
brary at Greenfield. See *Jim,* Vol III, p. 365.

Mr. Riley has never read elsewhere the lines
quoted from the old engraving, nor has he ever
learned their authorship.

p. 98   A HUMBLE SINGER

Written about September 2, 1899; printed in
The Topeka State Journal (Kansas), September 15,
1899; published in MORNING—1907, THE LOCKER-
BIE BOOK—1911. Eugene Ware's *Old Kansas Vet-
eran,* which appeared in *The Indianapolis Journal,*
September 2, 1899, inspired the writing of these
lines. See note on *The Rhymes of Ironquill,* Vol.
IV, p. 527, for further information about Eugene
Ware.

p. 99   THE NOBLEST SERVICE

Written at the death of Dr. Wyckliffe Smith, of
Delphi, Indiana, December 28, 1899, and dated
December 29; published in HOME-FOLKS—1900,
THE LOCKERBIE BOOK—1911. Dr. Smith, one of
the poet's best of friends, was killed at a railroad
crossing while making a professional call in the
country near Delphi. His daily life was filled with
deeds of kindliness and service. For the story of

his friendship with Mr. Riley compare the following poems and their notes in Vol. III: *Herr Weiser,* p. 172; *From Delphi to Camden,* p. 174; *On the Banks o' Deer Crick,* p. 290.

p. 100 OLD MAN WHISKERY-WHEE-KUM-WHEEZE

Printed in *The Century Magazine,* February, 1900, with the four poems that follow under the general title, *The Hoosier Youngster;* published in THE BOOK OF JOYOUS CHILDREN—1902.

p. 102 LITTLE-GIRL-TWO-LITTLE-GIRLS

Printed in *The Century Magazine,* February, 1900, with the title, *The Little Girl That Was Two Little Girls;* published in THE BOOK OF JOYOUS CHILDREN—1902.

p. 103 THE PENALTY OF GENIUS

Printed in *The Century Magazine,* February, 1900; published in THE BOOK OF JOYOUS CHILDREN—1902.

p. 104 A PARENT REPRIMANDED

Printed in *The Century Magazine,* February, 1900; published in THE BOOK OF JOYOUS CHILDREN—1902.

p. 105 IN FERVENT PRAISE OF PICNICS

Printed in *The Century Magazine,* February, 1900; published in THE BOOK OF JOYOUS CHILDREN—1902.

p. 106 THE HOME-VOYAGE

Printed in *The Indianapolis Journal,* February 6, 1900; published in HOME-FOLKS—1900, THE LOCKERBIE BOOK—1911. General Henry W. Lawton, a veteran of the Civil War, the Indian campaigns in the West, and the Spanish-American War, was born at Toledo, Ohio, March 17, 1843, and was killed by a shot fired from ambush at San Mateo, near Manila, P. I., December 18, 1899. His body was brought back to America and lay in state at Indianapolis, February 6, 1900, before being taken to its last resting place, the soldiers' national cemetery at Arlington. At the time of his death he was a great national hero.

p. 108 TO THE QUIET OBSERVER

Dated March, 1900, printed in the first issue of *The Quiet Observer,* a small magazine edited by Erasmus Wilson, May 3, 1900; hitherto unpublished in book form. See *Erasmus Wilson,* Vol. IV, p. 113.

p. 109 PROEM TO "HOME-FOLKS"

Published, without title, as the proem in HOME-FOLKS—1900.

p. 110 OUR BOYHOOD HAUNTS

Published in HOME-FOLKS—1900, SONGS OF HOME—1910, THE LOCKERBIE BOOK—1911.

p. 112 UNCLE SIDNEY'S LOGIC

Published in HOME-FOLKS—1900.

p. 113   HIS LOVE OF HOME

Published in HOME-FOLKS—1900.

p. 114   TO "UNCLE REMUS"

Published in HOME-FOLKS—1900. Between Mr. Riley and Joel Chandler Harris there was an affectionate friendship. On Christmas day, 1904, the latter sent him his new book, *The Rhymes of Uncle Remus,* written at Mr. Riley's suggestion. In this volume Mr. Harris inscribed the following poem, in appreciation of that inspiration, and reminiscent of delightful companionship on summer evenings in Mr. Harris' home, Wren's Nest, near Atlanta, during Mr. Riley's visits. These verses are now published for the first time. The last stanza refers to the dedication of his novel of *Gabriel Tolliver* to Mr. Riley.

TO JAMES WHITCOMB RILEY

It's ho-my-Riley! kaze all thu my dreams
You er allers a-skippin' dat Jim-along-Jeems
Wid Jim-along-Joe twel it natchally seems
You er here sho 'nough, whar you oughter be,
A-bangin' aroun' an' a-loafin' wid me—
An' I wish you wuz—Yes-sir-eee!

Well, dish yer book, it b'longs ter you,
Kaze you up'd an' tol' me what to do,
An' when ter blow on my fil-a-ma-loo:
An' I went an' done it, des *ez* you say,
Sometimes in de night, sometimes in de day,
An' when folks *pestered,* I had um sont away.

Now ol' Gabe Tolliver, he was a shame,
A little too long, an' a little too tame,
An' dish yer's de book dat oughter have yo' name
Den it's ho-my-Riley! I hope you feelin' fine,
But you'd feel lots better wid me an' mine,
A watchin' dat mocker in de honeysuckle vine!
           Affectionately yours,
Christmas, 1904.   JOEL CHANDLER HARRIS.

p. 115 THE BALLADE OF THE COMING RAIN

Published in Home-Folks—1900, Songs of Summer—1908.

p. 116 TO THE JUDGE

Published in Home-Folks—1900, Songs of Home—1910, The Lockerbie Book—1911. The poem was intended for Mr. Riley's old friend, Judge Grandison Offut, of Greenfield.

Stanza 5, ll. 3-4: "Hans Breitmann," the pseudonym of Charles Godfrey Leland; Artemus Ward, Mark Twain, Robert J. Burdette, Edgar Wilson Nye, all favorite humorists of the two friends.

p. 118 A WHOLLY UNSCHOLASTIC OPINION

Published in Home-Folks—1900.

p. 119 A SHORT'NIN' BREAD SONG—PIECED OUT

Published in Home-Folks—1900. The chorus is adapted from an old negro song and fiddle tune.

p. 122 THE UNHEARD

Published in Home-Folks—1900, The Lockerbie Book—1911.

p. 124 EQUITY—?

Published in Home-Folks—1900.

p. 125 MOONSHINER'S SERENADE

Published in Home-Folks—1900.

p. 127   THE EDGE OF THE WIND

Published in HOME-FOLKS—1900, THE LOCKER-
BIE BOOK—1911.

p. 128   THE HIRED MAN'S FAITH IN CHILDREN

Published in HOME-FOLKS—1900, SONGS o'
CHEER—1905, THE RAGGEDY MAN—1907. See *The
Raggedy Man,* Vol. IV, p. 102.

p. 129   THE LOVELY HUSBAND

Published in *Spirk and Wunk Rhymes, Rounds
and Catches* in THE FLYING ISLANDS OF THE NIGHT
—1900. Stanza 1 of this poem first appeared in
1898 in the final revision of the poem, *The Flying
Islands of the Night,* Vol. I, p. 287, ll. 3-14. At the
same time appeared another stanza not included in
this version of *The Lovely Husband.* [Cf. Vol. I, p.
302, l. 15 to p. 303, l. 2.] Neither the music nor
stanzas 2 and 3 were produced until the 1900 edition of the volume, THE FLYING ISLANDS OF THE
NIGHT, where they were published in the sec-
tion called *Spirk and Wunk Rhymes, Rounds and
Catches.*

p. 133   THREE SEVERAL BIRDS

Published in *Spirk and Wunk Rhymes, Rounds
and Catches* in THE FLYING ISLANDS OF THE NIGHT
—1900, THE LOCKERBIE BOOK—1911.

p. 137   THE BED

Printed in *The Century Magazine,* October, 1900,
published in HOME-FOLKS—1900, THE LOCKERBIE
BOOK—1911. This is one of Mr. Riley's favorite
poems.

p. 140   HOME-FOLKS

Printed in *The Indianapolis Journal,* October 28,
1900; published in HOME-FOLKS—1900. The early
version consisted of five stanzas only: 1, 2, 4, 8
and 10.

p. 142   AMERICA'S THANKSGIVING

Printed in *The World* (New York), November
25, 1900; hitherto unpublished in book form.

p. 144   TO EDMUND CLARENCE STEDMAN

Written for the reception to Edmund Clarence
Stedman given by The Authors' Club in New York
City, December 6, 1900; published in MORNING—
1907, THE LOCKERBIE BOOK—1911. Edmund Clarence, Stedman [1833-1908] journalist, scholar, poet,
banker, was president of the National Institute of
Arts and Letters, 1904-1905. There was a long and
cordial friendship between him and Mr. Riley.

p. 146   WHEN WE FIRST PLAYED "SHOW"

Written early in January, 1901; published in
THE BOOK OF JOYOUS CHILDREN—1902. Mr.
Charles Vergil Tevis reports the following from an
interview with Mr. Riley, in *The Indianapolis Sentinel,* June 28, 1903:—

I determined to become a showman—a man who paraded
golden chariots, cages of ferocious wild beasts, possessed
of a large tent, a lot of stunning horses for the beautiful
princesses to ride, with knightly followers who sold pea-
nuts and red lemonade. If fortune deserted me short of
this ideal I would be a clown or a bareback rider, who helps
the beautiful lady with the diamonds all over her like salt
on onions, away and on her bounding steed. Oh, I would
be the funniest clown that ever was! How I would make

the folks laugh! Especially the ones that had been crying. And maybe I would be a clown who could ride a horse my own self; and then when all the people thought I couldn't ride, I would fool 'em, for that's a clown's business. I had it all planned out, exactly as a thousand other boys have planned it all. During the inception part of this epoch the five-pin-admission-fee-back-yard-circus was my training quarters. Where is the man who will be ignorant of my meaning?

p. 149   WILLIAM PINKNEY FISHBACK

Printed in *The Indianapolis Journal,* January 17, 1901; hitherto unpublished in book form. With the poem appeared this notice:—

William P. Fishback died suddenly at his home in Indianapolis, January 15, 1901. He was one of the best-known lawyers in the state, a partner of General [Benjamin] Harrison and [Governor] Albert G. Porter.

Mr. Fishback, a man of remarkable wit and brilliance, was a close friend of Mr. Riley and, accompanied by Myron W. Reed, made a trip to England with him in the summer of 1901.

p. 151   A GOOD MAN

Written after the death of James A. Mount, January 16, 1901; printed in *The Indianapolis Journal,* January 18, 1901, with the subtitle, *James A. Mount;* published in Morning—1907, Songs of Home—1910, The Lockerbie Book—1911. James A. Mount [1843-1901], farmer and orator, was twenty-fourth governor of Indiana.

p. 152   JOHN CLARK RIDPATH

This tribute, hitherto unpublished in book form, was prepared for the exercises held in memory of Mr. Riley's friend, John Clark Ridpath, at De-Pauw University, January 20, 1901, on which occasion it was read by Miss Hope Erwin, in Mr. Riley's absence. Dr. Ridpath had died on the thirty-first day of the previous July. Writing to Mrs. Ridpath, February 26, 1901, Mr. Riley said:—

How little we can do for those we so deeply love, after they have gone from us! To me the loss—or, rather, the continued absence—of the doctor is deeply felt, and my world of friends is grown a small world indeed since his presence of old so filled and made it populous.

See *Lines to Perfesser John Clark Ridpath,* Vol. IV, p. 130, and note.

p. 154   HIS HEART OF CONSTANT YOUTH

Written at the death of Major Charles L. Holstein, January 22, 1901; printed in *The Indianapolis Journal,* January 25, 1901; published in MORNING—1907, THE LOCKERBIE BOOK—1911. Major Holstein [1843-1901], soldier, lawyer and student, was one of the poet's most congenial and helpful friends. In 1892 he invited Mr. Riley to make his home with him on Lockerbie Street, since which time the poet has resided there. The quotation beneath the title, not printed with the first version, is from Major Holstein's poem, *The Drums.*

p. 157   THE PATHS OF PEACE

Written February 15, 1901; printed in *The Indianapolis News,* February 21, 1901, with the title, *Maurice Thompson;* published in HOME-FOLKS (Homestead Edition)—1902, HIS PA'S ROMANCE—1903, THE LOCKERBIE BOOK—1911. Maurice Thompson [1844-1901], naturalist, lawyer, poet, and soldier in the Confederate army, was the au-

thor of *Songs of Fair Weather, The Witchery of
Archery,* etc. For the greater part of his life he
lived at Crawfordsville, Indiana. Mr. Riley admired
and delighted in his poetry.

p. 159   THE TRIBUTE OF HIS HOME

Written following the death of President Benjamin Harrison at Indianapolis, March 13, 1901; published in HOME-FOLKS (Homestead Edition)—1902,
HIS PA'S ROMANCE—1903, THE LOCKERBIE BOOK
—1911. At the time of Harrison's death, Mr. Riley
gave the press a statement here partly quoted:—

My first meeting with General Harrison dates back to the
time when he appeared as an attorney at the Greenfield
bar. Among the members of that bar was my father, Reu-
ben Riley, who was among his ardent admirers. So my
affectionate admiration for General Harrison was fixed in
my boyhood.

A man more universally esteemed than General Harrison
will not be found within the boundaries of our common
country. He was a man who inspired the deepest respect
of all those with whom he came in contact, and particu-
larly of those who knew him best here in his own home
city, where his long life has been passed. We have nothing
but praise, honor and affection for our great friend and
fellow. This adds to the very distinguished greatness
which he so justly earned by his upright, intellectual life.

See *Benjamin Harrison,* p. 430.

p. 160   AMERICA

Dated September 14, 1901, the day President
McKinley died, and printed in *The Chicago Evening Post, Annual Book Number,* November 30,
1901, with the title, *O Thou America—Messiah of
Nations;* published in MORNING—1907, THE LOCK-
ERBIE BOOK—1911. President McKinley had been
shot at Buffalo, September 6, 1901.

With the title, *The Messiah of Nations,* the poem was set to music by John Philip Sousa, and sung by a chorus at the dedication of the Indianapolis Soldiers' and Sailors' Monument May 15, 1902. On May 10, 1902, the music was published with the poem in *The Indianapolis News.*

See the following poem and note.

p. 162	EVEN AS A CHILD

Written at the burial of President McKinley, September 19, 1901; published in MORNING—1907, LOCKERBIE BOOK—1911. See preceding note and poem; also *William McKinley,* p. 409.

p. 163	THE HOOSIER IN EXILE

Read at a banquet of The Indiana Society of Chicago, December 17, 1901; printed in *The Indianapolis Journal,* December 18, 1901; published in MORNING—1907, THE LOCKERBIE BOOK—1911.

p. 165	THE QUEST OF THE FATHERS

Read by the author before the New England Society of Detroit, December 20, 1901; printed in *The Detroit Free Press* of the same date; published in MORNING—1907, THE LOCKERBIE BOOK—1911.

p. 168	TO THE MOTHER

Written at the death of Mrs. Sarah J. Hays, December 26, 1901; hitherto unpublished in book form. Mrs. Hays was the mother of Dr. Franklin W. Hays, Mr. Riley's early friend.

p. 169   NEW YEAR'S NURSERY JINGLE

This poem was found on the back of an old envelope with the subheading, *1902;* hitherto unpublished in book form.

p. 170   FOOL-YOUNGENS

Printed in *The Century Magazine,* January, 1902: published in THE BOOK OF JOYOUS CHILDREN —1902.

p. 172   A GUSTATORY ACHIEVEMENT

Printed in *The Century Magazine,* January, 1902; published in THE BOOK OF JOYOUS CHILDREN —1902.

p. 173   BILLY AND HIS DRUM

Printed in *The Century Magazine,* January, 1902; published in THE BOOK OF JOYOUS CHILDREN —1902.

p. 175   A DIVERTED TRAGEDY

Printed in *The Century Magazine,* January, 1902; published in THE BOOK OF JOYOUS CHILDREN —1902.

p. 176   THOMAS THE PRETENDER

Printed in *The Century Magazine,* January, 1902; published in THE BOOK OF JOYOUS CHILDREN —1902.

p. 178   TO MY SISTER

Written February 10, 1902, for Mrs. Henry Eitel; hitherto unpublished in book form.

p. 179 THE SOLDIER

Read by the author at the dedicatory exercises of the Soldiers' and Sailors' Monument, Indianapolis, May 15, 1902, for which occasion the poem was written; printed in *The Indianapolis Journal,* May 16; published in MORNING—1907, THE LOCKERBIE BOOK—1911. See *A Monument to the Soldiers,* Vol. III, p. 148, and its note.

p. 182 A CHRISTMAS GLEE

Written in June, 1902, printed in *The Reader,* December, 1905; published in MORNING—1907. Mr. Riley composed music for these verses and this accompanied the words when printed in *The Reader.*

p. 184 NO BOYS KNOWS

Mr. Riley completed this poem just prior to the exercises at Yale University, June 25, 1902, when the honorary degree of A. M. was conferred upon him, and read it that day at the Alumni Dinner; published in THE BOOK OF JOYOUS CHILDREN—1902, THE LOCKERBIE BOOK—1911.

p. 186 HIS PA'S ROMANCE

Written during the summer of 1902, printed in *The Ladies' Home Journal,* January, 1903; published in HIS PA'S ROMANCE—1903, Christy Edition with the title, WHEN SHE WAS ABOUT SIXTEEN—1911. The latter edition was dedicated "To Jap Miller," about whom the poem *Jap Miller,* Vol. IV, p. 17, was written.

The narrative is true in all essential particulars. It was briefly communicated to Mr. Riley in a letter dated January 20, 1902, by A. C. Fishback, of Brazil, Indiana, who had read the story in the early eighties in a newspaper. He vouched for the fact of the incident, but could not recall where it happened.

p. 198   TO JOEL CHANDLER HARRIS

Published as a dedicatory poem in THE BOOK OF JOYOUS CHILDREN—1902, "gratefully and affectionately inscribed to Joel Chandler Harris." See *To "Uncle Remus,"* p. 114, and note; and also *Ef Uncle Remus Please ter 'Scusen Me,* p. 360.

p. 199   THE BOOK OF JOYOUS CHILDREN

Introductory poem in THE BOOK OF JOYOUS CHILDREN—1902, published in THE LOCKERBIE BOOK—1911.

p. 201   ELMER BROWN

Published in THE BOOK OF JOYOUS CHILDREN—1902.

p. 203   THE RAMBO-TREE

Published in THE BOOK OF JOYOUS CHILDREN—1902. The Rambo apple has an unusually delicious flavor.

p. 205   FIND THE FAVORITE

Published in THE BOOK OF JOYOUS CHILDREN—1902. The incident is true, even to the names of the three cats; and occurred at Mr. Riley's present home. "Katy" Kindell, the housekeeper, reported it to the poet.

p. 208 THE BOY PATRIOT

Published in THE BOOK OF JOYOUS CHILDREN—
1902, THE LOCKERBIE BOOK—1911. These aspira-
tions were vividly experienced by the boy Riley
while his father was at the front in the sixties. Even
more than saber and rifle, the drum appealed to
him, as witness the interview with Charles Virgil
Tevis, in *The Indianapolis Sentinel*, June 28,
1903:—

[One of my earliest aspirations] was to be the man who
thumps the snare-drum in the band. I wanted to dangle
my feet over the tail-board of the band wagon and beat that
drum. In my dreams the wagon was all gold and pictures,
like the one in the show parade. The man who puffed
over the biggest horn didn't inspire such admiration and
envy in my mind as did the snare-drummer. In time I real-
ized this treasured ambition. I dangled my legs over the
back of the band wagon and rattled noisy symphonies and
abused the sheepskin to my heart's content, and the public's, too! But the reality somehow destroyed the inspiration of my dreams. After a while (a short time) I forgot
that the consummate joy of living depended upon a tenor
drum.

p. 210 EXTREMES

Published in THE BOOK OF JOYOUS CHILDREN—
1902.

p. 211 INTELLECTUAL LIMITATIONS

Published in THE BOOK OF JOYOUS CHILDREN—
1902.

p. 212 A MASQUE OF THE SEASONS

Published in THE BOOK OF JOYOUS CHILDREN—
1902, THE LOCKERBIE BOOK—1911.

p. 215   LITTLE DICK AND THE CLOCK

Published in THE BOOK OF JOYOUS CHILDREN—
1902.

p. 217   THE KATYDIDS

Published in THE BOOK OF JOYOUS CHILDREN—
1902.

p. 219   THE NOBLE OLD ELM

Published in THE BOOK OF JOYOUS CHILDREN—
1902.

p. 220   EVENSONG

Published in THE BOOK OF JOYOUS CHILDREN—
1902, THE LOCKERBIE BOOK—1911.

p. 221   AN IMPROMPTU FAIRY-TALE

Published in THE BOOK OF JOYOUS CHILDREN—
1902.

p. 223   THE TWINS

Published in THE BOOK OF JOYOUS CHILDREN—
1902. The jargon of the refrain is from Burns'
Verses on Captain Grose, beginning:—

> Ken ye ought o' Captain Grose?
> Igo and ago,
> If he's amang his friends or foes?
> Iram, coram, dago.

p. 225   THE LITTLE LADY

Published in THE BOOK OF JOYOUS CHILDREN—
1902, THE LOCKERBIE BOOK—1911.

p. 227   "COMPANY MANNERS"

Published in THE BOOK OF JOYOUS CHILDREN—
1902.

p. 228   **THE GOOD, OLD-FASHIONED PEOPLE**

Published in THE BOOK OF JOYOUS CHILDREN—
1902.

p. 230   THE BEST TIMES

Published in THE BOOK OF JOYOUS CHILDREN—
1902.

p. 231   "HIK-TEE-DIK"

Published in THE BOOK OF JOYOUS CHILDREN—
1902. "Hik-tee-dik" was the youthful war-cry of
"Billy" (Dr. William Morris Pierson), and
"Buddy," the boy Riley. See Vol. I, p. 408.

p. 233   "OLD BOB WHITE"

Published in THE BOOK OF JOYOUS CHILDREN—
1902.

p. 234   A SESSION WITH UNCLE SIDNEY

Published in THE BOOK OF JOYOUS CHILDREN—
1902.
One of His Animal Stories: The poem is founded
on fact. The incident was told the poet by his lecture manager, John Marcus Dickey, who related it
as his own experience.
    p. 236, l. 21: "Waumus," a knit coat.
The second stanza of *Uncle Brightens Up,*
printed in *The Century Magazine,* February, 1900,

with the title, *A Pet of Uncle Sidney's;* the third
stanza printed in *The Century Magazine*, January
1902, with the title, *In the Kindergarten of Noble
Song.*

And Another of Our Betsy, with the title, *Our
Betsy*, published in HIS PA'S ROMANCE (Green-
field Edition and Red Series only)—1903, WHILE
THE HEART BEATS YOUNG—1906.

The Imperious Angler written in a letter to a little friend, Edith Thomas Medairy (called "Dory-
Ann"), September 25, 1901.

p. 246   A SONG OF SINGING

Published in THE BOOK OF JOYOUS CHILDREN—
1902, THE LOCKERBIE BOOK—1911. Stanza 2, entitled *Sing,* appears in HOME-FOLKS (Homestead
Edition)—1900, where lines 3-4 read:—

> Sing! robin on the garden-wall
> Or redbird by the woodland spring.

p. 247   THE JAYBIRD

Published in THE BOOK OF JOYOUS CHILDREN—
1902.

p. 248   A BEAR FAMILY

Published in THE BOOK OF JOYOUS CHILDREN—
1902.

p. 251   SOME SONGS AFTER MASTER-SINGERS

Published in THE BOOK OF JOYOUS CHILDREN—
1902, THE LOCKERBIE BOOK—1911. The initials as
sub-headings refer to the authors in whose fashion
the verses were written: William Shakespeare,

Robert Herrick, William Wordsworth, Alfred
Tennyson, Robert Browning, William Morris. See
the third paragraph, on p. 548, Vol. II.

p. 257   CLIMATIC SORCERY

Published in THE BOOK OF JOYOUS CHILDREN—
1902.

p. 258   THE TREASURE OF THE WISE MAN

Published in THE BOOK OF JOYOUS CHILDREN—
1902, THE LOCKERBIE BOOK—1911.

p. 259   OLD GRANNY DUSK

Written September-October, 1902; published in
THE BOOK OF JOYOUS CHILDREN—(second edition)
—1902, HIS PA'S ROMANCE—1903.

p. 260   FIRE AT NIGHT

Written September-October, 1902; published in
THE BOOK OF JOYOUS CHILDREN (second edition)
—1902, HIS PA'S ROMANCE—1903.

p. 261   THE YOUNG OLD MAN

Written September-October, 1902; published in
THE BOOK OF JOYOUS CHILDREN (second edition)
—1902, HIS PA'S ROMANCE—1903, THE LOCKERBIE
BOOK—1911.

p. 263   SOME CHRISTMAS YOUNGSTERS

Written September-October, 1902; published in
THE BOOK OF JOYOUS CHILDREN (second edition)
—1902, HIS PA'S ROMANCE—1903.

p. 266 TWILIGHT STORIES

Written September-October, 1902; published in THE BOOK OF JOYOUS CHILDREN (second edition) —1902, HIS PA'S ROMANCE—1903.

p. 267 "GO READ YOUR BOOK!"

Written July-October, 1902; published in THE BOOK OF JOYOUS CHILDREN (second edition)—1902, HIS PA'S ROMANCE—1903, THE LOCKERBIE BOOK —1911.

p. 269 WHEN UNCLE DOC WAS YOUNG

Written September-October, 1902; published in THE BOOK OF JOYOUS CHILDREN (second edition) —1902, HIS PA'S ROMANCE—1903.

p. 271 THE LISPER

Written September-October, 1902; published in THE BOOK OF JOYOUS CHILDREN (second edition) —1902, HIS PA'S ROMANCE—1903, WHEN THE HEART BEATS YOUNG—1906, CHILD-VERSE—1908.

p. 273 A MOTTO

Written probably early in 1903; hitherto unpublished in book form. These lines were written in answer to a request from a college fraternity for a motto.

p. 274 A SIMPLE RECIPE

Written in a letter to a young friend, Thomas Whitcomb Hays, February 3, 1903, with the subtitle, *Showing How to Make the Right Kind of a*

Man Out of the Right Kind of a Boy; printed in *Collier's Weekly,* February 28, 1903; published in His Pa's Romance—1903. See *Busch and Tommy,* Vol. IV, p. 59, and its note.

p. 275   HER LONESOMENESS

Printed in *The Youth's Companion,* February 26, 1903; published in While the Heart Beats Young—1906, His Pa's Romance (Homestead Edition)—1908, Child-Verse—1908. Elizabeth, the little daughter of President Harrison, was the occasion of these verses. She said to her father one morning, "I get so lonesome about you."

In a lecture often delivered in the early eighties Mr. Riley made this comment on child utterance :—

There are unconscious poets all about us: men and women, who, in their most commonplace duties and avocations, are unconsciously sweetening their lives and our own with the poetic drippings of their melodious natures. And if we but analyze the incoherent lispings of the children—our own Paul Dombeys—how often may we find the virgin ore of poetic thought. I recall an instance of this character, furnished by a little fellow yet in dresses, who was caught staring absently from the window at the sky one day, and softly crooning over and over to himself the words : "Lonesome as a pale daylight moon—lonesome as a daylight moon!" And I know many ambitious writers of verse who would be proud to lay claim to that simple utterance; for it is poetry, so pure and perfect, in even technical construction, that it might have adorned the song of any master.

p. 277   ALMOST BEYOND ENDURANCE

Printed in *The Ladies' Home Journal,* March, 1903; published in His Pa's Romance—1903, While the Heart Beats Young—1906, Child-Verse—1908.

p. 279   THE TOY-BALLOON

Printed in *The Ladies' Home Journal,* March, 1903; published in His Pa's Romance—1903.

p. 281   THE OLD DAYS

Written about April, 1903; printed in *Collier's Weekly,* December 5, 1903, with the title, *Old Days;* published in Morning—1907, Songs of Home—1910, The Lockerbie Book—1911.

The following, from an undated manuscript fragment, touches on the same theme in dialect:—

> In the old days 'at's past and gone,
> As dead as where yer walkin' on
> The graves of them you loved and lost
> In Spring o' life, afore the frost
> O' death set in—In the old days
> I face around and gaze and gaze.

p. 282   TO A POET ON HIS MARRIAGE

Written in June, 1903; hitherto unpublished in book form. Mr. Riley sent these lines to his good friend, Mr. Madison Cawein, on the occasion of the latter's marriage to Miss Gertrude McKelvey, at Louisville, June 4, 1903. See *A Southern Singer,* Vol. IV, p. 36; and note.

p. 283   LOCKERBIE FAIR

Written in June, 1903, for the second Lockerbie Street Fair held June 24-26; published in His Pa's Romance—1903, The Lockerbie Book—1911. The poem was sold in pamphlet form in one of the booths at this neighborhood fair, whose purpose was to pay for a cottage at the Summer Mission for Sick Children. In appreciation the cottage was named for Lockerbie Street.

p. 285 THE OLD MAN OF THE SEA

Printed in *Collier's Weekly,* September 26, 1903; published in His Pa's Romance—1903.

p. 287 PROSE OR VERSE?

Published in His Pa's Romance—1903.

p. 288 BILLY MILLER'S CIRCUS-SHOW

Published in His Pa's Romance—1903, Songs o' Cheer—1905, The Orphant Annie Book—1908, Ef You Don't Watch Out—1911. See *When We First Played "Show,"* p. 146, and its note.

p. 290 IT'S GOT TO BE

Printed in *Success Magazine,* December, 1903; published in Morning—1907, Songs of Home—1910.

p. 293 CHRISTMAS SEASON

Written for Christmas, 1903; published in His Pa's Romance (Homestead Edition)—1908. The verses were sent in a Christmas letter to the poet, Miss Edith M. Thomas, and her niece, Miss Edith Thomas ("Dory-Ann") Medairy, with this additional stanza as a postscript:—

A MANHATTAN CHRISTMAS VOICE

What!—Talk of Shakespeare's English!—Pshawr!—
  Were it a New York man's,
'Twere "Marian's nose looks red and rawr,
  And so does Dory-Ann's!"

p. 295   ART AND POETRY

Written for The Press Artists' Exhibition held at the Claypool Hotel (Indianapolis) the last week in January, 1904; hitherto unpublished in book form. The lines were addressed to the famous cartoonist, Homer C. Davenport [1867-1912].

p. 296   THE CHILDREN OF THE CHILDLESS

Printed in *Collier's Weekly,* April 2, 1904; published in MORNING—1907, THE LOCKERBIE BOOK—1911.

p. 298   HOOSIER SPRING-POETRY

Printed in *The Century Magazine,* June, 1904; published in MORNING—1907, SONGS OF SUMMER —1908, A SUMMER'S DAY AND OTHER POEMS—1911.

p. 300   THE VOICE OF PEACE

Dated November 17, 1904, on which day the Independence Bell was exhibited in Indianapolis to the school children; printed in *The Reader,* July, 1905; published in MORNING—1907, THE LOCKERBIE BOOK—1911. For the early form of the lines see Vol. I, pp. 255-6.

p. 302   A DEFECTIVE SANTA CLAUS

Printed in *Collier's Weekly,* December 3, 1904; published in A DEFECTIVE SANTA CLAUS—1904, HIS PA'S ROMANCE (Homestead Edition)—1908. The poem is dedicated "To Hewitt Hanson Howland, with halest Christmas greetings and fraternal," and to him the first four lines are addressed.

p. 313   WHAT LITTLE SAUL GOT, CHRISTMAS

Printed in *The Cosmopolitan,* December, 1904;
published in WHILE THE HEART BEATS YOUNG—
1906, MORNING—1907, THE RUNAWAY BOY—1908.

p. 315   GENERAL LEW WALLACE

Written at the death of General Lew Wallace,
February 16, 1905; printed in *Collier's Weekly,*
March 4, 1905; published in MORNING—1907, THE
LOCKERBIE BOOK—1911. General Lew Wallace was
born at Brookville, Indiana, April 10, 1827, and
served throughout the Civil War. At the unveiling
of the Wallace monument in the Hall of Fame,
Washington, January 11, 1910, Mr. Riley read this
poem, preceded by the following four stanzas written for the occasion.

> Even as his sculptured counterpart
>   Shall here endure through dateless time,
> So lives he still, in soul and heart,
>   Heroic and sublime—
> A kinsman of us all, and yet
>   A prince of high and heavenly strain,
> The world's love as his coronet,
>   Throughout an endless reign.
>
> Ay, still he lives—where harvests hum
>   And days of bounteous peace are ours;
> Or at the sudden whirring drum
>   When battle tempest lowers—
> He lives and moves, through war's alarm,
>   A sensate spirit, leading still
> His legions with a wavering arm
>   And an unwavering will.
>
> What heights of inspiration he
>   Awakens in each patriot brave
> Who follows him to victory,
>   Above the very grave—

Who meets and smites the impious foe
 That strikes the banner we so love:
It shields our every home below
 Or hope of home Above.

Shall ever, in the coming years,
 The Spirit of the Soldier fail
To fire men's lips with answering cheers
 And prayers while arms prevail?—
And shall not art forever shrine
 Him living in her record thus,
And History, in glowing line,
 Prolong his life for us!

p. 317
ON READING DR. HENRY VAN DYKE'S VOLUME OF POEMS—MUSIC

Printed in *The Reader,* March, 1905; published in
MORNING—1907, THE LOCKERBIE BOOK—1911. Mr.
Riley's friend, Dr. Henry van Dyke, author and
poet, and long an effective teacher at Princeton
University, is now minister to The Hague. It may
be interesting to know that he has written a tribute
To James Whitcomb Riley, Gardener.

p. 319 HER SMILE OF CHEER AND VOICE OF SONG

Printed in *The Indianapolis News,* April 3, 1905,
with the title, *Spring Fails;* published in SONGS O'
CHEER—1905. This poem is a tribute to Mrs. Anna
Randall, written at the time of her death, March 30,
1905. Mrs. Randall was the daughter of Mr. and
Mrs. Lee O. Harris, and a schoolmate of Mr. Riley.
See *To Annie,* Vol. I, p. 135, and its note.

p. 320   **THINKIN' BACK**

Printed in *The Reader,* April, 1905; published in
MORNING—1907, SONGS OF HOME—1910.

p. 322   SIS RAPALYE

Printed in *Collier's Weekly,* April 15, 1905; published in Morning—1907, The Lockerbie Book—1911.

p. 324   TO BLISS CARMAN

Published as the dedicatory poem to Songs o' Cheer—1905, also published in The Lockerbie Book—1911. Mr. Carman has long been a friend of Mr. Riley's; and one evidence of his regard may be found in an appreciation of Mr. Riley's work written by him for *The Atlantic Monthly,* September, 1898.

p. 326   A SONG O' CHEER

Published as the proem to Songs o' Cheer—1905; published in His Pa's Romance (Homestead Edition)—1908.

p. 327   CHILD'S CHRISTMAS CAROL

Published in Songs o' Cheer—1905, His Pa's Romance (Homestead Edition)—1908, The Lockerbie Book—1911.

p. 328   I' GOT TO FACE MOTHER TO-DAY!

Printed in *The Reader,* September, 1905; published in Morning—1907.

p. 330   NAME US NO NAMES NO MORE

The first two stanzas written about September 1, 1905, the last stanza added in March, 1906; published in Morning—1907. A poem of like humor is *By Any Other Name,* Vol. IV, p. 30.

SOME IMITATIONS

The next poems in the order of composition are
Pomona, The Passing of a Zephyr, and *Ef Uncle
Remus Please ter 'Scusen Me,* all published in *The
Reader,* October, 1905, and grouped with some later
poems under the general heading, *Some Imitations,*
in this volume, p. 357.

p. 332   HENRY IRVING

Written at the death of Sir Henry Irving, October 13, 1905; printed in *Collier's Weekly,* October
28, 1905; published in MORNING—1907, THE LOCK-
ERBIE BOOK—1911. Mr. Irving and Mr. Riley met
many times, both in America and on the latter's
visit to England in 1891. Through all his asso-
ciations with the actor, the poet was never able to
separate his real personality from the gentle character played by him when he first saw him on the
stage. This was in the play *Olivia,* and the part
was the kindly Vicar of Wakefield, whose character Irving lived throughout the play in an all-
perfect subtlety. Mr. Riley was impressed not
alone with the great actor's art, but with his kindness to all about him and his consideration for even
the humblest helper, in consequence of which he
was loved and revered by every soul who knew him.

p. 333   LINCOLN—THE BOY

Printed in *Collier's Weekly,* February 10, 1906;
published in MORNING—1907, THE LOCKERBIE
BOOK—1911. See *Lincoln,* Vol. III, p. 201.

p. 334   NICHOLAS OBERTING

Written just after February 25, 1906, at which
time the item quoted below the title appeared in

The Indianapolis Star; published in MORNING—
1907.

p. 337 RABBIT

Printed in *The Reader,* May, 1906; published in
MORNING—1907.

p. 339 A SPRING SONG AND A LATER

As indicated by the original manuscript, written
late in August, 1906, with the title, *The Two Songs;*
published in MORNING—1907, SONGS OF HOME—
1910, THE LOCKERBIE BOOK—1911.

p. 340 OURS

As explained by the subheading, read at a banquet given Henry Watterson, December 8, 1906;
published in MORNING—1907, THE LOCKERBIE
BOOK—1911. In the original the following stanzas
precede those of the present version:—

> By more than his great State—
> By more than all the great
> United States, we rate
>   Our love for one
> Whose home is anywhere
> His hat's off and the air
> Of heaven strokes his hair:—
>   Our Watterson!
>
> And even though he goes
> To Spain—and finds, in *rows,*
> His "castles"—grand as those
>   Of Cervantes,—
> Kings, courtiers, could but fill
> Him with unrest—until
> He struck old Louisville
>   And friends like these!

To his State, then, we do
Like loving homage to.—
It nurtured Boone; it grew
    Us Prentice,—Clay;
The Crittendens (You know 'm!)
'Twas Lincoln's native loam—
Their "Old Kentucky Home"
    The World's, to-day!

As all the glorious list
Swings back, through Fancy's mist,
We see the hands they kissed—
    The maids—the wives—
The mothers—of a race
We meet here, face to face:
Their lives, by highest grace,
    Heroic lives.

Henry Watterson is the editor of the *Louisville Courier-Journal,* and a distinguished orator, writer and politician. The occasion of this poem gave the poet an opportunity to show appreciation for his friend's tribute to him before the Indiana State Teachers' Association, December 28, 1905, at Indianapolis.

p. 342   OLD INDIANY

Written early in December, 1906; hitherto unpublished in book form. In preparing these lines Mr. Riley had in contemplation a banquet of the Indiana Society of Chicago, December 11, 1906, but he did not use them. On this occasion Mr. George Ade, referred to in the last lines, was toast-master.

p. 345, l. 21: The quotation is adapted from Lowell.

p. 345   LONGFELLOW

Written for the centennial anniversary of Longfellow's birth, February 27, 1907; published in

MORNING—1907; THE LOCKERBIE BOOK—1911.
See Notes, Vol. I, p. 412; *Longfellow's Love for
the Children*, Vol. III, p. 25; *Longfellow*, Vol. IV,
p. 205.

p. 346   WITH A CHILD-BOOK

Written in March, 1907; published in HIS PA'S
ROMANCE (Homestead Edition)—1908. These
lines were written in a volume of *The Tailor of
Gloucester* sent by Mr. Riley as a birthday gift to
Mr. Madison Cawein's little son, Preston, March 18,
1907.

p. 347   THE DOCTOR

Printed in *The Indianapolis Star*, April 29, 1907;
published in MORNING—1907, THE LOCKERBIE
BOOK—1911. Of this poem Dr. A. W. Brayton,
of Indianapolis, said in *The Indianapolis Medical
Journal*, May, 1911 :—

And at last in the full ripeness of years Mr. Riley made
his last and greatest tribute to the whole medical profes-
sion in full appreciation of the knowledge of the great
progress in the sciences of chemistry and biology which
physicians have applied to the curing and prevention of
disease. For this purpose he took the occasion of the death
of an old friend—the most romantic figure of his genera-
tion of physicians; a scientist, a soldier, a philanthropist,
a combination of the scientific mind and the artistic tem-
perament; a worker, a teacher, a helpful citizen, a loving
father and brave soldier; one who knew not fear, cared
not for tradition and was not deceived by names or phrases.
Mr. Riley did not dwell upon science or philosophy; he saw
the great field and purpose of medicine as expressed in and
dominating the general practitioner and surgeon, rather
than the man of science and so he "idealized the doctor
some" in the poem, *The Doctor*, which appeared in *The Indianapolis Star* the morning of Dr. W. B. Fletcher's funeral
and burial, April 29, 1907. Five stanzas there are—forty
lines, each ringing clear and true as those in Kipling's

Recessional, and like that poem which was the crowning
and unexpected—even unasked for climax of the great
English exhibit of her power and glory, calling the proud
and haughty to the stern and essential things of natural
life and duty, "lest we forget"—so this tribute to the doctor
calls him to his great function of a minister to the minds
and souls as well as to the bodies of his patients.

Two other stanzas to the doctor, both inscribed
by Mr. Riley in books presented Dr. Joseph Eastman in the early eighties, are here given :—

> Take the best man ever wuz
>   At Death's door, with Heaven in sight;
>   He don't want no Infinite.
> He wants health, that's what he does,
>   And the doctor, and he's right.

This second inscription was afterward used by
the family upon the monument over Dr. Eastman's
grave :—

> First laureate of humanity,
> Lo, science is his poetry!
> With noblest master hand sweeps he
> The harp-strings of Anatomy.

p. 349   ABE MARTIN

Written in the spring of 1907; hitherto unpublished among Mr. Riley's works. This poem was
used by Mr. F. Kinsey Hubbard (Kin Hubbard),
whose cartoons appear in *The Indianapolis News,*
as the introductory poem to his first book, *Abe Martin of Brown County, Indiana,* printed in 1907.

p. 351   MORNING

Published in Morning—1907, The Lockerbie
Book—1911.

p. 352   THE LOVELINESS

Published in Morning—1907, The Lockerbie Book—1911.

p. 354   A PARTING GUEST

Published in Morning—1907, The Lockerbie Book—1911.

p. 355   "OUT OF REACH"

Published in Morning—1907, Songs of Home—1910, The Lockerbie Book—1911.

p. 356   MY FOE

Published in Morning—1907, The Lockerbie Book—1911.

p. 357   SOME IMITATIONS

Published in Morning—1907.

I POMONA

Printed in *The Reader,* October, 1905, with the pseudonym John Challing; published also in Songs of Summer—1908. See *A Southern Singer,* Vol. IV, p. 36; *To a Poet on His Marriage,* p. 282.

II THE PASSING OF A ZEPHYR

Printed in *The Reader,* October, 1905, under the pseudonym John Challing.

III EF UNCLE REMUS PLEASE TER 'SCUSEN ME

Printed in *The Reader,* October, 1905, under the pseudonym John Challing. The following clipping

from *The Indianapolis News* of July 14, 1903, the
immediate inspiration of these verses, was sent to
Joel Chandler Harris with the manuscript, which
is reproduced in facsimile in this volume:—

FIGHTING RABBIT HAS DOG FOR A COMPANION

SHOALS, IND., July 14.—A familiar sight in the streets
here is a white rabbit and white bird dog belonging to T.
V. Allbright, which are inseparable companions. Occasionally the dog wanders away from the rabbit, and the rabbit
then comes into the business portion of the town in search
of the dog. The rabbit is a fighter, and has whipped several strange dogs that attacked it. It never runs from a
dog; instead, it strikes its assailant so hard on the nose
with its forefeet that the dog generally turns tail and flees.

See *To Joel Chandler Harris,* p. 198, and its note.

V VAUDEVILLE SKITS

From old darky songs in general, but not from
any particular ones.

p. 366   THE ROSE-LADY

Published in MORNING—1907, THE LOCKERBIE
BOOK—1911.

p. 367   A HOOSIER CALENDAR

Published in MORNING—1907, as special edition,
illustrated by Gustave Baumann, ALL THE YEAR
ROUND—1912. Stanza 2, l. 6: *Hosler Joe* is a poem
by Oscar Wild.

p. 372   THE LITTLE WOMAN

Published in MORNING—1907, THE LOCKERBIE
BOOK—1911.

p. 375   WHAT TITLE?

Published in Morning—1907, The Lockerbie Book—1911. This is a tribute to Theodore Roosevelt.

p. 376   YOU MAY NOT REMEMBER

Published in Morning—1907, The Lockerbie Book—1911. The three lines introducing this poem as though by quotation are Mr. Riley's own. The inspiration expressed itself in this form.

p. 378   THE REST

Published in Morning—1907, The Lockerbie Book—1911. The poem is written to a fancied character,—hence the initials.

p. 380   WE MUST BELIEVE

Published in Morning—1907, Songs of Home—1910, The Lockerbie Book—1911.

p. 382   THE HIRED MAN'S DOG-STORY

Published in Morning—1907. The poem is dedicated to Dr. James Newton Matthews. See the note, *James Newton Matthews*, Vol. IV, p. 537.

p. 389   PERVERSITY

Published in Morning—1907.

p. 390   HER POET-BROTHER

Published in Morning—1907.

p. 392 GRAMPA'S CHOICE

Published in MORNING—1907.

p. 393 A LITTLE LAME BOY'S VIEWS

Published in MORNING—1907.

p. 395 A VERY TALL BOY

Published in MORNING—1907.

p. 396 THE RAGGEDY MAN ON CHILDREN

Published in MORNING—1907, THE RAGGEDY MAN—1907.

p. 397 'LIZABUTH-ANN ON BAKIN'-DAY

Published in MORNING—1907, THE ORPHANT ANNIE BOOK—1908, THE BOY LIVES ON OUR FARM—1911.

p. 398 GOLDIE GOODWIN

Published in MORNING—1907.

p. 399 SYMPTOMS

Published in MORNING—1907. Stanza 3, l. 2: "Old Blue" river. There is a stream of this name near Greenfield.

p. 400 BUB SAYS

Published in MORNING—1907.

p. 402 THE POOR STUDENT

Published in MORNING—1907.

p. 404   UNCLE SIDNEY'S RHYMES

Published in Morning—1907.

p. 405 "BLUE-MONDAY" AT THE SHOE SHOP

Printed in Morning—1907. See the note on *Jim*,
Vol. III, p. 365.

p. 407   THE THOUGHTS OF YOUTH

Published in Morning—1907.

p. 408   O. HENRY

Written August 15, 1907; hitherto unpublished
in book form. Mr. Riley inscribed these lines in
a set of his works presented to O. Henry [Sidney
Porter (1867-1910)], the short-story writer. The
subtitle refers to Sherrard Plummer, a character
in *A Madison Square Arabian Night* [in *The
Trimmed Lamp*], a story Mr. Riley took particular
pleasure in.

p. 409   WILLIAM McKINLEY

Dated September 30, 1907, printed in *The Indianapolis Journal,* October 1, 1907; hitherto unpublished in book form. Mr. Riley read this poem
when the monument to William McKinley was un-
veiled at Canton, Ohio. See *Even as a Child,* p. 162;
America, p. 160.

p. 411   "MOTHER"

Published in Morning—1907.

p. 414   THE BOYS OF THE OLD GLEE CLUB

Printed in *The Reader,* November, 1907; published in a special edition, THE BOYS OF THE OLD GLEE CLUB—1907, HIS PA'S ROMANCE (Homestead Edition)—1908. The poem is dedicated "To Newton Booth Tarkington." The *Indianapolis News* of November 2, 1907, said:—

James Whitcomb Riley's latest poem, *The Boys of the Old Glee Club,* appears in the November issue of *The Reader Magazine.* The glee club of which the Hoosier poet writes will be better known to residents of Indianapolis, and of Indiana, as the "Bald-Headed Glee Club." All its members, those who survive as well as those who have passed away, were personally acquainted with Mr. Riley and beloved by him. For years the singers appeared at various entertainments, giving freely of their services to assist in numerous worthy causes, singing at the reunions of old soldiers, at church fairs and sociables, for friends, for social gatherings, for their own amusement and for charity. The origin of the club can be traced to the first Harrison campaign in which it performed gallant service for the "favorite son" of Indiana. But it did not long remain a political glee club. Its members, all well known in the city and the State, found other calls for their talents, and to these responded freely and gladly.

As the years passed, however, age set its quaver upon their voices and it was not often that the old glee club could be mustered in strength to appear at public entertainments. Some of the younger members moved from the city and those of older years passed, one by one, to their long rest. As Mr. Riley recites, John Blake is no longer a resident of Indianapolis; Colonel Dan M. Ransdell is in Washington, sergeant-at-arms of the United States Senate; Macy and Weaver have both moved away; Bob Geiger lives in Georgia; Henry C. Adams, Mahlon Butler, David Wallace, Burgess Brown—these four alone remain. Sabold was the first to die, then came the deaths of John Slauson and Ward, and next Doctor Woodward and Edward P. Thompson followed those who had gone before. It was a cruel blow to those who had loved the men, as these old members of the old glee club had loved them, but it came with far less crushing weight than did the death of Col. Will Tarkington, the next to pass beyond the gate. "Ever' one," says Mr. Riley, "loved to love Will Tarkington."

The incident which the poet makes ūse of is no idle fiction of the romanticist. The phonograph record was taken, as Mr. Riley recites, and, at the home of John T. Brush, following the death of Mr. Tarkington, it was placed in the machine. The voices that came back to the old members of the club, now gray with age, holding dear the memories of the past, came to them as voices of the dead—

> "*Not* the *machine* a-singin'—No,
> Th' Old Glee Club o' long ago!
> Seeming to call, with hail and cheer,
> From Heaven's high seas down to us here."

p. 420, l. 11: Dick Thompson, mentioned in *Regardin' Terry Hut* and its note, Vol. III, p. 325.

p. 425, l. 9: Rear Admiral George Brown [1835-1913], a Hoosier born, and a veteran of the Civil and Spanish-American Wars, who lived at Indianapolis after his retirement.

The songs mentioned in the poem are described as follows: *Larboard Watch,* an old sailors' song, music composed by T. Williams; *Uncle Ned,* a negro song, words and music by Stephen Foster; *The Sword of Bunker Hill,* words by William Ross Wallace, set to music by Covert; "Billy Magee-Magaw,"—*Crow Song,* an old college song, author and composer unknown (can be found in *College Songs* compiled by Henry Randall Waite); *Tenting on the Old Camp Ground,* words and music by Walter Kittredge; "A Thousand Years, My Own Columbia!",—*Song of a Thousand Years,* words and music by Henry C. Work; "The Joys We've Known,"—*Joys That We've Tasted,* author and composer unknown; *Hear Dem Bells,* words and music by D. S. McCosh; *Hi-lo, Hail!,* not obtainable; *Hold the Fort,* words and music by P. P. Bliss.

p. 425 "MONA MACHREE"

The manuscript, in a presentation volume, is
dated May 20, 1908, with this inscription: "To T. A.
Daly, Esq., with hale greetings of his old contem-
porary, James Whitcomb Riley"; hitherto unpublished in book form. *Mona Machree* is a poem by
Mr. Daly which Mr. Riley greatly admires.

p. 426 SONG DISCORDANT

Published in HIS PA'S ROMANCE (Homestead
Edition)—1908.

p. 427 LARRY NOOLAN'S NEW YEAR

Published in HIS PA'S ROMANCE (Homestead
Edition)—1908.

p. 428 LISPING IN NUMBERS

Published in HIS PA'S ROMANCE (Homestead
Edition)—1908. The "little poetry-piece" here produced was preserved by Mr. Riley's sister, whose
little son, Edmund H. Eitel, had written it.

p. 430 BENJAMIN HARRISON

Written for the unveiling of the Harrison monument at Indianapolis, October 27, 1908, when Mr.
Riley read these two sonnets and the sonnet entitled
The Tribute of His Home, p. 159; the three sonnets
printed as one poem, with the title, *The Tribute of
His Home,* in *The Indianapolis Star,* October 28,
1908; these two sonnets hitherto unpublished in
book form.

492 *NOTES*

p. 432   LEE O. HARRIS—CHRISTMAS DAY, 1909

Written December 25, 1909; printed in *The Indianapolis Star,* December 27, 1909; hitherto unpublished in book form. Captain Lee O. Harris, the poet's old friend and teacher, died at Greenfield, December 23, 1909, aged seventy. The friendship that began when the boy Riley was his pupil deepened with the years as the latter came the better to understand and appreciate the fine qualities of his old master and the service he had rendered. They often counseled together over their poetical endeavors and always maintained the most affectionate friendship. See *James Whitcomb Riley—A Sketch,* Vol. I, pp. 370, 377; *Three Singing Friends,* Vol. IV, p. 272, and its note.

p. 434   TO BENJ. S. PARKER

Written on the day of the death of Benjamin S. Parker, March 14, 1911; printed in *The Indianapolis Star,* March 15, 1911; published in THE LOCKERBIE BOOK—1911. When Mr. Riley wrote this poem he was himself very ill. The death of his old comrade, one of his first literary friends, moved him to disregard his physician's command to abstain from writing. The news of Parker's death was communicated to him about midday and during the afternoon he composed the poem.

See *Three Singing Friends,* Vol. IV, p. 272, and its note.

p. 435   THE HIGHEST GOOD

Written for *The Shortridge High School Annual,* June, 1912, which was dedicated to Mr. Riley; hitherto unpublished in book form.

p. 436   MY CONSCIENCE

Completed April 17, 1913; printed in *The Century Magazine*, July, 1913; hitherto unpublished in book form. This poem was begun about November, 1888, and the unfinished manuscript was lost to view until discovered in the work of preparing this edition. Mr. Riley completed and revised the verses on April 17, 1913.

TO THE CHILDREN

On September 29, 1913, Mr. Riley learned that the school children of Indianapolis had planned to honor him on his birthday, October 7, with exercises in the schools, a poetry shower, and a parade past his home. In appreciation he wrote the following stanza, which appeared on a souvenir he presented to the children on the occasion :—

> O CHILDREN, so mild
> In pure worth, and so wild
> With delight, take the love of
> An "Elderly child."

The quotation in the last line is from Frederick Locker-Lampson.

Date Due

	PRINTED	IN U. S. A.	